THE HERO OF THE WAVERLEY NOVELS

LITERATURE IN HISTORY

SERIES EDITORS

David Bromwich, James Chandler, and Lionel Gossman

The books in this series study literary works in the
context of the intellectual conditions, social
movements, and patterns of action
in which they took shape.

Other books in the series:

Lawrence Rothfield, *Vital Signs: Medical Realism
in Nineteenth-Century Fiction* (1992)

David Quint, *Epic and Empire* (forthcoming)

THE HERO OF THE
WAVERLEY NOVELS

WITH NEW ESSAYS ON SCOTT

Alexander Welsh

PRINCETON UNIVERSITY PRESS

PRINCETON, NEW JERSEY

PUBLISHED BY PRINCETON UNIVERSITY PRESS, 41 WILLIAM STREET,

PRINCETON, NEW JERSEY 08540

IN THE UNITED KINGDOM: PRINCETON UNIVERSITY PRESS, CHICHESTER, WEST SUSSEX

COPYRIGHT © 1963, 1968 BY ALEXANDER WELSH;

NEW MATERIAL FOR THE PRINCETON UNIVERSITY PRESS EDITION © 1992

BY PRINCETON UNIVERSITY PRESS

ALL RIGHTS RESERVED

LIBRARY OF CONGRESS CATALOGING-IN-PUBLICATION DATA

WELSH, ALEXANDER

THE HERO OF THE WAVERLEY NOVELS:

WITH NEW ESSAYS ON SCOTT

INCLUDES BIBLIOGRAPHICAL REFERENCES AND INDEX.

ISBN 0-691-06958-1 (CL.)

ISBN 0-691-01533-3 (PBK.)

1. SCOTT, WALTER, SIR, 1771–1832. WAVERLEY NOVELS.

2. SCOTT, WALTER, SIR, 1771–1832—CHARACTERS—HEROES.

3. SCOTLAND IN LITERATURE. 4. HEROES IN LITERATURE.

PR5342.A2W4 1992 823'.7—DC20 92-15744 CIP

FIRST PRINCETON PAPERBACK PRINTING FOR THE

LITERATURE IN HISTORY SERIES, 1992

PRINCETON UNIVERSITY PRESS BOOKS ARE PRINTED

ON ACID-FREE PAPER, AND MEET THE GUIDELINES FOR

PERMANENCE AND DURABILITY OF THE COMMITTEE ON

PRODUCTION GUIDELINES FOR BOOK LONGEVITY

OF THE COUNCIL ON LIBRARY RESOURCES

1   3   5   7   9   10   8   6   4   2

1   3   5   7   9   10   8   6   4   2

(PBK.)

PRINTED IN THE UNITED STATES OF AMERICA

For Katharine Welsh

CONTENTS

BIBLIOGRAPHICAL NOTE

IN *The Hero of the Waverley Novels* and in the essays that follow, quotations are from the Centenary Edition of the novels, 25 vols. (Edinburgh: Black, 1885–1887). The publishers printed the first chapters of *Old Mortality*, *The Heart of Mid-Lothian*, and *The Bride of Lammermoor* as preliminary matter, however, and thus shifted the numbering of chapters by one throughout. To facilitate reference to other editions, I have silently restored the standard chapter numbers for these three novels.

PREFACE

IT IS THIRTY YEARS since *The Hero of the Waverley Novels* was written. When the book first appeared, Scott's novels were rarely studied in universities on either side of the Atlantic, and his vast popular readership had been shrinking since the end of the nineteenth century—though *Ivanhoe* lingered in the school curriculum and some notable films had been based on that novel and others. Furthermore, novel criticism at the time was typically formalist, or hovered about the art of writing, and *The Hero* sought to demonstrate a close relation of Scott's achievement to the political and social assumptions of his time. Combined literary and historical study is far more common today, and at least in universities Scott is enjoying something of a revival. Thirty years since, it is strange to think back on decades when critics imagined that great social fictions could be analyzed by themselves, divorced from history, and during which it was largely forgotten that Scott was the most widely read and imitated novelist of the nineteenth century—very possibly of all time.

I myself had not read Scott before I became a graduate student in English, when two things awoke my attention. First, I grew curious about those novels which few people read any more but which the Victorians, great and small, knew intimately. Second, in a course I took with Perry Miller on American romanticism, Miller started talking about the Waverley Novels and couldn't seem to stop. The influence of Scott is perhaps still better understood by students of American literature than by students of the English novel, but Miller's comparisons extended not only to Cooper and Hawthorne but to such Americana as the character Daisy in *The Great Gatsby* and the actor Gary Cooper in *High Noon*. Indeed the film, which had just been released and greeted as the epitome of the Western, could be shown to comply point by point with the conventions of Scott. Years later in Los Angeles I met the screenwriter, Carl Foreman, and told him of Miller's theories. It was news to Foreman, who told me what every film buff knew, that *High Noon* was about Foreman's own struggle with the House Un-American Activities Committee. Still, that this purpose could find its expression in conventions reaching back more than a century was itself testimony to Scott's power. If Foreman drew upon the Waverley Novels without knowing it, he would not have been alone in this respect.

The Hero of the Waverley Novels is a thematic study of the claims of landed society and a passive code of honor. It is not a book about

Scott's purported realism, therefore, but about the shaping of reality by fiction—a shaping that nonetheless plays a part in our history. Strictly speaking, themes are such principles as are confirmed by the action of a narrative or dramatic work. It won't do merely to point to some discussion of a certain matter in a novel, as historians too often do when they use literature as evidence: the principles have to be explicated as rules governing behavior in such a way as to produce a desired outcome. The prescriptive doctrine of property, easily documented from the political theory of Scott's day, is still the best explanation of his heroes' passive stance—their quite proper determination not to act for themselves. Mary Poovey, for example, in her excellent book on the same period, *The Proper Lady* (University of Chicago Press, 1984), put forward similar arguments apparently without knowledge of Scott or of my book, which frequently refers to the "proper hero" and "proper heroine" of property. Rather than revise *The Hero*—and risk spoiling its symmetry or dulling its wit in the process—I have added to it three essays designed to complement the argument of the original and present my recent thoughts. A few prefatory words may help situate these essays for the reader.

An account of European realism as the emergence of a single level of style was brilliantly set forth by Erich Auerbach in *Mimesis* (1946; Princeton University Press, 1953). Precisely because of his focus on classical decorum, the medieval mixture of high and low styles, and the modern adoption of a serious style for "low" matter, Auerbach could not cope directly with the great period of English realism. For the English novel, Scott's example—or his novelization of Shakespeare's example—assured the continuation, throughout the nineteenth century, of a mixture of styles. A book about heroes necessarily addressed the high style in the Waverley Novels, and only after editing *Old Mortality* for the Riverside series (Houghton-Mifflin, 1966), did I begin to appreciate Scott's use of a variety of low styles, in the use of Scottish dialect and the astonishing pastiche of Biblical quotations for the speech of the Covenanters. (It would be fair to say that I had never actually *read* the dialect passages until I had looked up each word in the *Oxford English Dictionary* and decided whether and how to gloss it.) When shortly thereafter I was asked to introduce a bicentennial program on Scott at Lawrence University—the only such celebration in the United States—my topic was "The Contrast of Styles in the Waverley Novels." The lecture was subsequently published by the journal *Novel* in the form in which it appears here. Since then, of course, a number of studies of Scott's language have appeared, including Graham Tulloch's *The Language of Walter Scott* (Andre Deutsch, 1980).

Scott's realism began to be understood differently after the translation into English of Georg Lukács's books, which were virtually unknown in America before the 1960s. Thanks to René Wellek, who
loaned me his copy of the Berlin edition, I was able to read the first
part of *Der Historische Roman* while preparing *The Hero* for the press. I
scarcely realized the extent to which Scott was Lukács's hero until I
studied the entire book in translation. In the essay on "History and
Revolution in *Old Mortality*," which also draws on my edition of that
novel, I have tried to recapture and rethink my own responses to
Lukács, who wrote about the Waverley Novels in the 1930s from the
common view that they were part history, part fiction—historical novels, in short. Lukács also wrote of the novels as a Marxist; I wrote of
them, I suppose, as a democrat determined to expose a myth about
property that went well beyond the covers of a few books—"Scott's reality," I claimed, was "a construction of society" (p. 93). In *The Historical Novel*, Lukács addressed a form of representation, literary realism,
which he regarded as a good thing, whereas I was expounding a the-
matics, trying to formulate what the novels said to their readers.
These approaches are complementary, though at some high theoretical level you might take me for the Marxist critic and Lukács for a
popularizer of the bourgeois novel. For a fuller understanding of the
use of history in Scott, one should turn to Ina Ferris, *The Achievement
of Literary Authority* (Cornell University Press, 1991), especially the second part.

The third essay here has also to do with Scott's contribution to history, but on the conceptual level. In it I return to the themes of *The
Hero*, especially the second half, in order to amplify some discontent
with society observed in the book. "The idea of society as a collective
resistance to individual passions," I had written, "inspires a political
fiction like the social contract, or a literary fiction like the passive
hero" (p. 95). In Scott's time, the notion of a social contract was supposedly antithetical to conservative thinking, which appealed to prescription, or existing entitlements to property in land. But in a wider
sense, all political theory had become contractual and, strangely,
more deeply committed to repression than patriarchy itself. The lesson of real property discouraged heroes, and all who identified with
heroes, from even inwardly transgressing: "transactions of getting and
spending advertise one's motives," whereas the passive possession of
estates implies "no motive whatever" (p. 80). Explicit motives, as contrasted with possession, are a bad thing for this vision of society,
which begins to demand self-inspection and an inward suspicion of
guilt. Since writing *Strong Representations* (Johns Hopkins University
Press, 1992), I have been concerned with the attribution of motives

by criminal prosecutors in the late eighteenth and early nineteenth centuries. If one consults Waverley's experience of the law and compares the risks encountered by Tom Jones—both actions supposedly taking place in 1745—one may conclude that psychological guilt was on the increase in Scott's lifetime. I believe that, with respect to guilt of this order, also, a change was occurring that can be associated with the idea of contract, or a devotion to society that has no other basis than a self-regulating contract. The burden of responsibility assigned to individuals is one that cannot readily be eased.

Psychological guilt, insofar as it is commonplace and chartable in the modern world—and nineteenth-century novels may be the best documentation we have—would seem to result from living with the contract rather than with patriarchy. Fathers may be propitiated, and even may forgive, but contracts can only be binding. Fielding's *Tom Jones* is the prime example of a patriarchal novel in English, but Scott's novels embrace a contractual ideal for society, frequently contrasted with feudal and patriarchal custom. This development does not mean that a parent can no longer make a child feel guilty, but it goes a long way toward explaining why unconscious guilt has become an object of concern. Modern society—at least the modern bourgeois family in the West—does not live in conscious fear of elders. Freud discovered that he harbored many hostile feelings toward his father, but the discovery did not diminish the propriety or economic sense of surpassing his father in whatever way he could. If one places psychoanalysis in historical perspective—and that means placing it alongside novels, among other things—then its interest in the Oedipus complex seems like a projection of the accumulated guiltiness of a new independence, or a nostalgia for patriarchalism.

Michel Foucault may have done more than any other single writer to historicize Freud. Foucault, of course, took repression for granted as a condition of modern life, and in a series of dazzling books he showed that repression has a history. Especially in *Discipline and Punish* (1975; Pantheon, 1978), he linked repression to pervasive techniques of social control and the suppression of crime—to the police and the prison, in short, as those institutions represent a thickly adumbrated system of power and obedience. In the 1980s, Foucault's expressive theories were readily exploited in such studies of the English novel as D. A. Miller's *The Novel and the Police* (University of California Press, 1988) and John Bender's *Imagining the Penitentiary* (University of Chicago Press, 1987). Miller is concerned with Victorian novels as they silently engage in policing, and Bender with eighteenth-century novels, including Fielding's, which in language and organization possibly anticipate the modern penitentiary; yet both might have hit upon more obvious material in Scott's novels, written in the era of transition to surveillance and imprisonment that Foucault highlights. Some of this imbalance of historical criticism has already been righted by Bruce Beiderwell's *Power and Punishment in Scott's Novels* (University of Georgia Press, 1991), a book that engages Foucault's work without being Foucauldian.

My book on Scott spoke metaphorically of heroes "searching about for the police" (p. 106) and noted that "an uneasy fear of jails runs all through the Waverley Novels" (p. 116), but these observations were not Foucauldian either, since the relevant works by Foucault had not yet been published. When it occurred to me that "Scott introduced the kind of anxieties that only very well behaved persons can entertain for customs officials or traffic signs that they do not intend to disobey" (p. 117), I was thinking of my own family—especially of my father, and not of our differences or Oedipal rivalry, but of feelings that we shared about civil authority, feelings already evidenced by the heroes of Scott. The present essay on "Patriarchy, Contract, and Repression" extends the emphasis on Scott's realism of my *Reflections on the Hero as Quixote* (Princeton University Press, 1981) and is another expression of my belief that historical studies matter insofar as they finally bear on present history, present society, present lives.

This new edition of *The Hero of the Waverley Novels* follows the first edition, published by Yale University Press in 1963, as silently corrected in the paperback edition by Atheneum in 1968. A good many teachers and friends contributed in particular ways to the writing and first publication of the book. Most were thanked in the original preface, and I would like to name them again here: Max Bluestone, Cleanth Brooks, Ross Dabney, Gordon Haight, David Horne, Howard Mumford Jones, Harry Levin, Harold C. Martin, Benjamin C. Nangle, Martin Price, and Katharine T. Welsh. It is less easy to comprehend my indebtedness, and express my gratitude, to the many persons who have influenced my thinking about Scott's novels since that time, but here's a try: Bruce Beiderwell, Barbara Bishop, David Bromwich, Frederick Burwick, Marilyn Butler, Patrice Caldwell, James Chandler, Steven Cohan, Thomas Dale, Ian Duncan, Ina Ferris, Robert Gordon, Russ Hart, Frederic Jameson, Karl Kroeber, George Levine, Jane Millgate, D. A. Miller, Max Novak, Morse Peckham, Judith Wilt, and Ruth Yeazell. Finally, I wish to thank Jeanette Gilkison for typing the new essays published here and Timothy Mennel for his copyediting.

CHRONOLOGICAL LIST

OF THE WAVERLEY NOVELS

Waverley.   1814.
Guy Mannering.   1815.
The Antiquary.   1816.
Tales of My Landlord: *The Black Dwarf* and *Old Mortality.*   1816.
Rob Roy.   1818.
Tales of My Landlord, Second Series: *The Heart of Mid-Lothian.*   1818.
Tales of My Landlord, Third Series: *The Bride of Lammermoor* and
    A Legend of Montrose.   1819.
Ivanhoe.   1820.
The Monastery.   1820.
The Abbot.   1820.
Kenilworth.   1821.
The Pirate.   1822.
The Fortunes of Nigel.   1822.
Peveril of the Peak.   1822.
Quentin Durward.   1823.
St. Ronan's Well.   1824.
Redgauntlet.   1824.
Tales of the Crusaders: *The Betrothed* and *The Talisman.*   1825.
Woodstock.   1826.
Chronicles of the Canongate: *Two Drovers, The Highland Widow,*
    and *The Surgeon's Daughter.*   1827.
Chronicles of the Canongate, Second Series: *The Fair Maid*
    of Perth.   1828.
Anne of Geierstein.   1829.
Tales of My Landlord, Fourth Series: *Count Robert of Paris* and *Castle*
    Dangerous.   1832.

I

ROMANCE

From the minuteness with which I have traced Waverley's pursuits, and the bias which these unavoidably communicated to his imagination, the reader may perhaps anticipate, in the following tale, an imitation of the romance of Cervantes. But he will do my prudence injustice in the supposition. My intention is . . . [to describe] that more common aberration from sound judgment, which apprehends occurrences indeed in their reality, but communicates to them a tincture of its own romantic tone and colouring.

—*Waverley*

1. Fiction as Projection

THE PRACTICE of fiction in the lifetime of Sir Walter Scott (1771–1832) generally differed from the main tradition of the English novel in both the eighteenth and nineteenth centuries. Dickens and Thackeray, Fielding and Smollett viewed the world about them with critical eyes. Even when they were patently imagining things, they appeared to report what they saw. They successfully conveyed the impression of real life. Scott, too, filled his works with a sense of life. But he differs from these other great novelists in that he never criticizes his own society. During Scott's lifetime writers of fiction were not always chiefly concerned with the imitation of reality. The wild passions of villains and the horrific predicaments of heroines could be imagined and expressed, perhaps, but not seen and reported. The extravagant practice of fiction in this period (and the novel of manners could be as fantastic in its way as the novel of terror) tempered the earlier theory of the mimetic nature of fiction. The novelistic program for "the spontaneous overflow of powerful feelings" meant surrendering some of the novel's pretensions to reality. Prose fiction was once again referred to as *romance*. Neglecting the knowledge of the world, romancers aspired to "the knowledge of the heart." As moralists, instead of exposing to view actual human behavior, they invented images of ideal behavior. As psychologists, they forewent the study of man's daily actions and discovered the dreamlike evidence of his bright hopes and darkest imaginings. The departures in practice reflect a new theory that fiction is in its own right a peculiarly satisfying and natural human activity.

Eighteenth-century assertions of the nature and purpose of fiction, whether or not they were entirely sincere, were highly moralistic.[1] In the romantic period fiction was still called upon to perform a moral duty, but morality was supposed to be conveyed in a fashion somewhat different from that of the age of reason. In the previous century morals had been interpreted in terms of practice. In fiction, precepts were illustrated by example. Inviting the reader to "see" good or bad behavior and its consequences, the moral reference of eighteenth-century fiction depended upon the real world, or a world assumed to be real. The realities glossed over by hypocrisy and affectation would be exposed: the thrust of fiction could cut through illusion toward objective reality. The new age, on the other hand, tended to express morality in terms of ideal motive or attitude rather than precept tested by act. The heart dictates to the man, and the man consults his heart faithfully. Morality was sought in an ideal world, not through watchful observation of the real. Fiction therefore abounded in good examples and gazed upward. Illusion, rather than disillusionment, was sometimes tenderly respected. A soft "moral of the whole" replaced the sharp revelation of vice. Seeing was no longer sufficient. When fictions "speak only to the eyes," urged Madame de Staël, "they can only amuse: but they have a high influence over all moral ideas when they move the heart."[2]

A theory of fiction appealing so frequently to "the heart" does not seem intellectually promising. The phrase implied, however, that fiction was in some emotional, ideal, or moral sense an expressive or projective activity rather than a critical instrument sensitive to external reality. In an essay on fiction prefaced to a collection of *British Novelists* in 1810, Anna Letitia Barbauld, the biographer of Richardson, entrusted her case for the dignity of the novel "above all" to "the power exercised over the reader's heart by filling it with successive emotions of love, pity, joy, anguish, transport, or indignation, together with the grave impressive moral resulting from the whole."[3]

---

[1] For summaries of eighteenth-century theories of fiction see Joseph Bunn Heidler, *The History, from 1700 to 1800, of English Criticism of Prose Fiction*, University of Illinois Studies in Language and Literature 13 (1928); and Arthur J. Tieje, "The Expressed Aim of the Long Prose Fiction from 1579 to 1740," *Journal of English and Germanic Philology* 2 (1912): 402–32.

[2] Anne Louise Germaine de Staël, "Essai sur les fictions," *Œuvres* (17 vols. Paris, 1820), 2: 162.

[3] Mrs. [Anna Letitia] Barbauld, ed., *The British Novelists, with an Essay, and Prefaces, Biographical and Critical* (50 vols. London, 1810), 1: 3.

Scott employed the same kind of language in his review of *Emma*, which we do not ordinarily regard as a novel of sentiment. Authors are most to be respected, he wrote, when, as in the case of Jane Austen, they "proclaim a knowledge of the human heart, with the power and resolution to bring that knowledge to the service of honour and virtue." In the same review, with characteristic honesty, Scott observed that, in fiction, even Peregrine Pickle and Tom Jones were "studiously vindicated from the charge of infidelity of the heart," and heroines were only more so.[4]

On behalf of the heart, or in obedience to morality, fiction could even set out to counter reality instead of emulating it. By observing in the *Quarterly Review* that a novel should be "in some degree a lesson either of morals or conduct," John Wilson Croker uttered a commonplace. But he arrived at this conclusion from the reflection that the picture of life in *Tom Jones, Peregrine Pickle*, and *Amelia* was "*too* real."[5] Clara Reeve's similar misgivings about Fielding were revealed by Euphrasia's remark in *The Progress of Romance* that "he certainly painted human nature as *it is*, rather than as *it ought to be*."[6] Mrs. Barbauld was very much aware that fiction could distort reality, and that ideal goodness was easily supplied in a make-believe world—but that is as it should be: "It costs nothing, it is true, to an author to make his hero generous, and very often he is extravagantly so; still sentiments of this kind serve in some measure to counteract the spirit of the world, where selfish considerations have always more than their due weight."[7]

Just as reality was acknowledged to yield to morality, the pretense to factual certainty might be surrendered to mystery. When, in *The Apparition of Mrs. Veal*, Defoe undertook to convey a mystery, he skillfully rendered his account as matter-of-fact as possible. The premium in his time was on the detailed impression of fact. By the end of the century mystery had become a commodity in its own right. "Curiosity and a lurking love of mystery" explain, according to Scott, the vogue of Ann Radcliffe: these are "more general ingredients in the human mind, and more widely diffused through the mass of humanity, than either genuine taste for the comic or true feeling of the pathetic." Because certainty is never so fearsome as uncertainty, "sublime emotion" originates in obscurity and suspense, "the dark and the doubtful."[8]

[4] *Quarterly Review* 14 (1815): 189, 191.

[5] Ibid., 7 (1812): 331.

[6] *The Progress of Romance*, 1785 (New York, Facsimile Text Society, 1930), 1: 141.

[7] Barbauld, *The British Novelists*, 1: 49.

[8] *Miscellaneous Prose Works* (6 vols. Edinburgh, 1827), 3: 436, 440.

The notion of fiction as an expressive or projective activity of mind gained strength from a belief in its primitive origins. Fiction was now supposed to be a practice as natural and universal as language itself. Miss Reeve declared that "romances are of universal growth, and not confined to any particular period or country."[9] The origin of fiction was associated with primitive mythology. Mrs. Barbauld also asserted the prevalence of fictitious adventures in all ages and nations: "These have been grafted upon the actions of their heroes; they have been interwoven with their mythology."[10] Sydney Owenson, author of *The Wild Irish Girl*, declared that works of fiction are to be found everywhere, "from the hut of the savage to the closet of the sage." As an example of the mythic and ritualistic origins of her trade she cited the "system of good and evil spirits" of the savages of America. "Thus in the remotest ages, and in the most opposite extremities of the earth, the source of fictitious narrative has existed; a source which can only be exhausted when the heart ceases to feel, the memory to record, and the imagination to combine, to modify, and to adorn."[11]

The most ambitious historical approach to fiction in this period was John Dunlop's *History of Fiction*, a three-volume work that appeared in 1814, the year of *Waverley*. In the introduction to his history Dunlop wrote not a word of the imitation of nature or of the strictly moral usefulness of fiction but instead drew an elaborate analogy between the origin of fiction and a savage planting a garden:

> The art of fictitious narrative appears to have its origin in the same principles of selection by which the fine arts in general are created and perfected. Among the vast variety of trees and shrubs which are presented to his view, a savage finds, in his wanderings, some which peculiarly attract his notice by their beauty and fragrance, and these he at length selects and plants them round his dwelling. In like manner, among the mixed events of human life, he experiences some which are peculiarly grateful, and of which the narrative at once pleases himself, and excites in the mind of his hearers a kindred emotion. Of this kind are unlooked-for occurrences, successful enterprise, or great and unexpected deliverance from signal danger and distress. . . . In the process of forming the garden, the savage finds that it is not enough merely to collect a variety of agreeable trees or plants; he discovers that . . . it is also essential that he should grub up from around his dwelling the shrubs which

[9] Reeve, *The Progress of Romance*, 1: xv–xvi.

[10] Barbauld, *The British Novelists*, 1: 1.

[11] "On the Origin and Progress of Fictitious History," *New Monthly Magazine and Universal Register* 14, Pt. II (1820): 22–23.

are useless or noxious, and which weaken or impair the pure delight which he derives from the others. . . . The collector of agreeable facts finds, in like manner, that the sympathy which they excite can be heightened by removing from their detail every thing that is not interesting, or which tends to weaken the principal emotion, which it is his intention to raise. He renders, in this way, the occurrences more unexpected, the enterprises more successful, the deliverance from danger and distress more wonderful.[12]

The savage thus derives the substance of his fiction from the external world but reworks it according to the lights of his inner mind. Dunlop stresses the motive of this process. Our savage takes pleasure in his fictions, but not the pleasure of imitation for its own sake. He gains his pleasure from improving reality, by exaggerating danger and distress and by flattering himself with his escape. The significance of this activity obviously lies in the disparity of romancing and reality rather than in the correspondence. To complete his thought Dunlop translates from Francis Bacon the following argument:

"As the active world," says Lord Bacon, "is inferior to the rational soul, so *Fiction* gives to mankind what history denies, and, in some measure, satisfies the mind with shadows when it cannot enjoy the substance: For, upon a narrow inspection, *Fiction* strongly shows that a greater variety of things, a more perfect order, a more beautiful variety, than can any where be found in nature, is pleasing to the mind. And as real history gives us not the success of things according to the deserts of vice and virtue, *Fiction* corrects it, and presents us with the fates and fortunes of persons rewarded or punished according to merit. And as real history disgusts us with a familiar and constant similitude of things, *Fiction* relieves us by unexpected turns and changes, and thus not only delights, but inculcates morality and nobleness of soul. It raises the mind by accommodating the images of things to our desires, and, not like history and reason, subjecting the mind to things."[13]

"Accommodating the images of things to our desires," fiction is satisfying in some sense. Fiction comes into being because human beings not only perceive an external world but project their emotions and ideals upon it. This idea of fiction amounts to a modern definition of romance, which, according to Northrop Frye, is "nearest of all literary forms to the wish-fulfilment dream."[14]

[12] *The History of Fiction* (3 vols., London, 1814), 1: v–vii.
[13] Ibid., 1: vii–viii. Cf. Bacon, *The Advancement of Learning*, Bk. II, ch. 4.
[14] *Anatomy of Criticism* (Princeton, 1957), p. 186.

2. Novel or Romance

The novelist's view of man and of society is traditionally a critical view. But in the romantic period man and humanity were more often applauded than berated. Even when the depravity of man was dwelt upon, it was explored with fascination rather than with despair. This was not a critical era, and the fiction of this period, including the Waverley Novels, lies outside the main tradition of the novel. Edwin Muir, a sympathetic and perceptive critic of Scott, endorsed this view. Scott's direct influence on subsequent fiction, according to Muir, was "trivial." Nor did Scott carry on the tradition of earlier fiction. "Fielding's and Sterne's criticism of life was intelligent and responsible. Scott substituted for this criticism a mere repetition of the moral clichés of his time. In his stories the public got the upper hand of the novelist, and it has kept its advantage, with few setbacks, ever since."[15] In Scott's lifetime the novel reverted to the romance, which expresses, rather than criticizes, the desires of the mind. In Scott's hands romance projected publicly acceptable desires—"the moral clichés of his time."

When Mark Twain indicted Scott—on a host of charges, including responsibility for the American Civil War—he appealed to a contrast with Cervantes: "A curious exemplification of the power of a single book for good or harm is shown by the effects wrought by *Don Quixote* and those wrought by *Ivanhoe*. The first swept the world's admiration for the medieval chivalry silliness out of existence; and the other restored it."[16] The popularity of *Don Quixote* did not abate in the romantic period—Scott's own writings are filled with tags and allusions from this favorite book.[17] At the same time, however, *Amadis of Gaul* had made a reappearance: in 1803 Robert Southey brought out an adaptation in English, curtailing the original romance to four volumes. This and another version of the romance were the subject of Scott's first periodical essay in the *Edinburgh Review*.[18]

Don Quixote has been interpreted in many ways. In the romantic era the antiromantic character of Cervantes' novel was played down. Hazlitt declared of it that "the whole work breathes that air of romance,—that aspiration after imaginary good,—that longing after

[15] "Walter Scott," in *The English Novelists*, ed. Derek Verschoyle (New York, 1936), p. 117.

[16] *Life on the Mississippi* (New York, 1944), pp. 271–73.

[17] Cf. Aubrey Bell, "Scott and Cervantes," in *Sir Walter Scott Today*, ed. H.J.C. Grierson (London, 1932), pp. 69–90.

[18] *Edinburgh Review* 3 (1803): 109–36.

something more than we possess, that in all places, and in all conditions of life,—'still prompts the eternal sigh, For which we wish to live, or dare to die.'"[19] Clara Reeve argued that Cervantes himself was not "cured" of romance, since he had not only written *Galatea* before *Don Quixote,* but wrote another serious romance, *Persiles and Sigismunda,* afterward. On another evening Euphrasia, who always speaks for the author of *The Progress of Romance,* rallies to the cause of the knight himself: "whenever this spirit, and this enthusiasm, become the object of contempt and ridicule, mankind will set up for themselves an idol of a very different kind." Romances inspire such spirit and enthusiasm—as they had inspired Don Quixote. "Let us suppose the character of Don Quixote realized, with all its virtues and absurdities. I would ask, whether such a man is not more respectable, and more amiable, than a human being, wholly immersed in low, groveling, effeminate, or mercenary pursuits . . .?"[20] One early nineteenth-century courtesy book severely chastises Cervantes for ridiculing his own hero—no less than six pages are devoted to a defense of the virtue of Don Quixote.[21] In general, because romantic critics pursued the origins of fiction to much earlier times, Cervantes appeared not so much the inventor of the novel as the specialist in "comic romance."

Scott's good sense saved him from associating too warmly with the Knight of La Mancha. The numerous tags from Cervantes in his letters and journal are generally borrowed from Sancho Panza. The same good sense, however, restricted Scott's understanding of Cervantes' parody. He does not seem to have understood, to the degree that Fielding and Sterne understood, the play between fiction and reality in *Don Quixote.* He neither practiced himself nor quite recognized the method of posing fiction against fiction in order to pass, in Harry Levin's phrase, "from the imitation of art through parody to the imitation of nature."[22] Instead, Scott's instinct was to rationalize Cervantes' parody. "In Spain," he wrote, "ere the ideas of chivalry were extinct amongst that nation of romantic Hidalgos, the turn of Don Quixote's frenzy seems not altogether extravagant, and the armour which he assumed was still the ordinary garb of battle."[23]

[19] William Hazlitt, *Complete Works,* ed. P. P. Howe (21 vols. London and Toronto, 1931), 16: 9.

[20] Reeve, *The Progress of Romance,* 1: 59, 101–3.

[21] [Kenelm Digby], *The Broad Stone of Honour: or, Rules for the Gentlemen of England* (2d ed. London, 1823), pp. 174–79.

[22] "The Example of Cervantes," *Contexts of Criticism* (Cambridge, Mass., 1957), pp. 79–96.

[23] *Miscellaneous Prose Works,* 3: 171.

Despite his sense of humor, irony seems foreign to Scott's mind. The mild irony with which Goldsmith infused *The Vicar of Wakefield* Scott read in an even softer light, discovering merely "a fireside picture of such a perfect kind, as perhaps is nowhere else equalled." The same taste for *Biedermeier*, as Mario Praz would call it, obscured from Scott the quixotry of the Vicar, whose "pedantry and literary vanity" simply "show that he is made of mortal mould, and subject to human failings."[24] Without question Goldsmith's novel has this *Biedermeier* quality; but even the most sentimental eighteenth-century novel generally owed a distant debt to Cervantes. Even in *The Man of Feeling* emotion is not easily distinguishable from the mockery of emotion—and Henry Mackenzie clearly borrowed more than sentiment from Sterne. Scott defended the manliness of Mackenzie's hero. He was eager, of course, to honor the reputation of this elder lawyer and writer who lived on in Scotland until 1831. "Sketched by a pencil less nicely discriminating, Harley, instead of a being whom we love, respect, sympathize with, and admire, had become the mere Quixote of sentiment, an object of pity, perhaps, but of ridicule at the same time."[25]

By the time *Waverley* was published criticism of fiction had gradually developed a distinction between novels and romances. Novels were characterized by a greater degree of realism than romances. Romances were characterized by a greater degree of invention. Projection was implicit in romance; novels were studied from real life. And romance, of course, was the older form. In his preface to the second edition of *The Castle of Otranto* (1765) Horace Walpole explained that his "Gothic Story" was "an attempt to blend the two kinds of romance: the ancient and the modern. In the former, all was imagination and improbability; in the latter, nature is always intended to be, and sometimes has been, copied with success."[26] Though *The Castle of Otranto* does not really answer to this description, the theoretical intention of combining the two forms was still important fifty years later.

In the preface to *The Progress of Romance* (1785) Clara Reeve promised "to mark the distinguishing characters of the Romance and the Novel"—a task that subsequently falls to Euphrasia on the seventh evening, when the discussion has proceeded as far as the modern novel:

> The word *Novel* in all languages signifies something new. It was first used to distinguish these works from Romance, though they have lately been

[24] Ibid., pp. 282–83.

[25] Ibid., pp. 346–47.

[26] *The Castle of Otranto*, in *Shorter Novels: Eighteenth Century*, ed. Philip Henderson (London, Everyman's Library, 1903), p. 102.

confounded together and are frequently mistaken for each other . . . The Romance is an heroic fable, which treats of fabulous persons and things. —The Novel is a picture of real life and manners, and of the times in which it is written. The Romance in lofty and elevated language, describes what never happened nor is likely to happen. —The Novel gives a familiar relation of such things, as pass every day before our eyes, such as may happen to our friend, or to ourselves; and the perfection of it, is to represent every scene, in so easy and natural a manner, and to make them appear so probable, as to deceive us into a persuasion (at least while we are reading) that all is real, until we are affected by the joys or distresses, of the persons in the story, as if they were our own.[27]

Scott drew roughly the same distinction between the novel and the romance in his "Essay on Romance" for the 1822 Supplement to the *Encyclopedia Britannica*. The romance is "a fictitious narrative in prose or verse; the interest of which turns upon marvelous and uncommon incidents." The novel is "a fictitious narrative, differing from the Romance, because the events are accommodated to the ordinary train of human events, and the modern state of society."[28] Neither word was used with any consistency in Scott's time. He generally referred to his own works as romances; but their collective title, of course, was "the Waverley Novels."

The realism accredited to the novel by Scott and Miss Reeve did not imply that the novel should indulge in a critique of reality. The purpose of increased realism, according to Miss Reeve, was to absorb the reader in the "joys and distresses" of the actors—to make romance more compelling. Scott's definition of the novel begins not with the critical representation of modern life but with the "accommodation" of romance to modern times and to a degree of probability. Elsewhere he refers to the novel as the "minor romance" and as "the legitimate child of romance."[29] These are distinctions of degree. Samuel Richardson, according to Scott, "threw aside the trappings of romance, with all its extravagance, and appealed to the genuine passions of the human heart." In his essay on Fielding he observed that "even Richardson's novels are but a step from the old romance, approaching, indeed, more nearly to the ordinary course of events, but still dealing in improbable incidents, and in characters swelled out beyond the ordinary limits of humanity."[30] The common assumption here is the gradual development of the novel out of romance—the

---

[27] *The Progress of Romance,* 1: 110–11.
[28] *Miscellaneous Prose Works,* 6: 156–57.
[29] Ibid., 3: 142; *Quarterly Review* 14 (1815): 189.
[30] *Miscellaneous Prose Works,* 3: 76, 117.

"progress" of romance. In the general preface to the Waverley Novels (1829) Scott explained that he had hoped, in creating *Waverley*, "that a romance founded upon a Highland story, and more modern events, would have a better chance of popularity than a tale of chivalry."[31] Thus the Waverley Novels themselves entered the tradition of modified romance, romance tempered by realism.

Another way of distinguishing between the romance and the novel was to say that the former stressed incident and the latter, character. In paraphrasing Horace Walpole's expressed intention for *The Castle of Otranto* Scott wrote simply that ancient romance was characterized by "the marvelous turn of incident," and the modern novel, by the "accurate display of human character, and contrast of feelings and passions."[32] In a prize essay of 1826 George Moberly, future headmaster of Winchester and Bishop of Salisbury, distinguished "fictions of incident" from "fictions of character" in such a way as to suggest that the two kinds of fiction were neither accidental nor historical, but scientific corollaries. Strong simple passions yield violent actions; subtle qualities of character are displayed by more minute actions. Romance is the earlier form because strong simple passions prevailed in earlier times. Moberly's essay closed with a promise that the union of the fictions of incident and of character would "raise fiction to the height of which it is capable."[33] Walpole's idea of a "blend" of the two kinds of fiction had become a prominent goal. In his general preface Scott professed to have emulated in *Waverley* the achievement of Maria Edgeworth: she was congratulated by the *Quarterly Review* in 1812 for successfully mediating between the extremes of novel and romance.[34]

Under the guise of "novel of incident" and "novel of character" the distinction between the romance and the novel has long been useful. Robert Louis Stevenson, who defended romance in theory and in practice, argued that it was "not character, but incident" with which a reader becomes emotionally embroiled.[35] Edwin Muir distinguished between novels of action and novels of character—and the highest form of fiction, the dramatic novel, combined features of these two forms. The plot of the novel of action "is in accordance with our wishes, not with our knowledge. . . . It is a fantasy of desire rather than a picture of life."[36] Both writers single out the affective quality of

---

[31] References to Scott's prefaces and introductions to the Waverley Novels are cited from the Centenary Edition (25 vols. Edinburgh, 1885–1887).

[32] *Miscellaneous Prose Works*, 3: 364.

[33] "Is a Rude or a Refined Age More Favourable to the Production of Works of Fiction?" *Oxford English Prize Essays* (5 vols. Oxford, 1830), 4: 131–54.

[34] [John Wilson Croker], *Quarterly Review* 7 (1812): 329–32.

[35] "A Gossip on Romance," *Longman's Magazine* 1 (1882): 77.

[36] *The Structure of the Novel* (London, 1949), pp. 19–23.

romance. The substance of romance corresponds to the internal world of its audience, not to the external world. Both Muir and Stevenson pointed to the Waverley Novels as illustrations of romance, or the novel of action.

In several contexts Scott contrasted the mischance and unmanageability of life with the studied pattern and enclosure of events in fiction. He was twice brought to this reflection in apology for what he regarded as the ungovernable course of his own plots. He censured *The Monastery* on the ground that the incidents of romance should always arise "out of the story itself."[37] The incidents of real life are linear or haphazard. "It is seldom that the same circle of personalities who have surrounded an individual in his first outset in life, continue to have an interest in his career till his fate comes to a crisis." One kind of fiction, the picaresque, emulates this natural order of events: examples of such works are *Gil Blas* and *Roderick Random*.

> But though such an unconnected course of adventure is what most frequently occurs in nature, yet the province of the romance-writer being artificial, there is more required of him than a mere compliance with the simplicity of reality,—just as we demand from the scientific gardener, that he shall arrange, in curious knots and artificial parterres, the flowers which "nature boon" distributes freely on hill and dale.

Tom Jones illustrates this more special art. Scott returned to the subject in the introduction to *The Abbot* and suggested that the arbitrary sequence of events in real life might excuse the "unintelligibility" of his narrative.

Scott's contemporaries shared this perception of the difference between art and life. His garden figure recalls John Dunlop's interpretation of fiction as a species of plant freed and separated from less attractive or satisfying varieties of life. Mrs. Barbauld contrasted the unfinished, ever continuing "chance-medley" of life with the completed, enclosed, and deliberate unity of fiction, where events always achieve some appropriate denouement.[38] Richard Whately remarked the same inherent conflict of imitation and harmony and declared that the two interests were reconciled by the art of Jane Austen.[39] Whately was actually repeating an argument of Scott's review of Jane Austen in 1815:

> Although it may be urged that the vicissitudes of human life have occasionally led an individual through as many scenes of singular fortune as are represented in the most extravagant of these fictions, still the causes

---

[37] Introduction to *The Monastery*.
[38] Barbauld, *The British Novelists*, 1: 55.
[39] *Quarterly Review* 24 (1822): 360.

and personages acting on these changes have varied with the progress of the adventurer's fortune, and do not present the combined plot, (the object of every skilful novelist,) in which all the more interesting individuals of the dramatis personae have their appropriate share in the action and in bringing about the catastrophe. Here, even more than in its various and violent changes of fortune, rests the improbability of the novel.[40]

The "improbability of the novel"—of any novel—reflects simply a difference in the quality of experience in fact and in fiction. No fiction corresponds exactly to fact because fiction organizes events into an enclosed pattern. Fictions are significant variants from life. Obviously something causes a fiction to be so organized: the organizing principle is projective—an emotion or an ideal that distorts reality to its own satisfaction. The revival of romance, and the rough differentiation between the romance and the novel, enabled writers in this period to recognize these truths, which had gone virtually unrecognized during the eighteenth century.

3. Moral Truth

Notwithstanding these advances in the theory of fiction, the novel was in low repute when Scott anonymously tested the market for prose fiction in 1814. For those who valued the material progress of the age, truth and useful knowledge put fiction to scorn. The notion of a significant kind of falsehood was somewhat too paradoxical for a people with a high moral reverence for truth. Fictions were dishonest, as it were. Not theory, certainly, but only the Waverley Novels themselves could bring about the compromise between truth and fiction that was evident by 1832, when the *Edinburgh Review* eulogized Scott for raising the novel to "a place among the highest productions of human intellect."[41]

In the preface to *The Journal of a Voyage to Lisbon* Henry Fielding confessed that he "should have honoured and loved Homer more had he written a true history of his own times in humble prose."[42] The *Quarterly Review* greeted *Waverley* in almost the same spirit in 1814. "We cannot but wish," wrote Croker, that the author of *Waverley* had written a history instead of a fiction—"had rather employed him-

---

[40] Ibid., 14 (1815): 190–91.

[41] *Edinburgh Review* 55 (1832): 64.

[42] *Journal of a Voyage to Lisbon*, in *Works*, ed. William Ernest Henley (16 vols. London, 1903), 16: 182.

self in recording *historically* the character and transactions of his coun-
trymen."[43] It must be said that Scott himself took a similar view. He
worried less than some of his contemporaries about the possible ill effects of the novel. Novels were chiefly for entertainment. But in his
essay on Fielding, Scott, too, observed that the habit of reading fiction was "apt to generate an indisposition to real history, and useful
literature."[44] James Beattie, the author of *The Minstrel* (1771), had concluded his essay on romance with almost the same words.[45] It was necessary at this time to acknowledge the superior importance of truth
and serious works of knowledge. The authors of imaginative literature
in particular were anxious to assure the public that they did not believe in their own fictions. The first words of Beattie's essay "On Fable
and Romance" were incongruous with the title: "The love of truth is
natural to man; and adherence to it, his indispensable duty."[46]

The word *vraisemblance*, borrowed from French criticism, seemed
to bridge the gap between fact and fiction. A compounded word
suited perfectly an age so rashly devoted to both history and fable.
"That 'le vrai n'est pas toujours vraisemblable,' we do not deny,"
wrote Croker in 1812, "but we are prepared to insist that, while the
'*vrai*' is the highest recommendation of the historian of real life, the
'*vraisemblable*' is the only legitimate province of the novelist who aims
at improving the understanding or touching the heart."[47] Madame de
Staël was probably responsible for the use of the word in British criticism. In 1795 she had defined the modern novel as that fiction
"where everything is at the same time invented and imitated, where
nothing is true, but where everything is *vraisemblable*."[48] The word
fiction ordinarily embraces the same paradox, but *vraisemblance* did
not convey such an explicit suggestion of falsehood. Yet it was argued, on behalf of truth, that *vraisemblance* might be a dangerous
thing. Richard Whately declared that "what are strictly called novels,"
because of their plausibility, are more likely to give a false picture of
life than romances.[49]

The devotion to truth was thought to be a peculiarly modern virtue. Not only were Britons devoted to truth: they imagined that they
were becoming more and more so. By the end of the eighteenth
century the nation was confident that material progress and enlight-

[43] *Quarterly Review* 11 (1814): 377.
[44] *Miscellaneous Prose Works*, 3: 121–22.
[45] "On Fable and Romance," *Dissertations Moral and Critical* (London, 1783), p. 574.
[46] Ibid., p. 505.
[47] *Quarterly Review* 7 (1812): 329.
[48] "Essai sur les fictions," *Œuvres*, 2: 182.
[49] *Quarterly Review* 24 (1822): 353–54.

enment were native British qualities. A social historian has recently characterized the period, on its own terms, as "the Age of Improvement."[50] The politeness and understanding of the age became the implied premise of most literary criticism. Expansive pride in the useful arts pretended to take satisfaction in "the decline of the imagination." When Macaulay made his debut in the *Edinburgh Review* in 1825, he gravely complimented Milton for writing a great poem in spite of his intelligence and education. As civilization progresses, knowledge eclipses the imagination: "We cannot unite the incompatible advantages of reality and deception, the clear discernment of truth and the exquisite enjoyment of fiction."[51] Macaulay denies neither the utility nor the pleasures of deception: we simply can no longer be deceived.

Bishop Hurd, a spirit friendly to romance, posed the conflict of civilization and fiction as the closing note of his *Letters on Chivalry and Romance* in 1762: "What we have gotten by this revolution, you will say, is a great deal of good sense. What we have lost is a world of fine fabling."[52] By the end of the century social refinements seemed to have brought about even nicer changes of fashion in works of fiction. The novel of manners was felt to be the special product of an actual improvement in manners. Striking a characteristic note of the *Quarterly Review*, Scott observed that "social life, in our civilized days, affords few instances capable of being painted in the strong dark colours which excite surprize and terror."[53] Moberly attributed the succession of the fiction of character to the fiction of incident to "the gradually diminishing influence of the imagination." The development of "law and its attendant institutions," in particular, had crippled the life of romance.[54] Nassau Senior objected to *The Bride of Lammermoor* on related grounds: "Ghosts have no business to appear to mortgagers and mortgagees."[55]

The practical solution to the dilemma of fiction was the historical romance. In the full range of history passion and incident were often free of civilized restraint. Scott dismissed pastoral romance as an absurdity in any age; but chivalric romance had once corresponded with the real thing: "If *Amadis de Gaule* was a fiction, the chevalier Bayard

[50] Asa Briggs, *The Age of Improvement* (London, 1959).

[51] [Thomas Babington Macaulay], *Edinburgh Review* 42 (1825): 309.

[52] *Letters on Chivalry and Romance*, in *The Works of Richard Hurd* (8 vols. London, 1811), 4: 350.

[53] *Quarterly Review* 14 (1815): 192.

[54] George Moberly, "Is a Rude or a Refined Age More Favourable to . . . Fiction?" *Oxford English Prize Essays*, 4: 133, 141.

[55] *Quarterly Review* 26 (1822): 123.

was a real person."[56] All of the passions and prejudices of an earlier age, and events that were then believed supernatural, might form the truthful subject matter of historical romance. History extended the limits of plausible subject matter. "Romantic narrative is of two kinds,—that which, being in itself possible, may be matter of belief at any period; and that which, though held impossible by more enlightened ages, was yet consonant with the faith of earlier times."[57]

As a man of his times Scott was more literal-minded and conservative than one imagines him to be. Though he once commented at length on his lifelong propensity for daydreaming and "castle-building," he disavowed the effect of such dreaming on his "actual life."[58] Scott's rationalization of Don Quixote's armor illustrates his critical impulse to refer all incident that fails the test of common sense to some idiosyncrasy of time or of place. When something in fiction seemed to him unreal, he willingly cast about for an explanation. The one-sided relationship of Strap to Roderick Random, for example, could be rationalized by recollecting "in Scotland, at that period, the absolute devotion of a follower to his master."[59] And "in England, where men think and act with little regard to ridicule or censure of their neighbours," Uncle Toby's battleworks were perhaps quite plausible.[60] When his own romances were criticized, Scott was little interested in defending himself except against charges of inaccuracy in matters of Scottish history or character.[61]

One of Scott's favorite sayings, usually offered as an excuse for poor plotting, he borrowed from Bayes in *The Rehearsal*: "What the devil does the plot signify, except to bring in fine things?"[62] The conflicting prestige of useful knowledge and of romance in this period readily invited a loose division of form and content in the novel. Interesting history could be attached to a romantic tale. Some such division of form and content is always implicit in the historical novel. Most critics of the Waverley Novels have followed Scott and do not examine what the plot signifies. But Scott's attitude toward his own achievement is sometimes too cavalier. He carefully forestalls the so-

---

[56] *Miscellaneous Prose Works*, 6: 253.

[57] Ibid., 3: 376.

[58] *The Journal of Sir Walter Scott*, ed. J. G. Tait and W. M. Parker (Edinburgh, 1950), entry for Dec. 27, 1825.

[59] *Miscellaneous Prose Works*, 3: 194.

[60] Ibid., pp. 330–31.

[61] Cf. James T. Hillhouse, *The Waverley Novels and Their Critics* (Minneapolis, 1936), p. 27.

[62] Introductory Epistle, *The Fortunes of Nigel*; cf. *Quarterly Review* 16 (1817): 431; *Journal*, Oct. 16 and 17, 1826; *Miscellaneous Prose Works*, 4: 58.

phisticated conclusion that the author might believe that dreams come true. The numerous editors and narrators, the laborious introductions stationed between the author and the reader, the very anonymity of the Author of *Waverley* are in part related to this elaborate disavowal of imagination. Coleridge lost patience with it, and wrote the following comment in his copy of *The Pirate*:

> Sir Walter relates ghost stories, prophecies, presentiments, all praeter-supernaturally fulfilled; but is most anxious to let his readers know, that he himself is far too enlightened not to be assured of the folly and falsehood of all he yet relates as *truth*, and for the purpose of exciting the interest and the emotions attached to the belief of their truth—and all this, not with the free life and most happy judgment of Ariosto, as a neutral tint or shooting light, but soberly, to save his own (Sir Walter's) character as an enlightened man.[63]

In the end the novel complied with the scorn for deception by presuming to convey only moral truth, and a certain number of extrinsic materials—manners, history, and landscape—that might be as true as one pleased. Bulwer-Lytton once pronounced this general directive for writers of fiction: "There is no great poetic artist, whether in Epic, Drama, or Romance, who, in his best works, ever presents a literal truth rather than the idealized image of a truth."[64] This rule answered both the awareness that fiction is not fact and the conviction that it is a significant projection of an idea. Those who are committed to literal truth, furthermore, are possibly the most fit persons to communicate a just and restrained ideal of truth. The selection of an idealized image of truth entails an even greater responsibility than the devotion to literal truth. Public idealizing requires a very sane man— and such a man was Sir Walter Scott. The greatness of the Waverley Novels for Bulwer-Lytton was their "moral beauty."[65]

The idealized image of truth in the Waverley Novels was fundamentally uncritical. Scott undertook his romance with no satirical or ironic intent. Nor did he strive to render an image of truth that would transform his society in any way. He shaped into romance certain public images of truth of his day. To admirers of the Waverley Novels Carlyle's famous review of Lockhart's *Life* is still an object of bitter controversy. But Carlyle had this to say:

[63] *Coleridge's Miscellaneous Criticism*, ed. Thomas Middleton Raysor (London, 1936), p. 332.

[64] "On Certain Principles of Art in Works of Imagination," *Miscellaneous Prose Works* (3 vols. London, 1868), 3: 375.

[65] Cf. *Pelham* (Boston, 1891), Ch. 52.

Somewhat too little of a fantast, this *Vates* of ours! But so it was: in this nineteenth century, our highest literary man, who immeasurably beyond all others commanded the world's ear, had, as it were, no message whatever to deliver to the world; wished not the world to elevate itself, to do this or that, except simply pay him for the books he kept writing. Very remarkable; fittest, perhaps, for an age fallen languid, destitute of faith and terrified at scepticism? Or, perhaps, for another sort of age, an age all in peaceable triumphant motion?[66]

Though Scott was a "medievalist," he frequently criticized the chivalric age. He was fond of pointing out not only that medieval apartments were cold but that medieval behavior was in some respects too warm: "The valour of the hero was often stained by acts of cruelty, or freaks of rash desperation; his courtesy and munificence became solemn foppery and wild profusion; his love to his lady often demanded and received a requital inconsistent with the honour of the object."[67] This appraisal was profoundly directed not against the immorality of a rude age but against acts of "rash desperation" and sentiments of "wild profusion" in any age. The present age vaunted its faith in prudent action and restrained thoughts. Prudery in the narrower sense, increased refinement and delicacy, the insistence that "the forms must be veiled and clothed with drapery," were small but significant improvements over the past: Scott speculated that such factors might be responsible for the high incidence of female novelists in recent times.[68] As applied to morals in this period, the word "masculine" underwent an inversion of meaning so pronounced that Scott could wish that *Gil Blas* "might perhaps have been improved by some touches of a more masculine, stronger, and firmer line of morality."[69] Masculinity meant self-control under the most trying circumstances.

The antithesis of rash desperation is prudence. Scott held that "the direct and obvious moral to be deduced from a fictitious narrative, is of much less consequence to the public, than the mode in which the story is treated in the course of its details."[70] Prudence governs the mode in which the Waverley Novels were designed. In practice it was a curious mode, because the hero's action was confined to an ideal

[66] Thomas Carlyle, "Sir Walter Scott," *Critical and Miscellaneous Essays* (5 vols. New York, 1901), 4: 54–55.

[67] *Miscellaneous Prose Works*, 6: 204. For the discomfort of medieval apartments see *Ivanhoe*, Ch. 6.

[68] Ibid., 4: 62–63.

[69] Ibid., 3: 496.

[70] Ibid., p. 41.

that all but prohibited activity. Moberly observed this difficulty to be one of the problems of fiction in a refined age:

> While the indulgence of the passions was unrestricted by legislative en-actments or the influence of public opinion, there was necessarily the greatest facility for the commission of every description of violence. Nor can anything be better adapted for fiction, than the splendid crimes which frequently raised the heroes of antiquity to the rank of demigods. This kind of ignorance offers likewise great room for the display of ex-traordinary virtue. The virtues of modern ages are for the most part of a quiet and retiring character.[71]

Present-day achievements contrast favorably with the ignorance of rude ages; but the rule of law and of public opinion depends upon a single necessary virtue: loyalty to one's own orderly society. The hero of civilization and refinement is a passive hero of "quiet and retiring" character.

The prudence celebrated by the Waverley Novels would not be "cal-culating prudence." Scott cautioned against calculating prudence at the end of his review of *Emma*. The heritage of *Pamela* was such that impulse and generous feeling seemed in danger of being ruled out of fiction altogether.[72] Scott's romances veered well away from this dan-ger but thereby incurred a further risk. Expelling calculation from prudence destroyed its one attribute as an active virtue. A prudent hero who cannot be deliberately prudent can have no active role. He can do no deeds of violence; nor can he survive by cunning. He is wholly at the mercy of the forces that surround him, and thus acted upon rather than acting.

The period of romantic literature in England coincided with an era of national conservatism and moral righteousness. The standard and estimate of progress was high among all who had voice to express it; and the rational virtues of good sense and self-restraint were exalted by reformers as well as by the ruling class. Something called "public opinion"—a political fiction—began to assume the sacrosanct posi-tion that it enjoys in our own day. If novels such as those of the days of Charles II and Louis XIV were to reappear, Miss Owenson ven-tured to say, "they would be hunted down by the common consent of society."[73] Official prudery was second only to willing patriotism, and patriotism pressed directly on literary judgment as well as indirectly on practice. When Scott reviewed *Gertrude of Wyoming* for the new-

---

[71] Moberly, in *Oxford English Prize Essays*, 4: 142.

[72] Cf. *Quarterly Review* 14 (1815): 200–201.

[73] Sydney Owenson, *New Monthly Magazine and Universal Register* 14, Pt. II (1820): 28.

born *Quarterly* in 1809, he hoped that henceforth Thomas Campbell would find a subject more creditable to his nation. "The historian must do his duty when such painful subjects occur; but the poet who may chuse his theme through the whole unbounded range of truth and fiction may well excuse himself from selecting a subject dishonourable to his native land."[74]

The war with revolutionary France and with Napoleon had more to do with the nature of fiction in this period than is implied by the small part it plays in the novels of Jane Austen or of Scott. War inflated the moral currency as well as the price of corn. Anti-Jacobinism and national feeling overrode not only political opposition in Britain but searching criticism of most kinds. The felt triumph of stability and status obscured the rapid and far-reaching social and industrial changes that were taking place beneath the surface of the victory. Never was there a war more readily construed as a struggle for peace against violence and change. The victory symbolized the triumph of a universal and political reality-principle over ambition and passion on the Continent. According to the *Morning Chronicle* of February 2, 1815, "It is to the cultivation of the moral qualities that England is indebted for her power and influence. For the want of them France may be mischievous, but she will never be great."[75]

Like every other public statement, the Waverley Novels were affected by this spirit. In France the novel could hardly escape the impact of the bewildering successions of national fortune. The reality that Stendhal encountered, writes Erich Auerbach, "was so constituted that, without permanent reference to the immense changes of the immediate past and without a premonitory searching after the imminent changes of the future, one could not represent it; all the human figures and all the human events in his work appear upon a ground politically and socially disturbed."[76] But in England the novel figured forth a vision of permanence and perpetuity, consigning the kinetic energies of life to a series of romantic episodes.

Past Stendhal's hero the action at Waterloo sweeps in total confusion, a turmoil of impression and fragmented reality. As if he were a typical hero of Scott, Fabrice del Dongo is supported in this scene by a selfless and knowledgeable guide, the old *cantinière*, and eventually finds himself in trouble simply for having been present at the battle. But Stendhal thrusts his hero into a world of flux that does not prom-

---

[74] *Quarterly Review* 1 (1809): 243.

[75] Quoted by Elie Halévy, *England in 1815*, trans. E. I. Watkin and D. A. Barker (London, 1949), p. 451.

[76] *Mimesis*, trans. Willard Trask (Princeton, 1953), p. 463.

ise to right itself. In the Waverley Novels violence and change are confined to a world separate from that of the hero. The public event never threatens, as it does in Stendhal, to expand and diminish without end, nor to overwhelm the account of itself by its enigmatic proportions. Henri Beyle actually took part in the Napoleonic campaigns; Scott was lame from childhood. The war was waged on the Continent, and the British force was an expeditionary force.

The exact personal or public significance of Waterloo, or even whether he had really been there, was never quite clear to Fabrice. When the news of Waterloo reached Scott, he experienced "the extreme desire to hear a British drum beat in the streets of Paris," and he hurried to the scene. He arrived at Waterloo in time to secure a few relics of battle too worthless to have been carried off by the scavengers who followed the army.[77] The implications of the event for literature were mischievously pointed by Stendhal, who instructed Fabrice, after his escapade, not to be seen reading anything published after 1720—"with the possible exception of the novels of Walter Scott."[78] In 1815, of course, Fabrice could hardly have known that *Waverley* and *Guy Mannering* were written by Walter Scott.

[77] *The Letters of Sir Walter Scott*, ed. H.J.C. Grierson (12 vols. London, 1932–1937), 4: 76, 79.

[78] Stendhal [Henri Beyle], *La Chartreuse de Parme* (2 vols. Paris, 1933), Ch. 5.

II

THE PASSIVE HERO

> One of the first motives to civil society, and which becomes
> one of its fundamental rules, is, *that no man should be judge
> in his own cause.* By this each person has at once divested
> himself of the first fundamental right of uncovenanted
> man, that is, to judge for himself, and to assert his own
> cause. He abdicates all right to be his own governor. He in-
> clusively, in a great measure, abandons the right of self-de-
> fence, the first law of Nature.
>
> —Burke, *Reflections on the Revolution in France*

> "Then, in the name of Heaven, Mr. Francis Osbaldistone,
> what *can* you do?"
> "Very little to the purpose, Miss Vernon."
>
> —*Rob Roy*

4. Two Soliloquies

A SOLILOQUY from *The Fortunes of Nigel* supplies the best introduction to the hero of the Waverley Novels. This romance is
set in the London of James I and is imbued with the spirit of
the public stage of that era: in the antics of his apprentices and in the
spirited behavior of his middle-class heroine Scott gives free play to
his fondness for the drama. Before introducing the reflections of his
hero, imprisoned in Whitefriars, he therefore digresses on the nature
of soliloquy. Though the device is more essential to drama than to
narrative, Scott argues, the soliloquy still offers "a more concise and
spirited mode" of conveying the thoughts of the hero (Ch. 22).[1] Scott
frequently resorts to this dramatic convention in his prose romance—
one habit that undoubtedly estranges modern readers of the Waverley Novels. The device, in fact, represents more than a technical convenience. Soliloquies are appropriate to the Scott hero because he
is always more eloquent in resolution than in action. The players in
Wilhelm Meister's Apprenticeship agreed that *Hamlet*, of all plays, was in

---

[1] References to the Waverley Novels are cited by chapter from the Centenary Edition (25 vols. Edinburgh, 1885–87). See above, Bibliographical Note, p. ix.

this respect closest to a novel, the species of fiction in which the hero "must be suffering."[2]

In a fit of angry discovery Nigel draws his sword, in the king's park, against the villainous Lord Dalgarno. He flees to Whitefriars for sanctuary. Having arrived in the dreary house of old Trapbois, he is unable to find a servant to lay his fire or to help him dress. Mistress Martha Trapbois informs him that she has no servant and advises Nigel to be more independent. "Unable as yet to reconcile himself to the thoughts of becoming his own fire-maker," the hero paces to and fro while composing the following "reflections and resolutions." Here is the soliloquy:

> She is right, and has taught me a lesson I will profit by. I have been, through my whole life, one who leant upon others for that assistance which it is more truly noble to derive from my own exertions. I am ashamed of feeling the paltry inconvenience which long habit has led me to annex to the want of a servant's assistance—I am ashamed of that; but far, far more, am I ashamed to have suffered the same habit of throwing my burden on others, to render me, since I came to this city, a mere victim of those events, which I have never even attempted to influence—a thing never acting but perpetually acted upon—protected by one friend, deceived by another; but in the advantage which I have received from the one, and the evil I have sustained from the other, as passive and helpless as a boat that drifts without oar or rudder at the mercy of the winds and waves. I became a courtier because Heriot so advised it—a gamester because Dalgarno so contrived it—an Alsatian because Lowestoffe so willed it. Whatever of good or bad has befallen me, hath arisen out of the agency of others, not from my own. My father's son must no longer hold this facile and puerile course. Live or die, sink or swim, Nigel Olifaunt, from this moment, shall owe his safety, success, and honour, to his own exertions, or shall fall with the credit of having at least exerted his own free agency. I will write it down in my tablets, in her very words,—"The wise man is his own best assistant." [Ch. 22]

Nigel is actually one of the most complex of Scott heroes. His rigid moral resistance and puritanic fear of gambling are transformed, with psychological justice, into a niggling and cautious consent to play—by which he calculates always to win, and never risks even odds. Scott stands sufficiently outside his hero to make the sequence interesting. But when Nigel moves, in this soliloquy, from self-chastisement of his immediate folly to a sweeping condemnation of his total situation, he

---

[2] Johann Wolfgang von Goethe, *Wilhelm Meister's Apprenticeship and Travels*, trans. Thomas Carlyle (London, 1899), Bk. V, ch. 7.

speaks generically for all the heroes of the Waverley Novels. Suddenly Nigel indicts not so much his own character as the entire fiction within which he finds himself. As we shall see, Scott himself reproached the inactivity of his heroes. Nigel's recriminations—"a victim of events" "passive and helpless"—define the customary stance of the Scott hero; his circumstances and "the agency of others" are the stuff of the Scott romance.

The soliloquy suggests certain details of Nigel's predicament. As the title of the romance implies, his fortunes are in the balance. In the appropriate language of ups and downs, therefore, he speaks of what has "befallen" and how it has "arisen"; and again, that he shall rise or "fall." More precisely, since "safety" and "honour" flank "success," he shall either recover his just deserts or be cheated of them. He is not altogether hopeful and speaks twice in the language of drowning. He asserts his identity by addressing himself in the third person, but reinforces the obligation of his new resolutions by naming himself also "my father's son." He commits himself ultimately to an abstraction—"his own free agency." He fears he is not only a victim of events but in the hands of good and bad agents, who both protect and deceive him.

The previous events of the story justify Nigel's assault on his own dependence. More embarrassed than hungry in his destitution, Nigel fears to petition the king in person for the payments owed to his deceased father. George Heriot, the goldsmith whose kindness is entirely unmotivated by personal gain, seeks out the hero in his hiding place in London; and it is clear that Heriot is better acquainted with Nigel's state of affairs than is the hero himself (Ch. 4). When the goldsmith has advanced him one hundred pounds, unasked, and tidied him up for presentation at court, the door to the presence chamber is barred by the deputy chamberlain—one of those instinctive enemies who invariably discountenance the merits of heroes. The way is opened by the Earl of Huntinglen, who recognizes Nigel by his resemblance to his father; and the Earl generously exchanges his annual royal boon for Nigel's favor with the king (Ch. 9). Just as Master Heriot knows more of Nigel's business than the hero himself, so Margaret Ramsay has mysterious intelligence of the plots against him. She enumerates the motives of his enemies as "avarice" and "vindictive ambition," but inspired by an "absolute and concentrated spirit of malice"—the last suggesting that the hero's enemies are as unselfishly motivated as his friends (Ch. 19). As soon as Nigel becomes aware of Dalgarno's duplicity, an "impatient passion" involves him in the abortive duel in St. James's Park; but he stands there in risk of having his hand chopped off by the Star Chamber until "a decent-looking elderly man" urges him to run off. Luckily, he runs into a casual acquaintance, Lowestoffe, who knowledgeably arranges his admission to Whitefriars (Ch. 16). There we have discovered him, "never acting but perpetually acted upon."

The excellent resolutions represented by the soliloquy do not alter the tendency of these adventures in the least. By the end of the same chapter Nigel's decision to become an active hero takes a strange turn: he decides to surrender himself. He learns that Lowestoffe has been arrested for his timely assistance, and is thus confirmed in his purpose. However, "he had, even before hearing of a reason which so peremptorily demanded that he should surrender himself, adopted the resolution to do so, as the manliest and most proper course which his ill-fortune and imprudence had left in his own power" (Ch. 22). When forced to translate his vow of independence into a specific act, Nigel can think only of giving himself up. He is guided by what is "manliest and most proper"—considerations that dictate his passive role. On the face of it his decision makes it more likely that he will die than live, sink than swim. Ordinarily when a character exclaims that he shall "live or die, sink or swim," he expresses an overpowering determination to live. The hero of Scott expresses by these terms a stubborn allegiance to his society.

The hero of the Waverley Novels is seldom a leader of men. He is always a potential leader, because of his rank as a gentleman. He represents, however, a social ideal, and acts or refrains from acting according to the accepted morality of his public. Law and authority are the sine qua non of his being. Nigel is emotionally justified in drawing his sword in the park, but by doing so he has broken the law. Because he represents the individual acceptance of law and authority, he can only surrender himself. The hero of the Waverley Novels stands at the beginning of a tradition of which Sean O'Faolain celebrates the close in a book called *The Vanishing Hero*. Instead of a commander, this hero is an ideal *member* of society. By Mr. O'Faolain's account, the hero vanishes when society no longer defines him: "the Hero is a purely social creation. He represents, that is to say, a socially approved norm, for representing which to the satisfaction of society he is decorated with a title."[3] On the other hand, Mario Praz' study of Victorian fiction, commencing with Scott, is entitled *The Hero in Eclipse*.[4] We are always in danger of a confusion of terms: it goes without saying that Mr. Praz' title refers to another person altogether, the romantic hero who is pitted *against* society. Such romantic charac-

---

[3] *The Vanishing Hero* (London, 1956), p. 14.
[4] *The Hero in Eclipse in Victorian Fiction*, trans. Angus Davidson (London, 1956).

ters figure large in the Waverley Novels, but the proper hero of Scott implicitly accepts his society. His nearly complete passivity is a function of his morality—the public and accepted morality of rational self-restraint.

Self-imposed respect for law and authority only partly explains the passive hero, however. His characteristic responses are more (or less) than moral. They have an interesting emotional content. This content may be demonstrated by an Alpine adventure in *Anne of Geierstein* (Ch. 2), an adventure that exaggerates the propensities of a typical hero by exposing him to very untypical surroundings.

The verse tags to the first two chapters of *Anne of Geierstein* are from *Manfred*, but the hero is not affected by the manners of his chief literary rival. Arthur Philipson and his father—the Earl of Oxford in disguise—have been led up a wrong and precarious path in the mountains. A storm is brewing, and the path suddenly disappears into a rock slide. Arthur proposes to make his way across the slide in order to seek help from a habitation that can be seen in the distance. The hero undertakes this dangerous effort in a significant fashion. He *reasons* his way past the abyss, by "estimating the extent of his danger by the measure of sound sense and reality." The reader overhears his thoughts:

> "This ledge of rock," he urged to himself, "is but narrow, yet it has breadth enough to support me; these cliffs and crevices in the surface are small and distant, but the one affords as secure a resting place for my feet, the other as available a grasp to my hands, as if I stood on a platform of a cubit broad, and rested my arm on a balustrade of marble. My safety, therefore, depends on myself. If I move with decision, step firmly, and hold fast, what signifies how near I am to the mouth of an abyss?" [Ch. 2]

The moral expressed in this soliloquy is also general. As with most accounts of mountain climbing, the exercise is supposed to be symbolic. Unlike most climbers, Arthur does not pretend to enjoy the sport.

When Arthur has almost reached safety on the far side of the slide, a huge rock teeters under the climber's weight and smashes into the valley below—leaving the hero clinging to a tree. He is overcome by an attack of vertigo. The peril of his situation, and his consequent trembling fits, are spun out at great length in the narrative. Scott casts in peculiar language Arthur's determination to hang on: "nothing, save the consciousness that such an idea was the suggestion of partial insanity, prevented him from throwing himself from the tree, as if to join the wild dance to which his disturbed brain had given motion." At this point a Swiss maiden appears out of the mist. She walks so close to the precipice that Arthur sinks back into his tree with a groan. It is Anne of Geierstein, and she points out to the hero that solid ground lies but one bold step from his perch. Arthur is ashamed of himself, and prepares to take the leap, but is again overcome by fear. In order "to restore his confidence," Anne herself hops lightly from rock to tree and back again. She stretches out her hand to Arthur: "'My arm,' she said, 'is but a slight balustrade; yet do but step forward with resolution, and you will find it as secure as the battlement of Berne.'" Arthur has set out by imagining "a balustrade of marble" for his support; here he is offered one of real substance. He is sufficiently embarrassed—"shame now overcame terror so much"— that he leaps to safety without further assistance. In the following chapter the native Swiss chide the hero about this incident several times, though the writer continues to characterize him, without irony, as "young and daring."

Scott draws out this scene so as to leave no doubt of his hero's terror and its embarrassing associations. He stresses the hero's qualms much more than his prowess. The cause of "sound sense and reality" would seem better served if Arthur kept his head when the rock bounds into the abyss—or if he rescued Anne instead of the other way around. In *Anne of Geierstein* she comes to *his* rescue three times. Prudential morality might account for the fact that the hero can seldom be a savior, but it does not account for the mixed pleasure of being saved. The episode in *Anne of Geierstein* indicates that the passive hero only partially admits of a rational explanation. Romance, of course, is not a rational exercise. Nigel Olifaunt's decision to surrender cannot adequately be explained in moral terms; and Arthur Philipson's terror and embarrassment have reverberations throughout the Waverley Novels. Ultimately I shall argue that a relation obtains between the moral scruples of the Scott hero and his demonstrable anxieties.

5. Possible Exceptions

We have a full account of the origin of the name *Waverley*. Scott explained that he skirted both chivalrous names like "Howard, Mordaunt, Mortimer, or Stanley," and sentimental names like "Belmour, Belville, Belfield, and Belgrave," in favor of a name without associations. "I have, therefore, like a maiden knight with his white shield, assumed for my hero, WAVERLEY, an uncontaminated name, bearing with its sound little of good or evil, excepting what the reader shall hereafter be pleased to affix to it" (Ch. 1). A similar account of the choice of *Ivanhoe* was given in the 1830 introduction to that romance. But who is not tempted to detect a subconscious premonition of Waverley's career in his very name? The word *waver* emerges in one very typical situation:

> The question indeed occurred, whither he was to direct his course when again at his own disposal. Two schemes seemed practicable, yet both attended with danger and difficulty . . . to go back to Glennaquoich, and join Fergus Mac-Ivor . . . [or] to take shipping for England. His mind wavered between these plans; and probably, if he had effected his escape in the manner he proposed, he would have been finally determined by the comparative facility by which either might have been executed. But his fortune had settled that he was not to be left to his option. [Ch. 37]

The condition contrary to fact—"if he had effected his escape in the manner he proposed"—is an amusing commentary on the passive hero, who never engineers his own escape. Waverley actually has no escape plan, "the manner he proposed" having no antecedent in the text except as given above. Walter Bagehot found all Scott's heroes commonplace with the possible exception of Waverley, "whose very vacillation gives him a sort of character."[5] While acknowledging the uniformity of the heroes, the *Edinburgh Review* in 1832 applied the same word in a different judgment: "A strong fraternal likeness to the vacillating Waverley does not raise them in our esteem."[6] The likeness holds throughout the long series of novels to which Waverley gave his name—unless one excepts, in the very last of the series, *Castle Dangerous*, an older hero, "Walton the Unwavering" (Ch. 13).

The distinctive inactivity of the passive hero may be appreciated simply by contrasting him with the popular hero who succors the unfortunate, who makes his own fortune and wins the girl he loves, or who changes the course of history. That kind of heroism occurs to Scott himself, for example, as he sets forth the predicament of Adam Hartley in *The Surgeon's Daughter*. Though the hero would willingly devote his entire life to Menie Gray, he can only lament his helplessness to save her:

> The consciousness of being in her vicinity added to the bitter pangs with which Hartley contemplated her situation, and reflected how little chance there appeared of his being able to rescue her from it by the

---

[5] "The Waverley Novels," *Literary Studies* (2 vols. London, Everyman's Library, n.d.), 2: 158.

[6] *Edinburgh Review* 55 (1832): 69.

mere force of reason and justice, which was all he could oppose to the selfish passions of a voluptuous tyrant. A lover of romance might have meditated some means of effecting her release by force or address; but Hartley, though a man of courage, had no spirit of adventure, and would have regarded as desperate any attempt of the kind. [Ch. 14]

The hero eschews the use of "address" as well as the use of force; he must depend wholly upon reason and justice. The opposite course of action he would characterize as romantic and desperate. Yet reason and justice are here inadequate. The rescue is finally accomplished from outside by the native wisdom and absolute power of Hyder Ali Khan Behauder and the help of a ceremonial elephant to crush the life out of the villain.

The hero can best be defined by the words of Nigel Olifaunt—"a thing never acting but perpetually acted upon." But he is nevertheless the protagonist. He stands at the center of the struggle. He may not move, but his chances, his fortunes, are at stake. He is a victim, at the mercy of good and bad agents alike. He never aspires to property, nor actively courts the heroine. But he does not remain a victim, and he receives the heroine and the property in the end. The adventures of Nigel, outlined above, may be taken as typical. Instead of tediously tracing the inactivity of such heroes, however, it is easier to allow the exceptions to prove the rule. Even those protagonists of Scott whom one remembers as particularly bold and independent actors prove, on closer examination, to be cast in a passive role. Quentin Durward, for example, comes immediately to mind. The *Quarterly Review* considered him "not so passive as Waverley and Redgauntlet."[7]

At the outset of *Quentin Durward* the hero, in a compassionate gesture, cuts down a corpse hung up by the king's provost, and he is forthwith attacked by friends of the deceased and by the executioners in rapid succession. With typical inadvertence he thus stumbles into a situation in which "life, death, time, and eternity, were swimming before his eyes"; and he is rescued only by the fortunate proximity of some Scottish Guards (Ch. 6). Quentin escapes from the consequences of this incident by reluctantly allowing himself to be pressed into service with the Guards. He has many qualms about service to Louis XI. "How did the youth know but he might be soon commanded on some offensive operation of the same kind?" (Ch. 11). Next he sets out on a mission—to escort the Countess Isabelle and Lady Hameline to Liège—without knowing the country or the route, and evidently without instructions. Far from delivering orders to the expedition he commands, Quentin is informed in a whisper by one

[7] *Quarterly Review* 35 (1827): 545.

of his retinue "that their guide was to join them beyond Tours." Another man guides them out through the "pitfalls, snares, and similar contrivances" that surround the castle of Louis (Ch. 14).

When Quentin suspects treachery, however, he acts with exceptional alertness, following Hayraddin to a secret rendezvous at night, and overhearing the plot against the Countess (Ch. 17). Such information generally reaches the ears of the passive hero by accident, and then he will listen most unwillingly. The following chapter opens with Quentin carefully inspecting the shoes of the horses "with his own eyes"—an action symbolic of his unusual role. Subsequently he rescues Isabelle from the castle at Liège and restrains De La Marck, the Boar of the Ardennes, by holding a knife to the throat of his son (Chs. 22 and 23). So lively is Quentin by this point that the reader anticipates with gusto the slaughter of De La Marck in the last chapter—the stated reward for which deed is the hand of Isabelle of Croye. But just as Quentin is about to conquer the monster, Lady Hameline runs by in distress, and the hero has to nip out to save her from a French soldier. His uncle Ludovic Lesly, *alias* Le Balafré, finishes De La Marck, and refers his right to Isabelle to Quentin. "It is all that is left of a bit of work which my nephew shaped out, and nearly finished, and I put the last hand to" (Ch. 37). This awkward contrivance, which saves Quentin the responsibility of killing someone outright, owes entirely to the rules of passive heroism. Quentin has "nearly finished" the villain; but even the foulest villains are safe from death at the hero's hand.

The prototype for Quentin Durward, in the Waverley Novels, is Captain Dalgetty of *A Legend of Montrose*. Significantly, this first soldier hero is not, strictly speaking, the protagonist of the romance. As danger increases Dalgetty becomes more and more outrageous. He overpowers the Marquis of Argyll and actually escapes from the dungeon with a bundle of military secrets in his pocket. Menteith, the proper hero of the romance, survives his part in the Civil Wars, as heroes are wont to, by contriving to be a party to both sides through his marriage. The survival of Dalgetty almost parodies this typical denouement. From two paragraphs at the end of the tale the reader hears that he is captured; that he refuses to change sides—an act that would violate his military enlistment; and that he is reprieved from death by friends, who point out that his enlistment will expire in two weeks. At the end of two weeks Dalgetty does change sides, and eventually he gains "his paternal estate of Drumthwacket" by marriage to the daughter of the Whig who has usurped it (Ch. 23).

Scott returned to a soldier hero for *Count Robert of Paris*. In that romance Hereward the Saxon displays a degree of initiative similar to Quentin Durward's and at a critical moment even employs deceit to protect the emperor (Ch. 19). Durward and Hereward act where the typical heroes of Scott would await events. Because these honest mercenaries fight for pay, it is as if their heroic role were also contractual. Their enterprise seems acceptable so long as the service they perform is formally owed to someone else. They are akin to certain of the ordinary heroes' retainers, who are often more alert to the main chance than their masters.

Edgar Ravenswood of *The Bride of Lammermoor* presents a special problem. He is the only hero of the several "tragic" romances who actually shares the unhappy fate of the heroine. Yet the Master of Ravenswood, as he is ironically called, suffers his fate passively, albeit passionately. Though the story takes place on his family estate, he often seems a complete stranger to the grounds. His one direct action, serving to introduce the principals of the romance, is to rescue Lucy Ashton and her father from a wild bull (Ch. 5). He leaves the possible recovery of his estate to the vague agency of the Marquis A——— and becomes the uneasy dependent of the Ashtons. At the climax of *The Bride of Lammermoor*, as the marriage deeds are signed, Ravenswood rushes into the room, sword in hand, pistol cocked, and threatening everyone in sight (Ch. 33). There is no comparable scene in the Waverley Novels. Yet his "fierce and free ideas" are never really enacted except in this scene, and here he does not go so far as to strike anyone. Nassau Senior, who thought Ravenswood exceptionally well drawn, found it "a blemish, that his faults are so remotely connected with his misfortunes. . . . His misfortunes spring from the enmity of Bucklaw and Lady Ashton; both arising from causes out of his own controul, and as likely to have arisen if he had been the meekest of mankind."[8] His temperament is different, but his posture is fundamentally the same as that of the other heroes. Ravenswood himself tentatively recognizes the incompatibility in temperament between his dark passionate nature and the pale Lucy. "He felt that his own temper required a partner of a more independent spirit, who could set sail with him on his course of life, resolved as himself to dare indifferently the storm and the favouring breeze" (Ch. 21). It is the temperament and want of deeds together that make Ravenswood distinctive, essentially unattractive, and therefore interesting.

The Fair Maid of Perth, finally, can boast the most active and energetic hero of the Waverley Novels: Henry Wynd, the armorer. The atmosphere of this romance, like that of *The Fortunes of Nigel*, derives from Elizabethan and Jacobean theater, though *The Fair Maid of Perth* takes place a century earlier in Scotland. Scott's title suggests

[8] *Quarterly Review* 26 (1822): 121.

Heywood; and Simon Glover, but for his different trade, recalls Dekker's Simon Eyre. There is a vigorous courtship in this romance, not merely an "affection" that achieves its fulfillment when events permit. Contrary to practice in the Waverley Novels, the hero kisses the heroine. It is the bride who must be won, not merely the permission to marry her. Simon Glover, Catharine's father, approves the match. In the two other romances in which the hero enjoys such wholehearted support from the heroine's father (*Kenilworth* and *The Surgeon's Daughter*) the lady loves elsewhere. Unique among Scott heroes, Henry even possesses sexual experience: "a certain natural wildness of disposition had placed him under the influence of Venus, as well as that of Mars," before his love for Catharine "had withdrawn him entirely from such licentious pleasures" (Ch. 12). In a climax of independent action Henry slaughters on Palm Sunday no less than five Highlanders in an extremely bloody (thirty against thirty) trial by combat (Ch. 34).

The extenuating circumstance for Henry's behavior is not far to seek. His social class is responsible: he is an artisan, whereas the proper hero is a gentleman. "A gentleman," according to Charles II in *Woodstock* (Ch. 24), "is a term which comprehends all ranks entitled to armorial bearings—A duke, a lord, a prince, is no more than a gentleman." But an armorer is not entitled to armorial bearings. Henry's role, like that of the soldier heroes, approaches the role of some of the retainers to proper heroes: a similar license both to kiss and to kill is granted only to Cuddie Headrigg in *Old Mortality* and to Joceline Joliffe in *Woodstock*. Henry Wynd is far too violent for an ordinary hero—though his spirited presence makes *The Fair Maid of Perth* one of the most enjoyable of Scott's inventions.

6. Rationale

This characteristic hero did attract the notice of Scott's contemporaries. In his *Letters to Richard Heber* (1821) John Leycester Adolphus set out to prove, by internal evidence alone, and without spying at Abbotsford to catch him at it, that the Author of *Waverley* was the same as the Author of *Marmion*. Pursuing very closely the question of authorship, Adolphus produced a highly critical account of his material. In Letter VII of his treatise he compiled the following summary of the hero of the Waverley Novels:

> One circumstance very common in the novels and poems, and highly disadvantageous to the principal personage, is, that during a great part of

the story, he is made the blind or involuntary instrument of another's purposes; the attendant on another's will; and the sport of events over which he exercises no control. Such, for example, is Waverley; a hero, who, from the beginning to end of his history, is scarcely ever left upon his own hands, but appears almost always in the situation of pupil, guest, patient, protégé, or prisoner; engaged in a quarrel from which he is unconsciously extricated; half duped and half seduced into rebellion; ineffectually repenting; snatched away by accident from his sinking party; by accident preserved from justice; and restored by the exertions of his friends to safety, fortune and happiness.... Henry Bertram might justly claim to be the hero of Guy Mannering, if perils, labours, and courageous achievements could of themselves confer such a dignity; but it is difficult to consider him in that light, because we see him the mere king of a chess-board, advanced, withdrawn, exposed, protected, at the pleasure of those who play the game over his head. The character of Francis Osbaldistone [in *Rob Roy*] is not too insipidly immaculate to engage sympathy or awaken curiosity; but it wants that commanding interest which should surround the first personage of a novel; and the reason is, that in almost every part of the story we find him played upon as a dupe, disposed of as a captive, tutored as a novice, and unwittingly exciting indignation as a Marplot.[9]

Adolphus offers no explanation of this phenomenon. He is merely doing the job of description that is essential to his detective work. But he speaks of this kind of hero as "disadvantageous" and clearly disparages a hero who is merely "pupil, guest, patient, protégé, or prisoner."

Though contemporaries of Scott disparaged the passive hero, they also, in effect, ruled out any alternative. Nassau Senior recognized the limitations of "perfect heroism" and averred that Scott had moved beyond these limitations in Jeanie Deans of *The Heart of Mid-Lothian.*[10] But in the same review Senior invoked a moral theory of fiction that compels perfect heroism. He cannot accept Roland Graeme, in *The Abbot*, as a proper hero:

In real life, all would forgive, some would even admire, his conduct; but a writer of fiction has no right to dress, what is fundamentally wrong, in a covering that can attract sympathy or admiration. *He* is not exposed to the same difficulties as his heroes, and has no right to make their reward *depend* on that part of their conduct which does not deserve unmixed approbation. Still less has he a right to sanction a parley between

[9] *Letters to Richard Heber* (Boston, 1822), pp. 137–38.
[10] *Quarterly Review* 26 (1822): 120.

duty and passion, and to countenance the sophistry that attacks the understanding through the heart.[11]

One can sympathize with the reviewer's dislike of Roland Graeme. Though Graeme shares the troubles and concerns of other heroes, he bears his lot pettishly and spitefully, with grossly conceited notions of his just expectations. Though the substance is familiar, his complaint is shrill: "Am I for ever . . . to be devoured with the desire of independence and free agency, and yet to be for ever led on by circumstances to follow the will of others?" (Ch. 9).

Senior's dicta would rule Graeme out of the heroic class. Though the critic exempts real life from his ruling, he sternly applies it to fiction. His standpoint forces an author to choose between an insipid and an unworthy hero. From a twentieth-century perspective Roland Graeme is more interesting. His youthful behavior would intrigue the clinical psychologist. He suffers from an aggressive compulsion to stab people (Chs. 4 and 14). In the first four chapters of *The Abbot* Scott traces this behavior to the excessive protection and affection of his adopted mother. The discussion of Roland culminates in Henry Warden's sermon (Ch. 4), which stresses the boy's fondness for his dagger—the "treacherous and malignant instrument, which is therefore fit to be used, not by men or soldiers, but by those who, trained under female discipline, become themselves effeminate hermaphrodites, having female spite and female cowardice added to the infirmities and evil passions of their masculine nature." Roland's reaction to the sermon is as clinical as the diagnosis: "His brow grew red, his lip grew pale, he set his teeth, he clenched his hand, and then with mechanical readiness grasped the weapon of which the clergyman had given so hideous a character." When the subject rushes out of the room, the preacher concludes, "the sick man hath been offended at the wholesome bitter of the medicine—the wounded patient hath flinched from the friendly knife of the surgeon."

In a highly interesting document Scott recorded his own opinion of his first prose heroes. In 1817 he opportunely reviewed the first series of Tales of My Landlord in the *Quarterly*. The anonymous review of his own work was favorable, but Scott charged the heroes as follows:

> Another leading fault in these novels is the total want of interest which the reader attaches to the character of the hero. Waverley, Brown, or Bertram in Guy Mannering, and Lovel in the Antiquary, are all brethren of a family; very amiable and very insipid sort of young men. . . . His

[11] Ibid., p. 141.

chief characters are never actors, but always acted upon by the spur of circumstances, and have their fate uniformly determined by the agency of subordinate persons. . . . Every hero in poetry, in fictitious narrative, ought to come forth and do or say something or other which no other person could have done or said; make some sacrifice, surmount some difficulty, and become interesting to us otherwise than by his mere appearance on the scene, the passive tool of the other characters.[12]

"Never actors, but always acted upon" are very nearly the words of Nigel Olifaunt's soliloquy. Elsewhere Scott criticized one of Clara Reeve's heroes in similar terms: "for if Fitzowen be considered the Old English Baron, we do not see wherefore a character, passive in himself from beginning to end, and only acted upon by others, should be selected to give a name to the story."[13] This opinion had not deterred Scott from writing *Waverley*, nor had it affected the title in any way. Yet the author's opinion of Waverley as a hero seems to have been consistent from the beginning, since the well known letter to John Morrit in July, 1814, registered the same sentiment:

> The heroe is a sneaking piece of imbecility and if he had married Flora she would have set him up on the chimney-piece as Count Boralaski's wife used to do with him. I am a bad hand at depicting a heroe properly so calld and have an unfortunate propensity for the dubious characters of Borderers Buccaneers highland robbers and all others of a Robin Hood description. I do not know why it should be so [as] I am myself like Hamlet indifferent honest but I suppose the blood of the old cattle-drivers of Teviotdale continues to stir in my veins.[14]

Scott's notion that he had a flair for a more romantic type of hero is recorded also in earlier letters on the metrical romances.[15] He cherished the thought that some of his own ancestors led romantic and extralegal careers on the border. For our purposes, these several statements imply at least that "a heroe properly so calld" can be distinguished from the various romantic or historical personalities in the Waverley Novels who may be of heroic stature but are not the protagonists. Lovel is correctly designated by his author as the hero of *The Antiquary*, even though he is perhaps the least colorful character—he does not even possess a Christian name.

We are confronted, then, with an author who professes to scorn his unheroic hero and yet repeats the same creation in romance after ro-

[12] *Quarterly Review* 16 (1817): 431–32.
[13] *Miscellaneous Prose Works*, 3: 388–89.
[14] *Letters*, 4: 478–79.
[15] Cf. ibid., 2: 312; 3: 221.

mance. Scott offers an explanation—a somewhat halting and uncon-
vincing explanation—in his review of Tales of My Landlord. The
passive hero supplies a medium for introducing historical and topographical detail. He is a kind of representative of the reader at the
scene of action. He is inactive because he shares the reader's unfamili-
arity with the scene. Without such a hero the instructive or informa-
tive content of the fiction would seem dull. This much must be
derived from two sentences of Scott: the passive role of the heroes

> arises from the author having usually represented them as foreigners to
> whom every thing in Scotland is strange,—a circumstance which serves
> as his apology for entering into many minute details which are reflec-
> tively, as it were, addressed to the reader through the medium of the
> hero. While he is going into explanations and details which, addressed
> directly to the reader, might appear tiresome and unnecessary, he gives
> interest to them by exhibiting the effect which they produce upon the
> principal person of his drama.[16]

Secondly, and serving the same general end, a weak hero may be ex-
peditiously dragged about by an author who is bent on immediate
and temporary effects. For, Scott continues, the author "hesitates not
to sacrifice poor Waverley, and to represent him as a reed blown
about at the pleasure of every breeze" simply in order to get from
one place to another. In sum, the virtues of a passive hero are that he
may be a stranger and that he is at the mercy of his author. The argument reflects the contemporary willingness to separate "content"
from "plot," as well as Scott's habitual allusion to the carelessness of
his efforts.

Hazlitt attacked the same problem in an essay entitled "Why the Heroes of Romances Are Insipid." He thus employs the same adjective
that Scott applies to his heroes. In the latter half of the essay Hazlitt
deals expressly with the Waverley Novels. He first observes that readers take it for granted that the hero *is* interesting—a fact that Scott
neglects. Heroes adopt the correct or approved stance in any given situation. Heroes are in the right, unless they have been duped. "If
there was any doubt of their success, or they were obliged to employ
the ordinary and vulgar means to establish their superiority over
every one else, they would no longer be those 'faultless monsters'
which it is understood they must be to fill their part in the drama."[17]
The heroes of old romance had the advantage of active feats to perform. The heroes of modern French romance had at least the "fences

---

[16] *Quarterly Review* 16 (1817): 432.
[17] *Complete Works*, ed. P. P. Howe (21 vols. London and Toronto, 1931), 17: 247.

of morality and scruples of conscience" to break through. The heroes of the Author of *Waverley* Hazlitt explains as follows:

> Instead of acting, they are acted upon, and keep in the back-ground and in a neutral posture, till they are absolutely forced to come forward, and it is then with a very amiable reservation of modest scruples. Does it not seem almost, or generally speaking, as if a character to be put in this responsible situation of a candidate for the highest favour of the public at large, or of the fair in particular, who is to conciliate all suffrages and concentrate all interests, must really have nothing in him to please or give offence, that he must be left a negative, feeble character without untractable or uncompromising points, and with a few slight recommendations and obvious good qualities which everyone may be supposed to improve upon and fill up according to his or her inclination or fancy and the model of perfection previously existing in the mind? . . . In fact, the hero of the work is not so properly the chief object in it, as a sort of blank left open to the imagination, or lay-figure on which the reader disposes whatever drapery he pleases![18]

Among the possible factors affecting the hero's shy neutrality, Hazlitt stresses the operation of the fiction on the reader, the point at which the book takes hold of the reader and the reader enters into the story. For it seems true that the hero, of whatever description, is the character with whom the reader confuses, or "associates," his own person. Whether a "blank" character is most efficient for this purpose is open to question. Hazlitt argues that an imaginative cipher can accommodate the greatest range of readers. Reading itself is a passive act—more so than aural attention to the same narrative, and presumably much more so than attending "old romance" expressly intended for the ear. Possibly readers of the long prose narrative by definition enjoy fancying themselves acted upon rather than acting.

Scott's rationale also implies a special relation of the hero and the reader. But according to Scott's argument the reader would be more concerned with where the hero goes, when he lived, and what he saw, than with what he feels; and therefore the reader cannot be said to associate with the hero in the modern psychological sense. In the same year that Scott reviewed his own romances, an unidentified reviewer of Maria Edgeworth's comedies held that the theory of association or "sympathy" with the hero was an adequate theory of fiction itself: he rejected the theories of Beattie and of Bacon in two sentences.[19] The most convinced advocate of the association of reader and hero has

---

[18] Ibid., pp. 252–53.
[19] *Quarterly Review* 17 (1817): 97.

been Robert Louis Stevenson: "When the reader consciously plays at being hero, the scene is a good scene." In the fiction of character, the reader's pleasure is critical and distant. But in the fiction of incident, "we forget the characters; then we push the hero aside; then we plunge into the tale in our own person and bathe in the fresh experience; and then, and then only, do we say we have been reading a romance."[20]

Herbert Grierson suggested that Scott projected in his hero something of his personal distrust of passion. "If he did not enter very deeply into the souls of the characters whom he drew, it was because he never entered very deeply into his own motives. . . . It is this dislike of analysing feeling that makes his heroes of so little interest."[21] Enough is known of Scott's life to make this a convincing argument. To an extraordinary degree, however, Scott kept his life's experience out of his romance. And the most striking aspect of his letters and journal is the poverty of reference to his art. Grierson scores a much more telling point when he notes that the Waverley Novels touch hardly at all on Scott's own experience. "What a novel Balzac could have made of Scott's ambitions and negotiations and reckless expenditures and labours, and the careless ease and expansion of the social life he was to all appearance chiefly interested in—and then the failure and the tragic end."[22]

A different approach consigns the Waverley Novels to the historical and political sphere. In the English-speaking world David Daiches is the chief modern proponent of this school. The romances do not represent the adventures of the hero but are about human history, "chronicling, with deliberate ambiguity of feeling, the transition from the age of heroic violence to the age of prudence."[23] The conception that abstracts from the romances of Scott an image of conflicting historical or political forces may be named Coleridgian, since Coleridge discerned in the "subject" of the Waverley Novels one of his own favorite ideas. In a letter to Thomas Allsop he defined this subject as follows:

The essential wisdom and happiness of the subject consists in this,—that the contest between the loyalists and their opponents can never be *obsolete*, for it is the contest between the two great moving principles of social humanity; religious adherence to the past and the ancient, the de-

---

[20] "A Gossip on Romance," *Longman's Magazine* 1 (1882): 76–77.

[21] *Sir Walter Scott, Bart.* (London, 1938), p. 68.

[22] Ibid., p. 218.

[23] "Scott's *Redgauntlet*," in *From Jane Austen to Joseph Conrad*, ed. Robert C. Rathburn and Martin Steinmann, Jr. (Minneapolis, 1958), p. 47.

sire and the admiration of permanence, on the one hand; and the passion for increase of knowledge, for truth, as the offspring of reason—in
short, the mighty instincts of *progression* and *free agency*, on the other.[24]

Thus Mr. Daiches is in good critical company. It may be demonstrated from the introductions to the Waverley Novels that Scott sometimes conceived of a romance in terms of an interesting "contrast" of
historical characters or groups—of Saxon and Norman, or Cavalier
and Roundhead. From this point of view Nigel Olifaunt's debate between dependence and the exercise of "free agency" reflects an omnipresent conflict of social humanity.

The Coleridgian thesis—the idea of a large historical conflict at the
center of the Waverley Novels—is generally valid. It has an impressive
Marxist counterpart in the writings of Georg Lukács.[25] Scott, himself,
it is true, saw this conflict in eighteenth-century rationalist terms, as a
conflict of civilization and the state of nature. He would certainly
agree to the contrast of "violence" and "prudence." What seems to be
mistaken is the idea that Scott's hero is helpless because he stands for
neither one historical force nor the other, neither violence nor prudence. In another essay Mr. Daiches claims that the heroes are "not
heroes in the ordinary sense, but symbolic observers."[26] This is a so-
phisticated version of Scott's own rationale of the hero as a vehicle
for nonfiction. It is a mistake to dismiss the passive hero because he
seems to initiate none of the action: he appears in every full-length
romance except one; he is the only coherent focus in most of the
plots; and he is therefore the best introduction to an understanding
of the Waverley Novels. It is doubly a mistake to lose sight of the hero
between the age of prudence and the age of violence, between the
civil state and the state of nature. Whatever one may think of Scott's
sympathies—I myself think that his "romantic" sympathies are those
of a man confident of the superiority of modern civilization—his
hero is not a neutral. He stands committed to prudence and the superiority of civil society. That commitment alone makes him a passive
hero. Not only are his manners confined, in George Moberly's words,
to the "quiet and retiring character" of modern virtues, but he represents the modern and conservative model of a member of civil society. The hero is not precisely Everyman, but every gentleman—not in
some supercilious social sense, but in the profound conviction that
society is a compact of independent owners of property. He is a pas-

[24] *Coleridge's Miscellaneous Criticism*, ed. Raysor, pp. 341–42.

[25] *Der Historische Roman* (Berlin, 1955), pp. 23–60.

[26] "Scott's Achievement as a Novelist," *Literary Essays* (Edinburgh and London,
1956), p. 93.

sive hero because, in the words of Edmund Burke, a member of civil society surrenders the right "to judge for himself, and to assert his own cause. He abdicates all right to be his own governor. He inclusively, in a great measure, abandons the right of self-defence, the first law of Nature."[27] He abandons, in other words, all these various possibilities of action. Burke's next sentence is that "man cannot enjoy the rights of an uncivil and of a civil state together." Scott surely concurs: but in fiction he can at least afford pleasurable glimpses of the uncivil state. In this sense his hero is an observer—even a vacationer—and so is the reader. He is committed to the civil state, and observes the uncivil.

[27] *Reflections on the Revolution in France*, in *Works* (12 vols. Boston, 1865–67), 3: 309–10.

III

CHARACTER AND TOPOGRAPHY

This natural liberty consists properly in a power of acting as one thinks fit, without any restraint or controul, unless by the law of nature. . . . But every man, when he enters into society, gives up a part of his natural liberty as the price of so valuable a purchase. . . . And this species of legal obedience and conformity is infinitely more desirable than that wild and savage liberty which is sacrificed to obtain it.
  —Blackstone, *Commentaries on the Laws of England*

"I am determined to read no more books where the blond-haired women carry away all the happiness. . . . I want to avenge Rebecca and Flora MacIvor, and Minna and all the rest of the dark unhappy ones."
  —Maggie Tulliver, in *The Mill on the Floss*

7. Dark Heroes

THE ACTIONS and commitment of the passive hero in the Waverley Novels are so restricted that any activity depends upon other sources of energy. Two sorts of agents supply the necessary impetus to the plot. Some romances depend upon out-and-out villains of melodrama—"a villain or two of all work," as Scott characterized them in the romance of Mrs. Radcliffe.[1] About half of the Waverley Novels exploit the energy of an agent who is not totally depraved. This agent characteristically operates outside the law. He acts with deep feeling, and his intentions are "good," though fierce and mistaken. The reader can associate, to a greater or less degree, with his plight, which is that of a man outside society—or of a man, as we may choose to believe, without reason. He therefore is also a kind of hero, and for students of romantic literature, a very familiar figure. Here is George Staunton, *alias* Robertson, in *The Heart of Mid-Lothian*, as he appears to the passive hero, Reuben Butler:

The fiery eye, the abrupt demeanour, the occasionally harsh, yet studiously subdued tone of voice,—the features, handsome, but now clouded

[1] *Miscellaneous Prose Works*, 3: 431.

with pride, now disturbed by suspicion, now inflamed with passion—those dark hazel eyes which he sometimes shaded with his cap, as if he were averse to have them seen while they were occupied with keenly observing the motions and bearing of others—those eyes that were now turbid with melancholy, now gleaming with scorn, and now sparkling with fury—was it the passions of a mere mortal they expressed, or the emotions of a fiend, who seeks, and seeks in vain, to conceal his fiendish designs under the borrowed mask of manly beauty? The whole partook of the mien, language, and port of the ruined archangel. [Ch. 11]

Staunton is the most consciously designed romantic hero in the Waverley Novels. The passive hero can in no sense be called a "romantic hero" except on the grounds that he is born in the romantic period: he is the representative of an apparently conservative and satisfied way of life. But Staunton is fundamentally a disturbed man, driven by waves of passion and remorse. Scott deliberately stresses his Satanic aspect. He threatens Jeanie Deans with the execution of her sister "unless you yield up to my guidance body and soul" (Ch. 15). And he looms up from behind a rock in that nocturnal scene much as if he were Lucifer himself. Staunton is patently a creation of romantic literature. But in the Waverley Novels such characters play a carefully circumscribed part, and are even depreciated by their author.

The dark heroes of Scott are of mixed kinds. They can only be arbitrarily listed: Fergus Mac-Ivor, Elshie the Dwarf, Rob Roy, George Staunton, Allan M'Aulay, the Earl of Leicester, Clement Cleveland, Hugh Redgauntlet, Saladin, Albert of Geierstein. Some of the historical personages of the Waverley Novels also seem to belong in this list: Prince Charles in *Waverley*, King Richard in both *Ivanhoe* and *The Talisman*, Charles the Bold in *Quentin Durward* and *Anne of Geierstein*, Charles II in *Woodstock*. But the role of such historical characters is dictated rather by history than by the moral situation in which Scott chooses to involve them; they are necessary but not sufficient causes of the story; and they tend to oversee the fortunes of the passive hero rather than interfere purposively. (Rob Roy, Leicester, and Saladin, who are also historical, compete more directly with the protagonists.) On the other hand, many of the villains in the Waverley Novels also merge with the dark heroes. Burley in *Old Mortality*, for example, is a selfish and fanatical villain, but he is also a romantic force of violence.

With a few exceptions, moreover, Scott actually reduces the invented "romantic" characters to villains. He typically taints their moral freedom of action with selfish motives. George Staunton, for example, is ridden by a "sense of guilt" (Ch. 18) and by "bitterness of self-upbraiding" (Ch. 11). As leader of the Porteous mob he displays the swift, sure energies of a Robin Hood, operating outside the law but in a popular cause. Within himself, his personal transgression gnaws at his conscience, until it threatens to overwhelm his reason. His proposals that Jeanie Deans perjure herself (Ch. 15), or that he trade his own life (Ch. 34) to save Effie Deans are naively arrogant with respect to the law. Scott diminishes Staunton's stature in his initial description of the man, which contains a curious mixture of qualifiers:

> His carriage was bold and somewhat supercilious, his step easy and free, his manner daring and unconstrained.... His features were uncommonly handsome, and all about him would have been interesting and prepossessing, but for that indescribable expression which habitual dissipation gives to the countenance, joined with a certain audacity in look and manner, of that kind which is often assumed as a mask for confusion and apprehension. [Ch. 11]

Later in *The Heart of Mid-Lothian*, the reader learns of Staunton's youthful acquaintance with "the turf, the gaming-table, the cock-pit, and every worse rendezvous of folly and dissipation" (Ch. 34). His bitter conscience does not redeem him. In later years Jeanie Deans decides that "even in his strongest paroxysms of remorse, [Staunton] had appeared too much a stranger to the feelings of real penitence" (Ch. 46). Scott demonstrates the slight falseness or insincerity of Staunton's character upon his corpse, whence it appears that he has become a Catholic: "It then appeared, from the crucifix, the beads, and the shirt of hair which he wore next to his person, that his sense of guilt had induced him to receive the dogmata of a religion, which pretends, by the maceration of the body, to expiate the crimes of the soul" (Ch. 52). But surely a more effective thrust at this dark hero is delivered by the Edinburgh magistrate: "I know no business any man has to swagger about in the King's Park, and call himself the devil, to the terror of honest folks, who dinna care to hear mair about the devil than is said from the pulpit on the Sabbath" (Ch. 16).

In *Kenilworth* the Earl of Leicester emerges on somewhat better terms with his public, but here too the reader is left with an aftertaste of weak selfishness. The Earl has secretly married Amy Robsart, but stands in essentially the same relation to her as Staunton to Effie Deans, since he refuses to acknowledge his wife. Before long (Ch. 16) he allows a deliberate misconstruction of his relation to Amy to pass uncontradicted, and from that point he appears in less and less favorable light. If it were not for his given historical tenure, Leicester would surely perish at the end of the romance. In *Redgauntlet* and *A Legend of Montrose* the black fatalism of Hugh Redgauntlet and of Allan M'Aulay threatens more danger than it promises romantic adventure. Redgauntlet jeopardizes the security of Darsie and Alan Fairford and other innocents. M'Aulay poses a bewildered but rough sexual threat to Annot Lyle. In *Waverley* the narrow prejudices of Fergus Mac-Ivor detract from his grand motives. He grows suddenly ambitious to marry Rose Bradwardine, and makes it all too evident that he is more interested in her property than in her affections (Ch. 53). There is a delicate sense in which the passive hero has more sensitive, if not more passionate, feelings than his dark counterpart.

Clement Cleveland, whose profession is celebrated in the title of *The Pirate*, suffers from certain petty faults of character. "There was an assumption of superiority about him which Mordaunt did not quite so much like" (Ch. 9). Yet Scott deflates his pirate rather gently. Under the influence of Minna Troil, Cleveland sincerely desires to reform. If it were possible for a character in the Waverley Novels to escape entirely from his past, Cleveland would survive as a close relative of the passive hero. He is now trapped by the past because the burghers of Kirkwall intend to hold him responsible for the actions of a wild pirate crew that he no longer commands (Ch. 35). Scott offers to trace his entire career of piracy to "the concurrence of external circumstances" (Ch. 39). In any case, as soon as the nature of Cleveland's past life dawns upon Minna, she decrees that, "if she still love him, it must be as a penitent, and not as a hero" (Ch. 22).

Two principal romantic heroes in the Waverley Novels escape this process of diminution more or less unscathed: Rob Roy and Saladin. Both are essentially Robin Hoods. What is more, their real historical existence relieves the romancer from some of the responsibility for their activities. As it is, Scott does not fail to linger over the "wrongs" and "errors" of Rob Roy and to explore (in vain) the possibilities of extricating him once and for all from the social consequences (Ch. 35). In the 1829 introduction to this romance, Scott wrote of the historical Rob Roy that "his ideas of morality were those of an Arab chief, being such as naturally arose out of his wild education." The comparison links the Scottish chieftain to Saladin of *The Talisman*, the one romantic character in the Waverley Novels about whom Scott has no reservations at all. For a contrast to the passive hero Hazlitt unerringly singled out Saladin:

> Of all Sir Walter's characters the most dashing and spirited is the Sultan Saladin. But he is not meant for a hero [i.e. a proper hero], nor fated to be a lover. He is a collateral and incidental performer in the scene. His

movements therefore remain free, and he is master of his own resplendent energies, which produce so much the more daring and felicitous an effect. So far from being meant to please all tastes or the most squeamish, he is not meant for any taste. He has no pretentions, and stands on the sole ground of his own heroic acts and sayings. The author has none of the timidity or mawkishness arising from a fear of not coming up to his own professions, or to the expectations excited in the reader's mind. . . . There is no idle, nervous apprehension of falling short of perfection, arresting the hand or diverting the mind from truth and nature. . . . Accordingly all is spontaneous, bold, and original in this beautiful and glowing design, which is as magnificent as it is magnanimous.[2]

As the active hero of romance Saladin wins all honors: dark in complexion, clever and courageous, skilled in the healing arts, wise in the ways of men, more chivalrous than a Christian knight, wary, swift, and agile, omnipresent in the wilderness, and the scourge of evil. Thus, for example, he destroys the Grand Master of the Templars before the villain can touch his lips to the cup of hospitality: "The sabre of Saladin left its sheath as lightning leaves the cloud. It was waved in the air,—and the head of the Grand Master rolled to the extremity of the tent, while the trunk remained for a second standing, with the goblet still clenched in its grasp, then fell, the liquor mingling with the blood that spurted from the veins" (Ch. 28). Scott is constrained to add in a note that such a scene has an actual basis in history.

If we set aside the author's moral reservations, a composite but sufficiently coherent image of a dark hero emerges. There is something of the Robin Hood in all these characters. As Jack Bunce tells Cleveland, "you were as gentle a thief as Robin Hood himself" (Ch. 31). Because the dark hero is a passionate individual, he is generous and compassionate. He is closer to nature than the civilized passive hero, and generally disports himself in a wild, natural setting. He is physically strong. His relationship to other men, friendly or unfriendly, is direct and warm. He is loyal to individual persons and places, and submits with little grace to the artificial strictures of polity and realty. He boasts an intuitive morality that is anterior to law and perhaps even independent of divine law. "Men who are disobedient both to human and divine laws," avows George Staunton, "are not always insensible to the claims of courage and generosity" (Ch. 33).

The dark hero seems rough and irregular. The restraining and leveling forces of society have not molded him. He is not of average size.

Rob Roy's shoulders are abnormally wide, his arms abnormally long—"Two points in his person interfered with the rules of symmetry" (Ch. 23). Redgauntlet bears an irregular mark on his brow; Elshie the Dwarf is altogether misshapen. The dark hero lacks balance. Passion is not sufficiently tempered by reason and society, and there are hints of insanity about Elshie, Staunton, and Allan M'Aulay. "You are of that temperament," says Norna to Cleveland in *The Pirate*, "which the dark Influences desire as the tools of their agency; bold, haughty, and undaunted, unrestrained by principle, and having only in its room a wild sense of indomitable pride, which such men call honour" (Ch. 38). The dark influences are also an internal force, passion threatening to overwhelm principle.

The dark hero's difficulties commence in earnest when he brushes with society. He must stand or fall on his pretensions to a morality of his own: otherwise, Minna Troil must love him as a penitent, not as a hero. But morality for Scott is neither natural nor individual; it is artificial and social. That is why Saladin dwells far away in the east. Scott cannot rationally accept the notion of spontaneously generated ethics. He is sometimes even emotionally pitted against that kind of theory. He has, for example, no use at all for the philosophical heroes of Robert Bage, and asks his readers

> to consider seriously whether a system of Ethics, founding an exclusive and paramount court in a man's own bosom for the regulation of his own conduct, is likely to form a noble, enlightened, and generous character, influencing others by superior energy and faultless example; or whether it is not more likely . . . to regulate morals according to temptation and to convenience, and to form a selfish, sophisticated hypocrite, who, with morality always in his mouth, finds a perpetual apology for evading the practice of abstinence, when either passion or interest solicit him to indulgence.[3]

The romantic hero has a part to play in the structure of the Waverley Novels, but he has no ethical currency. He represents, therefore, an emotional force. "Courage and generosity" are good qualities, but in Scott they are not moral qualities. When Scott thinks of morality, he speaks in terms of regulation and restraint—rational and social functions.

The appearance of *two* heroes in certain of the romances first opens to view the thematic lines of the Waverley Novels. The proper and passive hero adheres to law or accepted morality; the dark hero boasts his own morality and places himself outside the law. From the

---

[3] *Miscellaneous Prose Works*, 3: 554.

interior aspect, the proper hero submits to reason or prudence; and the dark hero acts from feeling or passion. The two heroes may ultimately represent a favorite dualism of critics of the novel, that of society and the individual. Adolphus long ago indicated several pairs of contrasting heroes in Scott—though three of his dark candidates, Bois-Guilbert in *Ivanhoe*, Hatteraick in *Guy Mannering*, and Rashleigh Osbaldistone in *Rob Roy*, should perhaps be classified as villains.[4] Eino Railo observed the parallel construction of light and dark heroines.[5] But even critics who do not specify two kinds of hero have recognized some sort of dualism running through the Waverley Novels. This can be observed in any of the Coleridgian interpretations. David Daiches has noted that Scott himself "was two men. . . . He was both the prudent Briton and the passionate Scot."[6] E.M.W. Tillyard agrees that "Scott habitually opposed two ideals or tempers."[7] Bagehot wrote of a "union of sense and romance" in the Waverley Novels.[8] And Grierson concluded that "there was in Scott's mind a dualism which he made no attempt to bridge, of which he was not himself fully conscious. In the novels it shows itself in the contradiction between his romantic sympathies and his sober judgment."[9] The unresolved "dualism" of Grierson suits the case somewhat better than the "union" of Bagehot, though the elements of the contrast, reason and romance, are the same.

The traditional assumption of the "romantic sympathies" of Scott in the Waverley Novels can also be misleading. In *Redgauntlet* the sympathies of both Scott and his reader are much more closely aligned with the passive Sir Arthur Redgauntlet (Darsie Latimer) than with his romantic uncle, Hugh Redgauntlet (Herries of Birrenswork). The romance of lost causes and the tyranny of the past, in the person of his scowling uncle, make an unjust claim on Darsie. Darsie is not strongly affected by the attraction of the past: rather he is embarrassed by it. In fact he is held prisoner by his uncle, who intends to use him in the service of emotional loyalties that Darsie does not share. This loyalty affects him in some sense, of course, because he sets out in the first place to discover his family, and because he is somehow unable to break away from his uncle. Waverley does not

---

[4] [John Leycester Adolphus], *Letters to Richard Heber* (Boston, 1822), pp. 143–44.
[5] *The Haunted Castle: A Study of the Elements of English Romanticism* (London, 1927), pp. 286–88, 290–92.
[6] *Literary Essays* (Edinburgh and London, 1956), p. 92.
[7] *The Epic Strain in the English Novel* (Fair Lawn, N.J., 1958), p. 99.
[8] *Literary Studies* (2 vols. London, Everyman's Library, n.d.), 2: 161.
[9] *Sir Walter Scott, Bart.*, p. 307.

wish to join Fergus Mac-Ivor except for the most superficial reasons—
reasons adequately summarized at the end of *Waverley* by the presentation of "a large and spirited painting, representing Fergus Mac-Ivor
and Waverley in their Highland dress; the scene a wild, rocky, and
mountainous pass, down which the clan were descending in the back-
ground" (Ch. 71). On the contrary, Fergus wants the use of Waverley;
and he procures it, as it turns out, only through the dishonest services of Donald Bean Lean. The center of activity in the Waverley
Novels at most proves to be the *resistance* to romantic energies. This
implies, in author and reader, a sympathy with resistance—with prudence, in fact—as well as a tribute to the force resisted.

Everyone recognizes which force consistently triumphs in the romances of Scott. "All of them," writes Mr. Daiches, "end with the reluctant victory of prudence over the seductive but in the last analysis
anachronistic claims of romantic action."[10] I question whether this victory can be described as "reluctant." At the end of *Redgauntlet*, as the
same critic suggests, Scott achieved in a single sentence his finest summary of the Jacobite cause in the eighteenth century. The conspirators are surrounded by troops and General Campbell walks into their
midst. To their complete surprise he offers everyone, including the
Wanderer, whom he politely refuses to recognize, a free pardon.

> "Is this real?" said Redgauntlet. "Can you mean this?—Am I—are all,
> are any of these gentlemen at liberty, without interruption, to embark in
> yonder brig, which, I see, is now again approaching the shore?"
>
> "You, sir—all—any of the gentlemen present," said the General—"all
> whom the vessel can contain, are at liberty to embark uninterrupted by
> me; but I advise none to go off who have not powerful reasons uncon-
> nected with the present meeting, for this will be remembered against
> no one."
>
> "Then, gentlemen," said Redgauntlet, clasping his hands together as
> the words burst from him, "the cause is lost forever!" [Ch. 23]

The generosity of the government wins over the reader entirely. Redgauntlet's cry is suffused with recognition. Fact triumphs over regret:
in the last few chapters of this romance Scott clearly implies that a Jacobite conspiracy in 1770 is a travesty of common sense. The emotion
of discovery, of revelation, of cure, bursts from the dark hero. Initially
he cannot believe Campbell's terms: "Is it real?" But the terms *are*
supposed to be real, and in this moment Redgauntlet conceives that

---

[10] "Scott's *Redgauntlet*," in *From Jane Austen to Joseph Conrad*, ed. Robert C. Rathburn
and Martin Steinmann, Jr. (Minneapolis, 1958), p. 46.

his scheme for the restoration of the Stuarts is quite the opposite. Campbell tenders reality to the conspirators—Hanoverian fact against Stuart fiction. Common sense and the Revolution of 1688 triumph together. The house of Hanover has found a way of taming Jacobite passions by acting as chivalrously as the forces of romance.

8. Blonde and Brunette

In certain important romances a dark heroine shares appropriate features of the dark hero. The female of the species, however, enjoys a certain immunity from criticism. She is altogether unselfish. In her the excess of feeling directs itself outward. Fergus Mac-Ivor's designs on the property of Rose Bradwardine and his scheme of marrying his sister Flora to Waverley demonstrate an unmistakable degree of selfishness. "In Flora's bosom, on the contrary, the zeal of loyalty burnt pure and unmixed with any selfish feeling; she would have as soon made religion the mask of ambitious and interested views, as have shrouded them under . . . patriotism" (Ch. 21). Far from attempting to exploit Waverley, Flora urges him to stay clear of the Jacobite rising (Chs. 26 and 27). At the end of *Peveril of the Peak* Fenella, or Zarah, repudiates her alliance with the devilish Edward Christian: "While a noble motive fired thee—ay, a noble motive, though irregular—for I was born to gaze on the sun which the pale daughters of Europe shrink from—I could serve thee—I could have followed, while revenge or ambition had guided thee—but love of *wealth*, and by what means acquired! —What sympathy can I hold with that?" (Ch. 47).

Heroines are similarly favored with respect to religion. Though the persuasion of Catholicism is a highly suspicious circumstance in George Staunton or Redgauntlet, or especially in a villain like Rashleigh Osbaldistone, in the case of Flora Mac-Ivor or Die Vernon the same religion signifies their depth of feeling and loyalty. Nor does the interest of Rebecca suffer from her being Jewish. The dark heroines all chafe against the bonds of decorum and social life, and they pay dearly for their emotional commitments. Yet only Effie Deans in *The Heart of Mid-Lothian* is appreciably diminished in stature because of her sins. She is a spoiled child (Ch. 10) and throughout her career betrays "a smothered degree of egotism" (Ch. 48). But Effie is also the one principal female in the Waverley Novels who has willingly consented to her seduction.

The proper heroine of Scott is a blonde. Her role corresponds to that of the passive hero—whom, indeed, she marries at the end of the tale. She is eminently beautiful, and eminently prudent. Like the passive hero, she suffers in the thick of events but seldom moves them. The several dark heroines, no less beautiful, are less restrained. They long to participate in events. They suffer also, but internally, from the pressure of their own feelings. They allow their feelings to dictate to their reason, and seem to symbolize passion itself. Madame de Staël employed the contrast of two such heroines for the design of *Corinne, ou Italie* (1807). The virtues of the passionate Corinne are vigorously extolled, but they are the virtues of deep suffering, somehow irreconcilable with the claims of the world. Lord Nevil's deceased parent has commanded that he attach himself to the person and property of a native blonde named Lucy Edgermonde; and Corinne perishes recommending love—and her lover—to Lucy. The impression of *Corinne* clearly stamped itself on the Waverley Novels. Just before the advent of *Waverley* Jane Austen, in her own fashion, employed essentially the same contrast of heroines for Elinor and Marianne Dashwood of *Sense and Sensibility* (1811). The "dualism" of Scott assured an extended life and moral significance to this literary design.

The distinct pairs of light and dark heroines in the Waverley Novels are Rose and Flora in *Waverley*, Rowena and Rebecca in *Ivanhoe*, Brenda and Minna Troil in *The Pirate*, Alice Bridgenorth and Fenella (Zarah) in *Peveril of the Peak*, Jeanie and Effie Deans in *The Heart of Mid-Lothian*, and Margaret Ramsay and Hermione in *The Fortunes of Nigel*. In all but the last two romances, the blonde and brunette rival each other for the affections of the passive hero. In *Rob Roy* Die Vernon usurps the role of solo heroine, which is customarily reserved for a blonde. Hair coloring is a convenient though not absolute measure of such heroines. Both the Deans sisters have light hair. Alice Bridgenorth has long dark brown hair, but not as dark as that of Fenella, the rather unsuccessful copy of Goethe's Mignon. The two heroines are physically distinguished, nevertheless, and the hair may have special significance. The brunette seems to have more of it. When we first see Miss Vernon in *Rob Roy*, "Her long black hair streamed in the breeze, having in the hurry of the chase escaped from the ribbon which bound it" (Ch. 5). As she and Frank enter Osbaldistone Hall, Scott amplifies this image:

"There is no great toilette kept at Osbaldistone Hall, you must know; but I must take off these things, they are so unpleasantly warm,—and the hat hurts my forehead, too," continued the lively girl, taking it off, and shaking down a profusion of sable ringlets, which, half laughing, half blushing, she separated with her white slender fingers, in order to clear them away from her beautiful face and piercing hazel eyes. If there was any coquetry in the action, it was well disguised by the careless indifference of her manner. [Ch. 5]

The escaping hair symbolizes her freedom from convention and restraint. As Scott acknowledges in the last sentence, such an action conveys a muted sexual suggestion. The blonde does not "take off these things" in front of the hero. Like the dark hero, the brunette is more direct in her relationship with others, and hence more accessible or intimate than a proper heroine. To her ultimate distress the brunette has that quality of "availability" which Hollywood demands of its dark or preternaturally blonde heroines.

There are also hints in the Waverley Novels that the body of the dark heroine is more voluptuous than that of the blonde. Though Effie Deans, for example, is not dark, she has "a laughing Hebe countenance" and "a shape, which time, perhaps, might be expected to render too robust" (Ch. 10). Having stood the test of time, she appears at the end of *The Heart of Mid-Lothian* as a fashionable lady "rather above the middle size, beautifully made, though something *embonpoint*" (Ch. 50). In *Ivanhoe* Scott lingers just a moment longer over the "lovely neck and bosom" of Rebecca than he would over the anatomy of a proper heroine: "It is true, that of the golden and pearl-studded clasps, which closed her vest from the throat to the waist, the three uppermost were left unfastened on account of the heat, which something enlarged the prospect to which we allude" (Ch. 7). The personality of the blonde also corresponds to a physical type, but features and coloring are granted more prominence than the figure. The disposition of the Saxon Rowena "was naturally that which physiognomists consider as proper to fair complexions, mild, timid and gentle. . . . Her haughtiness and habit of domination was, therefore, a fictitious character; induced over that which was natural to her" (Ch. 23). For descriptions both male and female Scott frequently has recourse to the pseudoscience of physiognomy.

The contrast of blonde and brunette is most elaborately drawn in the description of Brenda and Minna Troil in *The Pirate* (Ch. 3). At every point Scott moves from physical feature to character type. "The dispositions of these lovely sisters were not less different than their complexions." Minna Troil, with "raven locks," is yet so pale "that many thought the lily had an undue proportion in her complexion." Her features "seemed calculated to express a contemplative and high-minded character." From the "serious beauty" of her motions, her voice, and her eye, it "seemed as if Minna Troil belonged naturally to some higher and better sphere, and was only the chance visitant of a world that was not worthy of her." She is a kind of introvert, her pleasures being "those of a graver and more solitary cast." Yet her depths are most surely stirred by compassion, and her relation to those about her is charged with emotion. "When Minna Troil heard a tale of woe or of injustice, it was then her blood rushed to her cheeks, and showed plainly how warm it beat, notwithstanding the generally serious, composed, and retiring disposition, which her countenance and demeanour seemed to exhibit."

Her blonde sister Brenda is at once less deeply emotional and more civilized. The brunette is more serious, more intellectual, with "a naturally powerful memory," and can make excellent conversation when she pleases; but the blonde is gayer company for the average man.

> The scarcely less beautiful, equally lovely, and equally innocent Brenda, was of a complexion as differing from her sister, as they differed in character, taste, and expression. . . . A fairy form, less tall than that of Minna, but still more finely moulded into symmetry—a careless, and almost childish lightness of step—an eye that seemed to look on every object with pleasure, from a natural and serene cheerfulness of disposition, attracted even more general admiration than the charms of her sister, though perhaps that which Minna did excite, might be of a more intense as well as a more reverential character.

Brenda has a perfect shape. Minna is symmetrical, we are to understand, but not so symmetrical as her sister. Minna shares that slight irregularity of romantic heroes, as well as their height. Brenda is both "more finely moulded" and attracts "more general admiration" from society. We are told further that "the cheerfulness of Brenda mixed itself with the everyday business of life." Whereas the charms of Brenda are molded by society, Minna is affected more deeply by nature. "The ocean in all its varied forms of sublimity and terror—the tremendous cliffs that resound to the ceaseless roar of the billows, and the clang of the seafowl" are the aspects of nature that Scott here singles out. "The love of natural objects was to her a passion capable not only of occupying, but at times of agitating her mind. Scenes upon which her sister looked with a sense of transient awe or emotion, continued long to fill Minna's imagination." The sisters are, as it were, the sublime and the beautiful. One belongs to a state of nature, and the other to civilization.

With determined consistency Scott invokes the contrast of his two heroines throughout *The Pirate*. In defense of her love for Cleveland Minna herself reiterates the difference of the sisters' response to nature: "Remember, Brenda, that when your foot loved the calm sea-beach of the summer sea, mine ever delighted in the summit of the precipice, when the waves were in fury" (Ch. 20). When Cleveland and Mordaunt depart, the grief of the sisters is carefully distinguished: "It is probable, that though Brenda's tears were most abundant, the grief of Minna was most deeply seated" (Ch. 23). And Norna of Fitful Head scorns Mordaunt's growing preference for Brenda: "You cannot be so dull of heart, so poor of spirit, as to prefer the idle mirth and housewife simplicity of the younger sister, to the deep feeling and high mind of the noble-spirited Minna? Who would stoop to gather the lowly violet, that might have the rose for stretching out his hand?" (Ch. 33). In "housewife simplicity" Norna unwittingly summarizes the chief virtue of the blonde, who will make an excellent wife.

The denouement of the romance conveys the final and inexorable difference of dark and light-haired heroines. Brenda, Rowena, Alice, Jeanie, Margaret, and Rose inherit property, marry passive heroes, and live happily ever after. The passionate careers of Minna, Rebecca, Fenella, Effie, Hermione, and Flora burn out—in exile or the cloister, or upon the sands of Zetland. Only in the cases of Effie and Hermione has sexual transgression literally occurred. The false marriage practiced on Hermione is remedied by a forced marriage (not for the purpose of living together, of course) at the end of *The Fortunes of Nigel*. Staunton eventually marries Effie. But no children of dark heroines survive except the fatal child born to Effie in *The Heart of Mid-Lothian*. He returns in the final pages to shoot his father before disappearing into the American wilderness (Ch. 52).

In the world, though not of it, the dark heroine does outlive the dark hero: Scott prefers her resignation to life rather than her sudden death. Her energies come up point-blank against reality. She has intellectual passion, but no books; she has political passion, but no cause; and she has sexual passion, but too much of all three for the wary passive hero to approach too near. Minna Troil's melancholy, we are told, "had no ground in real sorrow, and was only the aspiration of a soul bent on more important objects than those by which she was surrounded" (Ch. 3). There was material here that Scott scarcely exploited. Not only the heroines of George Eliot but even some of her prose are anticipated in the last long paragraph of *The Pirate*:

> But Minna—the high-minded and imaginative Minna—she, gifted with such depth of feeling and enthusiasm, yet doomed to see both blighted in early youth, because, with the inexperience of a disposition equally

romantic and ignorant, she had built the fabric of her happiness on a quicksand instead of a rock,—was she, could she be happy? Reader, she *was* happy. . . . Like Norna, but under a more regulated judgment, she learned to exchange the visions of wild enthusiasm which had exerted and misled her imagination, for a truer and purer connection with the world beyond us, than could be learned from the sagas of heathen bards, or the visions of later rhymers. . . . Minna . . . thanked Heaven, even while the eyes which she lifted up were streaming with tears, that the death of Cleveland had been in the bed of honour; nay, she even had the courage to add to her gratitude, that he had been snatched from a situation of temptation ere circumstances had overcome his new-born virtue. . . . Her thoughts, however, were detached from the world, and only visited it, with an interest like that which guardian spirits take for their charge, in behalf of those friends with whom she lived in love, or of the poor whom she could serve and comfort. [Ch. 42]

In the 1830 introduction to *Ivanhoe* Scott defended the denouement of that romance against "some fair readers" who felt that the hero should have married Rebecca, "rather than the less interesting Rowena." Scott does not contest the opinion that Rebecca is more "interesting": the last few lines of the romance suggested that Ivanhoe may have thought so himself (Ch. 44). Scott contends that Ivanhoe could not have married a Jewess in that period in any case, and that "a character of a highly virtuous and lofty stamp is degraded rather than exalted by an attempt to reward virtue with temporal prosperity." He next supposes that virtue is not so rewarded in real life. The argument that follows defies paraphrase, because it verges on contradiction:

Such is not the recompense which Providence has deemed worthy of suffering merit, and it is a dangerous and fatal doctrine to teach young persons, the most common readers of romance, that rectitude of conduct and of principle are either naturally allied with, or adequately rewarded by, the gratification of our passions, or attainment of our wishes. In a word, if a virtuous and self-denied character is dismissed with temporal wealth, greatness, rank, or the indulgence of such a rashly-formed or ill-assorted passion as that of Rebecca for Ivanhoe, the reader will be apt to say, verily virtue has had its reward. But a glance on the great picture of life will show, that the duties of self-denial, and the sacrifice of passion to principle, are seldom thus remunerated; and that the internal consciousness of their high-minded discharge of duty, produces on their own reflections a more adequate recompense, in the form of that peace which the world cannot give or take away.

In defense of his treatment of Rebecca, Scott preaches against his own romance. "Rectitude of conduct and of principle" and "the sacrifice of passion to principle" are ordinarily rewarded by a handsome marriage and a large property in the Waverley Novels. Except for one phrase—"a rashly-formed or ill-assorted passion"—Scott might argue here that Ivanhoe and Rowena themselves ought not to be rewarded with material happiness. If we pressed the argument broadly, we should have to attack the good fortune of all the proper heroes and heroines. Scott's argument could then be reconciled to his works of fiction only by supposing that the marriages and inheritances of proper heroes and heroines do *not* supply a "gratification of our passions, or attainment of our wishes"—in other words, by supposing that Rowena and Ivanhoe were not gratified by their prosperity. Such is the proposition to which Thackeray committed himself—perhaps a more sweeping proposition than he realized—in *Rebecca and Rowena.*

The confusion arises from Scott's rhetorical liberty. He speaks of Rebecca throughout the paragraph; in concession to those fair readers, to his own sympathies, and perhaps to the lost love of Ivanhoe, Scott looses a flood of moral approbation. From "suffering merit" to "high-minded discharge of duty" Rebecca has it all her way. Naturally it is hard to understand why this implies the exile of the Jewess. In the midst of this adulation Scott insidiously suggests that if *the reader* would care to reward this virtue with "wealth, greatness of rank, or *the indulgence of . . . passion,*" why, "*verily* virtue has had its reward." The "indulgence of passion"—the one criticism he levies against Rebecca in the entire passage—is neatly inserted as a supposed reward of virtue, and thereby ironically subverts the foregoing congratulation of Rebecca. In the final analysis, no extenuating circumstances can atone for emotions that are "ill-assorted" with reality.

Apart from the moral lines constructed from the contrast of blonde and brunette, the romance with two heroines offers many attractions. The reader may imagine himself in the situation of Julian in *Peveril of the Peak,* striding through the streets of London with a striking and contrasting beauty on each arm, "both remarkably calculated to attract the public eye" (Ch. 32). In view of their separate natures, in fact, this imaginary happiness is tantamount to keeping a mistress as well as a wife. The possibilities are even enhanced by the chance that the two women are acquainted. Though the fire of the brunette must eventually be damped, it may burn convincingly enough to kindle something of the same ardor in the blonde. (The dark heroines actually seem willing to share their insight. Only Fenella is markedly unfriendly to her competitor. In *Waverley* Flora

Mac-Ivor regards Rose as her "pupil" [Ch. 52].) In his mind, at least, the hero may enjoy both heroines to himself. The imagination may escape the law of contradiction accepted by morality, and bridge the dualism of dark and light. Dreams may unite what the reason condemns as "ill-assorted."

Those who suppose that heroes and readers are immune to such fantasy must still allow that two heroines enlarge the traditional prospect at the end of a romance. To the happiness of living ever after is superadded the pathos of the brunette. The brunette is the more literary being of the two—since the blonde stands for the real, the possible, the morally tenable relationship with women. If not from dreams, the more impossible brunette is derived from books. When Hermione suddenly glides into the room in *The Fortunes of Nigel* (Ch. 7), all in white except for her long black hair and a zone of rubies, we know that we are reading romance. To Nigel she seems like an "apparition." In *Rob Roy* Frank Osbaldistone recalls his first meeting with Die Vernon with the same thought: "my beautiful apparition" (Ch. 5). A contemporary parody demonstrates the pre-existence of this vision in romantic literature—namely, the dazzling "female form and countenance" that materializes in the chambers of Scythrop in *Nightmare Abbey*. Peacock published this work in 1818—after Flora and Rose, but before Rebecca and Rowena, Minna and Brenda, and the others were invented by Scott. "Call me Stella," exclaims Scythrop's apparition.

> Stella, in her conversations with Scythrop, displayed a highly cultivated and energetic mind, full of impassioned schemes of liberty, and impatience of masculine usurpation. She had a lively sense of all the oppressions that are done under the sun; and the vivid pictures which her imagination presented to her of the numberless scenes of injustice and misery which are being acted at every moment in every part of the inhabited world, gave an habitual seriousness to her physiognomy, that made it seem as if a smile had never once hovered on her lips.[11]

The energy, imagination, compassion, masculinity, melancholy, and particular physiognomy of dark heroines are here registered. Apart from topical allusions, the joke of *Nightmare Abbey* is that Scythrop loves both Marionetta and "Stella" and cannot make up his mind between them until too late. In the Waverley Novels the hero always knows his mind by the end. As the hero of civil society he chooses the blonde heroine of society.

[11] Thomas Love Peacock, *Works* (10 vols. London, 1924–34), 3: 93–94.

9. The Highland Line

The topographical stress of the Waverley Novels complements the contrast of two basic character types. The face of the land as well as the features of heroes and heroines physically represent the dualism of law and nature, reason and passion, sobriety and romance. Physiognomy and topography together supply the primary symbols for the thematic structure of the Waverley Novels. The symbols are products of the theme: in the romance of Scott morality is more fundamental than geography. Yet in a real sense these works originate from the city of Edinburgh, and could not have been written by a citizen of any other land but Scotland. To the present day, from the window of a library or from the confusion of city traffic in Edinburgh, one can be shocked by the sudden prospect of sublime nature crowding in upon civilization. And in former days, in *The Chronicles of the Canongate*, Chrystal Croftangry also looked out upon "the gigantic slope of Arthur['s] Seat, and the girdle of lofty rocks called Salisbury Crags; objects so rudely wild that the mind can hardly conceive them to exist in the vicinage of a populous metropolis" (Ch. 6). Another passage in the same work renders explicit the symbolism of this contrast: "I have, as it were, the two extremities of the moral world at my threshold" (Ch. 5).

The ambulatory motion of the Waverley Novels is typically from south to north, from England to Scotland, from lowlands to highlands, and back again. Running east and west from the Firth of Forth to the Clyde, the Highland line locates an ideal difference in ways of life rather than an actual political barrier. In the 1829 introduction to *Rob Roy* Scott attributed the interest of that historical figure to "this strong contrast betwixt the civilised and cultivated mode of life on the one side of the Highland line, and the wild and lawless adventures which were habitually undertaken and achieved by one who dwelt on the opposite side of that ideal boundary." *Waverley* and *Rob Roy* exploit the contrast most deliberately. The structure of *Redgauntlet* is similar—though the action moves from Edinburgh to the south and west, suggesting that the Highland line exercises an ideal rather than literal influence on the Waverley Novels. The passive hero in each of these romances is appropriately an Englishman. In *A Legend of Montrose* and *The Fair Maid of Perth* Lowlanders journey into the lawless and primitive region.

Scott inherits this kind of motion from the picaresque tradition. But the direction of the journey in his romance differs from that of the picaresque novel. The protagonist of the eighteenth-century novel in England travels toward the city, to London or to Bath, where civilization becomes, in effect, the victim of the hero's or heroine's innocence. Instead of searching out and exposing actual human behavior, romance projects ideal values. Scott's traveler sets out from Edinburgh, or from England, to probe the lawless state that civilization has overcome. As in the old romance, which moved from court to country, the journey is undertaken with the ultimate expectation of affirming rather than criticizing existing values. The superiority of society Scott takes for granted.

Moreover, from a position of strength in organized and accepted morality, the journey of romance turns inward, exploring the instinctual life of man.

> It is the same with a great part of the narratives of my friend Mr. Cooper. We sympathise with his Indian chiefs and backwoodsmen, and acknowledge, in the characters which he presents to us, the same truth of human nature by which we should feel ourselves influenced if placed in the same condition. So much is this the case, that, though it is difficult, or almost impossible, to reclaim a savage, bred from his youth to war and the chase, to the restraints and the duties of civilised life, nothing is more easy or common than to find men who have been educated in all the habits and comforts of improved society, willing to exchange them for the wild labours of the hunter and the fisher. The very amusements most pursued and relished by men of all ranks, whose constitutions permit active exercise, are hunting, fishing, and, in some instances, war, the natural and necessary business of the savage of Dryden, where his hero talks of being
>
> > —'As free as nature first made man,
> > When wild in woods the noble savage ran.'[12]

Scott significantly chooses sport to illustrate this movement away from society toward nature. Hunting and fishing, and, hopefully, war, are characterized by their temporary interest. Similarly, the journey in the Waverley Novels proves to be designed as an excursion, by which the hero ventures to explore "the opposite side of that ideal boundary," but returns safely to peaceful society.

In the eighteenth century, especially in the years after 1745, the Highlands of Scotland were thoroughly "pacified" in the interests of legal and political security. Conditions in this period were in some ways analogous to the frontier of nineteenth-century America. The union of 1707 was commercially unfavorable to all parts of Scotland,

---

[12] 1830 introduction to *The Monastery*.

and Hanoverian rule made slower headway north of the border irrespective of Stuart sympathies. The public toleration of smuggling, as evidence of the resentment of this settlement, is frequently remarked in the Waverley Novels. The local history of the century preceding 1814 provided a concrete source for the contrast of civilization and lawlessness, just as the closing of the frontier in the nineteenth century continues to supply a theme for popular American literature today.

History, therefore, furnished the same kind of material as geography. According to Scott's general preface of 1829, visits to the Highlands and conversations with the veterans of 1745 were central to the inspiration of the Waverley Novels. "It naturally occurred to me that the ancient traditions and high spirit of a people who, living in a civilised age and country, retained so strong a tincture of manners belonging to an early period of society, must afford a subject favourable for romance, if it should not prove a curious tale marred in the telling." We often credit Scott, however, with modern historical notions that he did not possess. Though he freely contrasted the "manners" of civilized and primitive ages, he did not assume that men were fundamentally products of a particular age and economic condition. The test of the latter concept of history is the full sense of the present as a concrete and particular environment. Stendhal and Balzac were able to transform the "atmospheric Historism" of romanticism into "atmospheric realism," but this process was not accomplished in English fiction until the eighteen-forties.[13] Scott was convinced of the primary uniformity of human nature in all periods. He would agree with David Hume that "the same motives always produce the same actions," and that history discovers "the constant and universal principles of human nature."[14]

In the general preface Scott connected his venture into prose romance with his experience in completing a romance of the antiquary Joseph Strutt. He proposed to render "a similar work more light and obvious to general comprehension . . . [and] founded on . . . more

---

[13] Cf. Auerbach, *Mimesis*, trans. Trask, pp. 443–48; also his "Vico and Aesthetic Historicism," *Journal of Aesthetics and Art Criticism* 8 (1949): 110–18.

[14] *Essays Moral, Political, and Literary*, ed. T. H. Green and T. H. Grose (2 vols. London, 1875), 2: 68. For the opinion that Scott adheres to the eighteenth-century rationalist view of history rather than romantic historicism see Duncan Forbes, *The Liberal Anglican Idea of History* (Cambridge, England, 1952), pp. 136–37, and n. 202, pp. 190–91. Forbes cites the concurrence of Carlyle, Taine, Bagehot, Ruskin, A. W. Benn, Buchan, and Legouis and Cazamian on this point, against the dissent of G. M. Trevelyan. For the opposite view see Leslie Stephen, *Hours in a Library* (3 vols. London, 1892), 1: 162–65; and especially the Marxist reading of Georg Lukács, *Der Historische Roman* (Berlin, 1955), pp. 23–60.

modern events." His reservations about *Queenhoo Hall* are more explicit in the dedicatory epistle to *Ivanhoe*:

> The late ingenious Mr. Strutt, in his romance of Queen-Hoo-Hall [sic], acted upon another principle; and in distinguishing between what was ancient and modern, forgot, as it appears to me, that extensive neutral ground, the large proportion, that is, of manners and sentiments which are common to us and to our ancestors, having been handed down unaltered from them to us, or which, arising out of the principles of our common nature, must have existed alike in either society. . . . The passions . . . are generally the same in all ranks and conditions, all countries and ages; and it follows, as a matter of course, that the opinions, habits of thinking, and actions, however influenced by the peculiar state of society, must still, upon the whole, bear a strong resemblance to each other.

Scott hesitates, in this last sentence, as if he were aware of the impending surge of historicism. In *Waverley* he contended that "the object of my tale is more a description of men than manners," and further resolved to escape the "disadvantages" of recounting the manners of the previous century "by throwing the force of my narrative upon the characters and passions of the actors;—those passions common to men in all stages of society, and which have alike agitated the human heart, whether it throbbed under the steel corslet of the fifteenth century, the brocaded coat of the eighteenth, or the blue frock and dimity waistcoat of the present day" (Ch. 1). The dynamics of human nature are thus supposed to be the constant of history.

Because history, and the peculiar situation of the Highlands, must reflect "passions common to men," history and geography in the Waverley Novels converge with a topography of the mind. The conflict of individual "romantic" energies against the civilizing restraints of society conforms to the chief interior conflict of passion and reason. A reciprocal arrangement obtains between the external and internal conflict, so that it is difficult to speak of one conflict without drawing a metaphor from the other. (Treating history in terms of the passions has since gone out of fashion, though the use of topographical metaphors for the mind has become, if anything, more common.) The contrast of light and dark heroes and heroines contributes to Scott's image of Scotland in the eighteenth century. Conversely, the contrast of Highlands and Lowlands, or of Scotland and England, elaborates a philosophy of mind and ethics. In *The Highland Widow* Captain Campbell, a Highland officer, doubts if his superior officer will sympathize with the tragic crime of Hamish MacTavish: "General ———— is half a Lowlander, half an Englishman. He has no idea of the high and enthusiastic character which, in these mountains, often brings ex-

alted virtues in contact with great crimes, which, however, are less of-
fences of the heart than errors of the understanding" (Ch. 5). In the
less civilized Highlands emotions prevail over the understanding; and
each individual Highlander illustrates the rule.

Even the Scottish romances are more usefully interpreted as general studies of the conflict of nature and civilization than as particular
imaginative tales of Scottish history. Rob Roy rejects Frank Osbaldistone's offer to help settle his account with society on the grounds
that he cannot live without nature: "the heather that I have trode
upon when living, must bloom ower me when I am dead—my heart
would sink, and my arm would shrink and wither like fern in the
frost, were I to lose sight of my native hills; nor has the world a scene
that would console me for the loss of the rocks and cairns, wild as
they are, that you see around us" (Ch. 35). As if in direct response to
this feeling for nature, Rob Roy longs for the condition of man that
philosophers regularly characterized as the state of nature: "it was a
merry warld when every man held his ain gear wi' his ain grip, and
when the country side wasna fashed wi' warrants and poindings and
apprizings, and a' that cheatry craft" (Ch. 25). Law of property is the
principal civilizing force. On behalf of his English novices, Bailie
Nicol Jarvie paints a similar picture of the Highlands, substituting the
present geographical equivalent for the world which Rob Roy relegates to the historical past:

> "They are clean anither set frae the like o' huz;—there's nae bailie-
> courts amang them—nae magistrates that dinna bear the sword in vain,
> like the worthy deacon that's awa', and, I may sa't, like myself and other
> present magistrates in this city—But it's just the laird's command, and
> the loon maun loup [the fellow must leap]; and the never another law
> hae they but the length o' their dirks—the broadsword's pursuer, or
> plaintiff, as you Englishers ca' it, and the target is defender; the stoutest
> head bears langest out;—and there's a Hieland plea for ye."
>
> Owen groaned deeply; and I allow that the description did not greatly
> increase my desire to trust myself in a country as lawless as he described
> these Scottish mountains. [Ch. 26]

The basic contrast of nature and civilization, and of natives and citizens, made the romance of Scott peculiarly meaningful to the American audience. But the American frontier had already contributed
something to this romance before the Waverley Novels were imported
to the United States. For Europeans one of the symbols of man in a
state of nature was the American Indian. This symbol formed part of
Scott's own image of the Highlands: "It was not above sixty or seventy
years . . . since the whole north of Scotland was under a state of gov-

ernment nearly as simple and patriarchal as those of our good allies the Mohawks and Iroquois."[15] Rob Roy shares his symbolic stature with that of the Indian, and an Indian in close vicinity to modern society: "Thus a character like his, blending the wild virtues, the subtle policy, and unrestrained license of an American Indian, was flourishing in Scotland during the Augustan age of Queen Anne and George I."[16] The long factual and legendary account of Rob Roy that follows in the 1829 introduction does not remind us strongly of an American Indian, but that is his symbolic value.

The highly generalized cast of the conflict of law and lawlessness in the Waverley Novels may be discerned in an excursion that sets out in the very opposite direction from the Highland line. In her journey from Edinburgh to London in *The Heart of Mid-Lothian* Jeanie Deans may be seen moving out of the sphere of civilized life and then into it again. She meets persons who seem to originate from another moral world: "'In what strange school,' thought Jeanie to herself, 'has this poor creature been bred up, where such remote precautions are taken against the pursuits of justice? What would my father or Reuben Butler think if I were to tell them there are sic folk in the world?'" (Ch. 30). A little later she resolves to follow Madge Wildfire as long as her wandering steps seem likely to lead "into contact with law and legal protection" (Ch. 31). In the same romance Scott introduces Effie Deans, who transgresses the laws of society, as an "untaught child of nature, whose good and evil seemed to flow rather from impulse than from reflection" (Ch. 10). She belongs, if we pursue the geographical symbolism of the Waverley Novels, in the Highlands with Hamish MacTavish. Similarly, at the end of *The Heart of Mid-Lothian*, Staunton expresses grave apprehension at the approach of an unusual storm. Butler, the passive hero, scorns the notion that "the laws of nature should correspond in their march with our ephemeral deeds or sufferings," but Staunton believes implicitly in the prophetic character of natural events (Ch. 51). He is, indeed, fated to die in a few moments by the hand of his natural son. "The eyes of the lad were keen and sparkling; his gesture free and noble, like that of all savages" (Ch. 50). And the boy flees in the logical direction, westward to America, where he murders his inhuman master, and disappears among "the next tribe of wild Indians" (Ch. 52). The two worlds are distinguished therefore in the romance that is morally the most complex of the Waverley Novels.

The two extremities of the moral world set the passive hero in mo-

---

[15] Dedicatory epistle to *Ivanhoe.*
[16] 1829 introduction to *Rob Roy.*

tion. His allegiance, however, is firmly to one side. He may tour the dark, wild Highlands but never negotiate between that world and the achieved order of his own world. For him the Highland line is an ideal but rigid moral barrier that he cannot violate, though he may have pleasurable glimpses of the other side. If he were actually to participate in that other life, or attempt to negotiate a fresh settlement between its claims and the claims of "prudence and principle," then, in terms of this fable, he would have to depart forever into the west. The fable does not envision a compromise. Bailie Nicol Jarvie, himself a magistrate of Glasgow, does negotiate between the states of nature and civilization. He pays blackmail to certain Highlanders, including Rob Roy, for protection. But the consequent irony of his advice to Frank Osbaldistone mocks the moral predicament of heroes: "ye suldna keep ower muckle company wi' Hielandmen and thae wild cattle. Can a man touch pitch an no be defiled?—aye mind that" (Ch. 23).

IV

PROPERTY

The power of perpetuating our property in our families is
one of the most valuable and interesting circumstances belonging to it, and that which tends the most to the perpetu-
ation of society itself. It makes our weakness subservient to
our virtues; it grafts benevolence even upon avarice.
 —Burke, *Reflections on the Revolution in France*

[Property] is, in the last resort, the palladium of all that
ought to be dear to us, and must never be approached but
with awe and veneration.
 —Godwin, *Political Justice*

10. Nature and Convention

THE DENOUEMENT in the Waverley Novels obeys an economic motive: the passive hero and blonde heroine ordinarily
inherit a superabundance of real property. According to William Paley's *Principles* (1785), of which there were twenty-one editions
by 1814, "the real foundation of our right [to property] is, THE LAW
OF THE LAND."[1] For Paley, private property is ultimately sanctioned by
divine law; but neither divine law nor natural right is required to understand the practical foundation of property, which consists of the
existing legal "regulations" agreed upon by men. Property rests directly on the rational order of society, and is secure only by virtue of
an agreement among men to respect it—that is, to respect the existing titles to property, and ultimately to respect reality, or things as
they are. In the Waverley Novels, by adhering steadfastly to the law of
the land—so steadfastly that they may hardly act in any direction—
the passive hero and blonde heroine demonstrate their respect for
property and their fitness to possess and perpetuate the title to property for future generations.

In the second book of the *Commentaries* Blackstone warms to the
subject of *jura rerum*, the rights of things, with the observation that

---

[1] *Principles of Moral and Political Philosophy*, in *Works*, ed. D. S. Wayland (5 vols. London, 1837), 1: Bk. III, Pt. I, ch. 4.

"there is nothing which so generally strikes the imagination, and engages the affections of mankind, as the right of property; or that sole and despotic dominion which one man claims and exercises over the external things of this world, in total exclusion of the right of any other individual in the universe." In a subsequent sentence (reflecting on the general obscurity of property law) he unconsciously sketches both sides of the emotional stake in property: "Pleased as we are with the possession, we seem afraid to look back to the means by which it was acquired, as if fearful of some defect in our title."[2] The excitement of the idea of property derives from the expectation of material benefit and from the anxiety of loss, from the security of tangible things and the uncertainty of abstract titles.

Property is far from being a dry legal relation. Paley and Blackstone are the great rationalizing minds of their age; they accept things as they are with sometimes astonishing complacency. Yet the excitement, the possible irrationality, of the idea of property reveals itself in their pages. Paley's treatment of the subject begins with a famous but unresolved parable of pigeons:

> If you should see a flock of pigeons in a field of corn; and if . . . you should see ninety-nine of them gathering all they got into a heap; reserving nothing for themselves but the chaff and refuse; keeping this heap for one, and that the weakest, perhaps worst, pigeon of the flock; sitting round, and looking on, all the winter, whilst this one was devouring, throwing about, and wasting it; and if a pigeon more hardy or hungry than the rest, touched a grain of the hoard, all the others instantly flying upon it, and tearing it to pieces: if you should see this, you would see nothing more than what is every day practised and established among men.[3]

The analogy would be subversive in any age. As Paley writes in the following paragraph, "there must be some very important advantages to account for an institution, which, in the view of it above given, is so paradoxical and unnatural." He lists, in fact, four advantages of property as an institution: it increases production by securing the product; "it preserves the produce of the earth to maturity" for the same reason; it prevents war and confusion; and "it improves the convenience of living" by stimulating invention and division of labor.[4] But Paley can discover no fully satisfactory foundation of the *right* of property—

[2] William Blackstone, *Commentaries on the Laws of England* (15th ed. 4 vols., London, 1809), 2: 2.

[3] *Moral and Political Philosophy*, Bk. III, Pt. I, ch. 1.

[4] Ibid., ch. 2.

who should receive what—except the law of the land, the established system of distribution.

Property is an idea. This idea is distinct from the mere possession or use of a thing. The "rights of things" are not invested in the thing or land itself: property is an abstract relation between things and persons. According to Jeremy Bentham, "there is no form, or colour, or visible trace, by which it is possible to express the relation which constitutes property. It belongs not to physics, but to metaphysics: it is altogether a creature of the mind."[5] And William Godwin compares the proprietor to a factor or a warehouseman rather than a consumer: "Property implies some permanence of external possession, and includes in it the idea of a possible competitor."[6] The idea of property does not concern the actual activity of sowing and reaping, eating and sleeping, but the expectation of these things, the "right" to them. Property is a moral idea. It contains the idea of obligation; it expresses what *ought* to be occupied or used by whom, and not merely the fact of occupation or use. Statements about property obviously share in all the perplexity of ethical statements in general. For Godwin the right of property is rooted in those all-important "passive rights" of man, rights which impose an obligation on others.[7] Bentham, with his language of pleasure and pain, derives property from a "disappointment preventing principle." Disappointment is always more painful than surprise is pleasurable.[8] Even for these radical thinkers the relation of private property—which is also the central principle of the passive hero—is a defensive, a "passive" or "disappointment preventing," principle.

Theorists of property are seldom consistent. The failing is understandable in an area where moral ideas, sets of rights and obligations, are so inextricably and purposively attached to material interests—and when the idea of property, as Blackstone and Godwin both immediately observe, contains the "exclusion of the right of any other individual" and "the idea of a possible competitor." The history of the idea of property in every age reflects the confusion of the moral and material interests that it hopes to unite.[9] In the Christian era the caution of Christ against riches and the example of the apostles, who "had all things common" and divided their possessions among

[5] Quoted by Elie Halévy, *The Growth of Philosophical Radicalism*, trans. Mary Morris (London, 1928), pp. 46–47.

[6] *Enquiry Concerning Political Justice and Its Influence on Morals and Happiness*, facsimile of 3d ed. (1798), ed. F.E.L. Priestley (3 vols. Toronto, 1946), Bk. VIII, ch. 2.

[7] Ibid., and Bk. II, ch. 5.

[8] Halévy, *The Growth of Philosophical Radicalism*, p. 46.

[9] Cf. Richard Schlatter, *Private Property: The History of an Idea* (New Brunswick, 1951).

men,[10] have never become social practice. In the middle ages the Christian idea of stewardship, which has to some extent influenced all subsequent ideas of the responsibility of property, fused easily with the feudal idea of property as "dominion," property held in trust from some higher feudal rank. And from the teaching of Aristotle St. Thomas Aquinas was able to conceive of all social institutions, including that of property, as extensions of natural law.[11] But in the sixteenth and seventeenth centuries the revival of Stoic ideas, and the compelling interest of new kinds of wealth, began to replace the feudal and scholastic idea of conditional rights with a theory of natural rights and of a society founded by a contract among independent persons.

The great English philosopher of natural rights and the social contract, John Locke, wrote in 1690 as the exponent of newly secured political power: his justification of private property naturally focused on the acquisition of property; his theory was bound to suggest some dynamic principle. Locke argued that the right to property derived from human labor: "it is allowed to be his goods who hath bestowed his labour upon it." He attached no conditions to this right; presumably one may do entirely as one wishes with the things "he hath mixed his labour with." He did conceive of a limit to the amount of property that one man should possess: "As much as any one can make use of to any advantage of life before it spoils, so much he may by his labour fix a property in," and, "the measure of property Nature will set, by the extent of man's labour and the conveniency of life."[12] Locke's theory, therefore, is highly individualistic; it places great weight on labor and enterprise; it formulates a "natural" right to property; and it strikes one as revolutionary.

The considerable influence of this theory is more easily traced in France and in America than in England. David Hume could make no sense at all of founding a right of property by mixing one's labor with something—unless the expression were merely a metaphor.[13] Property is not a natural relation to Hume, but a highly conventional one, closely allied to the principal artificial virtue of justice. The laws of property may all be regarded as rationalizations, in a sense, but their primary tendency is simply to eliminate "indifference and ambi-

---

[10] Acts 2:44–45.

[11] A. J. Carlyle, "The Theory of Property in Medieval Theology," in *Property, Its Duties and Rights . . . Essays by Various Hands* (London, 1915), pp. 119–32.

[12] *The Second Treatise of Civil Government*, ed. J. W. Gough (Oxford, 1948), ch. 5.

[13] *A Treatise of Human Nature* (2 vols. London, Everyman's Library, 1952), Bk. III, Pt. II, secs. 2–3.

guity [of ownership] which would be the source of perpetual dissention." Hume is surprised at the difficulties that philosophers have made for themselves on this subject: "What other reason, indeed, could writers ever give, why this must be *mine* and that *yours*; since unobstructed nature, surely, never made any such distinction?"[14] Whereas Locke allows the ideal and original use of property, as he conceives it, to enhance the moral suasion of his theory, Hume attempts to describe the institution of property as it operates in society. The latter approach governs the thinking of the remainder of the eighteenth century in Great Britain—including the thought of Edmund Burke and Walter Scott. The moral and emotional enhancement of property always returns, merely reinforcing the existence of property instead of its origins. By the end of the century the main view of property is "realistic"—even antitheoretical; but the "reality," the way things are, becomes sacrosanct and rigid. For Burke it was "a sort of profaneness to talk of the use, as affecting the title of property"[15]—a position that places a higher value on private ownership per se than on the use that is made of it, and which therefore subverts the ideas of dominion and stewardship just as effectively as any theory of natural rights.

Insofar as Scott holds a theory of property, it is the theory of the law and of Hume. Property exerts and responds to a workable order in society and keeps individual passions in check. According to usages set down in the laws of the land, intelligent citizens agree to respect the lines of property as they find them. Scott's own career contradicts but also confirms this thesis. On extensive credit he himself acquired new property, with great speed and, one must say, with great passion. At the same time he can hardly be said to have acknowledged what he was doing: he kept his partnership in the Ballantyne firm a secret; and he undertook to build and extend Abbotsford in a situation of precarious financial unreality. Scott's idea of property is also highly colored with a sense of *noblesse oblige*; but fundamentally it is realistic and defensive. Those that have property, have it. In regard to a new anti-Jacobin paper in Edinburgh in 1819, Scott writes to Lord Melville that the current unrest of the populace would "be easily extinguished if men of property will be true to themselves and use their power." Who are the men of property? "It is the middle class which requires to be put on the guard—every man who has or cultivates a furrow of land or has a guinea in the funds or vested in stock, in trade or in

---

[14] *Essays Moral, Political, and Literary*, ed. Green and Grose, 2: 189–90.
[15] *Reflections on the Revolution in France*, in *Works*, 3: 383.

mortgage or in any other way whatsoever."[16] When Adam Smith suggests that civil government exists to defend the rich against the poor, he adds, on second thought, a similar distinction between "those who have some property against those who have none at all."[17] This definition of property is extremely broad—and extremely realistic: anyone with anything to lose has property. Property is the right to things as presently constituted; realty is practically the same thing as reality.

11. Property in 1814

In Great Britain the force and appeal of the labor theory becomes generalized, contributing to the prestige of private property without seriously infecting the realm with its logic. Locke's chapter on property is less straightforward than it seems. Locke recognizes but immediately corrects the radical implications of his argument: "every man should have as much as he could make use of . . . had not the invention of money, and the tacit agreement of men to put a value on it, introduced (by consent) larger possessions and a right to them."[18] This critical sentence extends the basis of property to include convention as well as a natural right, and the labor theory may apply only to the state of nature. The significance of the Second Treatise becomes difficult to assess: "The nearest approach to a definite statement of Locke's ultimate conclusions seems to be that this mysterious compact, which is the binding force of the whole social order, is in fact the tacit consent of mankind to the inequality of property, as implied in the use of money, and made necessary by the corruption which followed the golden age."[19]

Locke can hardly be scolded for confounding the idea of property in both natural and conventional causes—Grotius and the Roman jurists themselves committed similar ambiguities.[20] What this surplus of grounds for private property produces in the eighteenth century is a new and virtually suprarational idea of property as an absolute value—an idea with considerable impact on British society and with

---

[16] *Letters*, 6: 31. I have supplied the punctuation in the last sentence. Cf. 7: 198, to Byron. "I am not for one afraid of tumults which are to begin with those who have anything left to lose."

[17] *An Inquiry into the Nature and Causes of the Wealth of Nations*, ed. Edwin Cannan (New York, Modern Library, 1937), Bk. V, ch. 1, pt. ii.

[18] Second Treatise, ch. 5, par. 36.

[19] Leslie Stephen, *English Thought in the Eighteenth Century* (2 vols. London, 1876), 2: 142.

[20] Schlatter, *Private Property*, pp. 24–30, 130–31.

profound consequences for British fiction. The faith in an absolute right of property can be seen gathering force in the Second Treatise itself, when Locke suggests that inheritance of property is also a natural right; when he argues that the right of conquest in war extends to the lives of the enemy but "not to their estates," and, most obviously, when he discovers that the preservation of property is "the great and chief end" of commonwealths.[21] In one remark he even states that "government has no other end but the preservation of property."[22] In the eighteenth century the conviction that property precedes and occasions government was pronounced with increasing favor. "Till there be property there can be no government"—the sentiment was heard in the lectures of Adam Smith;[23] it could be read in the popular works of William Paley[24] and above all in the arguments of Edmund Burke, who entertained "a high opinion of the legislative authority; but . . . never dreamt that Parliament had any right whatever to violate property, to overrule prescription."[25]

With Burke property becomes an absolute without being a "natural" right. The institution of property is both the cause and the best defense of civil society. In his usage one of the legal titles to property—prescription—subsumes all others. "Prescription is the most solid of all titles, not only to property, but, which is to secure that property, to Government."[26] When not only property but government is morally identified with the existing state of things, the Revolution of 1688 has to be regarded in a particular manner. Burke regards the Revolution "as a final settlement, not as a precedent."[27] He goes to considerable lengths to argue that "the nation in that act was on the defensive" and repeats many times that this unique revolution was "*the case of necessity only.*"[28] It was brought about, as it were, by physical causes. Burke perhaps shares the uneasiness of Blackstone[29] in discussing the event of 1688, but the accomplishment of the Revolution is at the very base of his thinking. It took, of course, a century for Whig principles to become the Tory Reaction. In *Rob Roy* the hero declares

---

[21] Second Treatise, pars. 124, 182, 190.

[22] Ibid., par. 94.

[23] Adam Smith, *Lectures on Justice, Police, Revenue and Arms . . . Reported by a Student in 1763*, ed. Edwin Cannan (Oxford, 1896), p. 15. Cf. *The Wealth of Nations*, Bk. V, Ch. 1, pt. ii.

[24] *Moral and Political Philosophy*, Bk. III, Pt. I, ch. 3.

[25] *Reflections on the Revolution in France*, in *Works*, 3: 434. Cf. p. 373.

[26] Quoted by Halévy, *The Growth of Philosophical Radicalism*, p. 162.

[27] Alfred Cobban, *Edmund Burke and the Revolt against the Eighteenth Century* (2d ed. London, 1960), p. 58.

[28] *Appeal from the New to the Old Whigs*, in *Works*, 4: 80, 124. Cf. 3: 254.

[29] *Commentaries*, 1: 211–12.

to Justice Inglewood in firm tones that he "had been educated as a good subject in the principles of the Revolution, and as such now demanded the personal protection of the laws which had been assured by that great event" (Ch. 8).

According to A. V. Dicey, "the optimism which may well be called Blackstonianism . . . led in the sphere of law to contented acquiescence with the existing state of things."[30] Dicey's period of "contented acquiescence" and "legislative quiescence" (1760–1830) corresponds very nearly to Scott's lifetime (1771–1832), and Blackstone's *Commentaries* typify the new attitude toward property. Blackstone begins with the "design of Providence" and a "state of primeval simplicity" but argues more confidently in the style of Burke. "Necessity begat property: and, in order to ensure that property, recourse was had to civil society."[31] Blackstone thus joins the ranks of those who make property prior to government and even to society. The highest achievements of men, he continues, depend upon leisure "to cultivate the human mind, to invent useful arts, and to lay the foundations of science," and therefore such achievements also flow from property. The *jura rerum*, furthermore, peacefully and perpetually reinforce the society they have ordained. "And thus the legislature of England has universally promoted the grand ends of civil society, the peace and security of individuals, by steadily pursuing that wise and orderly maxim, of assigning to every thing capable of ownership a legal and determinate owner."[32] The emergence from a state of nature appears to depend on nothing less than the discovery that things can be assigned proprietors. Blackstone founds the right of property both in "necessity"—a natural cause that operates in every state of history—and in positive law—the accomplishment, in particular, of 1688. He infers, in short, that property is an absolute good. There are instances "in which the law of the land has postponed even public necessity to the sacred and inviolable rights of private property."[33] "So great moreover is the regard of the law for private property, that it will not authorize the least violation of it; no, not even for the general good of the whole community."[34]

It may be argued that the Author of *Waverley* was trained in the law of Scotland, not of England, and that even today Scottish property law retains more feudal vestiges than English law. But historically the

[30] *Law and Public Opinion in England* (London, 1930), p. 81.
[31] *Commentaries*, 2: 8.
[32] Ibid., p. 15.
[33] Ibid., 1: 140.
[34] Ibid., p. 139.

two systems of law respond together to the new attitude toward property. The parallel development of the idea of property as an absolute can be detected in the language of two great institutes of Scottish law, that of Lord Stair (1681) and that of John Erskine (1773). In the seventeenth century Stair approaches property as one of several relations, or "real rights," between individuals and the land. "The main real right is property, standing in the middle betwixt community and possession, which precede it, and servitude and pledge which follow it."[35] The right of property is still conceived as one of degree, taking a certain rank among a series of obligations, and adjoining the rights of those who have no title at all to dispose of the land or do as they please with it. This hierarchy of rights is also a feudal characteristic. "The way to distinguish betwixt property and servitude is, that the greatest interest retaineth the name of property, which hath in it the power of disposal of the substance of the thing, or alienation thereof; whereas servitude is a lesser right, and reacheth but the fruits or use in part, or for a time."[36] This language contrasts with that of Erskine, the eighteenth-century professor of law, whose discussion of real rights proceeds directly to the "sovereign" right of property:

> Things or subjects fall no otherwise under the consideration of law, than as persons may have a right to them . . . and the sovereign or primary real right is that of property; which is the right of using and disposing of a subject as our own, except in so far as we are restrained by law or paction. This right necessarily excludes every other person but the proprietor; for if another had a right to dispose of the subject, or so much as to use it, without his consent, it would not be his property, but common to him with the other. Property therefore implies a prohibition, that no person shall encroach upon the right of the proprietor; and consequently every encroachment, though it should not be guarded against by statute, founds the proprietor in an action of damages.[37]

Not only has property emerged as a supreme right, an absolute or near absolute right of individuals: the proprietor is firmly entrenched behind that right. No sooner is property defined, than it "implies a prohibition," corresponding to the "total exclusion of the right of any other individual in the universe" ascribed by Blackstone to English law and "the idea of a possible competitor" in Godwin's definition.

---

[35] James Dalrymple, first Viscount Stair, *The Institutions of the Law of Scotland* (2 vols. Edinburgh, 1826), Bk. II, Title 1.

[36] Ibid.

[37] John Erskine, *An Institute of the Law of Scotland* (2 vols. Edinburgh, 1812), Bk. II, Title 1.

And Erskine immediately anticipates the need for a law of torts. As the hero of *Rob Roy* declares to Rashleigh, "unless you instantly do justice to your benefactor, my father, by accounting for his property . . . until I have full satisfaction concerning the fraud you meditate—you shall go with me before a magistrate" (Ch. 25).

By the end of this century the absolute right of property becomes the premise rather than the conclusion of political argument. Other institutions were defended by analogy or in relation to the institution of property. Liberty itself was the chief of these. Even the most visionary reformers did not imagine that the political franchise should extend to those who owned nothing. Only independent means could ensure independent judgment. Godwin merely reversed the terms of the relation, making the idea of property "a deduction from the right of private judgment."[38] For his part, Burke opposed the arbitrary and dangerous doctrine of natural rights with a theory of inherited rights analogous to heritable property. The idea of inheritance "leaves acquisition free; but it secures what it acquires. . . . We transmit our government and our privileges, in the same manner in which we enjoy and transmit our property and our lives."[39] He could argue from the same premise against the legislation of farm wages or the public administration of charity. The interference of a magistrate in matters of charity "is a violation of the property which it is his office to protect."[40] The people of England have also wisely "identified the estate of the Church with the mass of *private property*," and thereby save the clergy from becoming the "ecclesiastical pensioners of the state."[41] The militia, likewise, could be depended upon to support the true interests of the country, since its officers were landed gentlemen, with a stipulated income for each rank.[42] Commissions in the army, purchased for cash, were also regarded as private property.[43] And there was a selection of other public offices to be regarded as the property of younger sons. Scott held two such sinecures himself, and his letters, though not his novels, are an excellent introduction to these practices. In all ages, finally, the institution of property must come to terms with the institution of taxes. We ordinarily find taxes and property opposed—measures threatening "the dissolution of all landed property . . . pregnant with alarm both to private property and

---

[38] *Political Justice*, Bk. VIII, ch. 2.

[39] *Reflections on the Revolution in France*, in *Works*, 3: 274–75.

[40] *Thoughts and Details on Scarcity*, in *Works*, 5: 146.

[41] *Reflections on the Revolution in France*, in *Works*, 3: 364–65.

[42] Halévy, *England in 1815*, p. 69.

[43] Ibid., p. 80.

public liberty."[44] But even taxes may be deduced by the logic of property. Blackstone defines the king's revenue as the "portion which each subject contributes of his property, in order to secure the remainder."[45]

These arguments reflect the actual history of property in land during the course of the eighteenth century. Private estates were becoming larger and more profitable. In the early years of the century Parliament enacted an average of one enclosure bill per year; in the first ten years of the nineteenth century 906 bills for the "dividing, allotting, and enclosing" of land were enacted.[46] But the statistics of enclosure tell only part of the story. The administration and legal expense of such acts fell to the petitioners themselves, who were the largest landowners and who emerged more powerful than ever. The enclosure of land required capital, and the large owners in a parish were left in a position to purchase the small holdings. The enclosure movement of the sixteenth and seventeenth centuries had been opposed by the crown, but that of the eighteenth century was virtually directed by a parliament representing the large and independent interests of the country.[47] Meanwhile, at the end of this period, as more and more land came under cultivation and with the price of corn at its wartime peak, the profits of land grew steadily higher. By the year in which *Waverley* appeared, agricultural rents in England and Scotland had risen 100 or even 150 per cent over the previous twenty or twenty-five years.[48] In the Highlands of Scotland the enclosure, engrossing, and improvement of estates had created a serious problem of overpopulation.[49]

The French Revolution, far from calling such theories and practices into question, confirmed in Great Britain the political, economic, and emotional prestige of private property. In fact, by a peculiar irony of history the absolute right of property became the rallying cry of both sides in the conflict that shook the world just prior to the publication of the Waverley Novels. In France the revolution was fought in the name of the right to property; in England the same rev-

---

[44] Pamphleteer's preface to a speech by Sir John Sinclair, *An Alarm to Land Holders; or the Consequences of the Bill for the Redemption of the Land Tax* (London, 1798), pp. 31–32.

[45] *Commentaries*, 1: 281.

[46] Paul Mantoux, *The Industrial Revolution in the Eighteenth Century*, trans. Marjorie Vernon (London, 1928), p. 146.

[47] Ibid., pp. 169–70.

[48] Halévy, *England in 1815*, p. 229 and n.

[49] See Thomas Douglas, Earl of Selkirk, *Observations on the Present State of the Highlands of Scotland* (London, 1804), chs. 2–4.

olution was abhorred as a threat to property. The first articles of the Declaration of the Rights of Man positively declared the right of property; yet for Burke the principal fallacy of the revolution can be expressed, "*that the political and civil power of France is wholly separated from its property of every description.*"[50] In the judgment of R. H. Tawney, "the dogma of the sanctity of private property was maintained as tenaciously by the French Jacobins as by English Tories; and the theory that property is an absolute . . . is identical . . . with that not only of the men of 1789, but of the terrible Convention itself."[51] In the aftermath of the French wars, British Tories easily equated any revolution or unrest with an attack on property. In 1821 Scott censured James Ballantyne for his support in the *Edinburgh Weekly Journal* of the revolt in Naples: "The general belief is that *property* is aimed at and that is a very feverish sensation for those that have it."[52] "In Scotland within this six or seven year," he writes in 1827, "nothing could have prevented a civil war of the horrid *servile* description except the power which is now no more of pouring three thousand horse . . . on the disturbed districts."[53]

During the lifetime of Scott, as the right of property was exercised more and more freely, certain radical thinkers returned to the egalitarian implications of Locke. Everyone mixed his labor with something. Or if property and society were so inextricably bound together, then every member of society would seem to have a natural right to property. In the Waverley Novels property tends to become consolidated: an ideal denouement unites the considerable estates of hero and heroine into an even larger estate. The system of primogeniture could operate to this effect even in real life. The radicals were interested in quite the opposite process of distributing property. Only if each man worked his own soil could productivity be assured. The meaning of Locke was clear: the institution of property was intended only to guarantee the laborer his reward. Locke had also intimated that in the state of nature no man's right of property would exceed what he could use in his lifetime. The modesty of this claim—Christian modesty, one might say—attracted more general notice. William Paley shared some of the logic, though not the active sentiments, perhaps, of the radicals: "Inequality of property, in the degree in which it exists in most countries of Europe, abstractly considered, is an evil: but it is an evil which flows from those rules concerning the

---

[50] *Thoughts on French Affairs,* in *Works,* 4: 350.

[51] *The Acquisitive Society* (London, 1952), pp. 55–56. Cf. Harold J. Laski, *The Rise of European Liberalism* (London, 1936), pp. 226–36.

[52] *Letters,* 6: 428.

[53] Ibid., 10: 337.

acquisition and disposal of property, by which men are incited to industry, and by which the object of their industry is rendered secure and valuable. If there be any great inequality unconnected with this origin, it ought to be corrected."[54] The affirmation of the right of property in the Waverley Novels and elsewhere must be viewed against the general uneasiness, implicit in both the natural-rights theory and in Christianity, over the inequality of privilege. What one man has and another has not is always a subject of interest. In these years it was a particularly absorbing interest.

Men like Thomas Paine, William Ogilvie, and Thomas Spence were willing to quarrel with the current distribution of property.[55] The idea of history in their radical thought bears a close resemblance to that of the Waverley Novels—that is, a distinction between a state of nature and a state of civilization. The emotional values of the Highland world intrigued Scott: in his romance he constructed a fable by which these values could be enjoyed in the very act of reaffirming the claims of society. The state of nature also intrigued the radicals. Having no reason to rationalize large holdings of property by imputing violence to the state of nature, and perhaps equipped with a better perspective on the strife and struggles of civilization itself, the radicals regarded the earlier age as rather more peaceful than warlike. They agreed with Scott that in this early time a man's independence was gauged by his own strength. Being closer to the tradition of Dissent, they equated strength with work rather than warlike deeds. Far from being committed to the present state of things, they proposed the one solution that the dualism of the Waverley Novels forbids: they proposed to negotiate an actual compromise between the best of two possible worlds. What this would mean, however, was suggested by William Ogilvie, a professor at Aberdeen: "If it be indeed possible to accomplish any great improvement in the state of human affairs, and to unite the essential equality of a rude state, with the order, refinements, and accommodations of cultivated ages, such improvement is not so likely to be brought about by any means, as by a just and enlightened policy respecting property in land."[56]

William Godwin may be thought of as the age's most exhaustive theorist of equality. No thinker could be further from the mind of Scott. Godwin's view of society is atomistic rather than organic; he believes in society but not in government; he is for democracy as op-

---

[54] *Moral and Political Philosophy*, Bk. III, Pt. I, ch. 2.

[55] The pamphlets of Paine, Ogilvie, and Spence are reprinted in *The Pioneers of Land Reform*, ed. Max Beer (London, 1920).

[56] *An Essay on the Right of Property in Land* (published anonymously in 1781; reprinted in *Pioneers of Land Reform*), Pt. I, sec. 3.

posed to monarchy, and science as opposed to custom; his philosophy is more Platonic than pragmatic; he regards even promises as evils. Godwin can write that the idea of inherited property is a "gross imposition." "The property is produced by the daily labour of men now in existence. All that [the owners'] ancestors bequeathed to them, was a mouldy patent, which they show, as a title to extort from their neighbours what the labour of those neighbours has produced." He scorns the flimsy rationale of large estates: "The country-gentleman who, by levelling an eminence, or introducing a sheet of water into his park, finds work for hundreds of industrious poor, is the enemy, and not . . . the friend of his species."[57] Yet no author of the Tory Reaction more clearly demonstrates the conviction that property is the "palladium" of society. Godwin's ideal state has merely been transferred from the golden age to the golden future. When the "revolution of opinions" has been accomplished, and the triumph of rationality and prudence is complete, perhaps men can live without property. Meanwhile, according to the same chapter of *Political Justice*, the system of property is probably "better than any other." "If, by positive institution, the property of every man were equalized to-day, it would be unequal tomorrow." The very worst thing would be to attempt "to correct the distribution of wealth by individual violence." Rather, it should be defended, "if need be, by means of coercion." Godwin concludes his argument with an eloquent defense of property as the adjunct of private judgment and the bulwark of public security. "Civil society maintains a greater proportion of security among men, than can be found in the savage state."

The right of private property would seem to be in good hands. In the summer of 1814, however, in the very months that *Waverley* was completed, a theoretical and political attack on property in land was launched that would eventually prove overwhelming. In an article in the *Eclectic Review* James Mill announced that the interests of landowners diverged from the general interest of the nation, and the discussions were under way that culminated in Ricardo's *Principles of Political Economy and Taxation* in 1817. The intention of landowners to maintain their rents in the postwar period, and the bad harvests of 1814, were direct influences on the theory of rent in its now classic form.[58] Rent, defined by Ricardo as "the difference between the produce obtained by equal portions of labour and capital employed on land of the same or different qualities,"[59] became a hard core of irrationality in the center of things, and the interests of proprietors of land

---

[57] *Political Justice*, Bk. VIII, ch. 2.
[58] Halévy, *The Growth of Philosophical Radicalism*, pp. 277–81.
[59] Quoted by Halévy, ibid., p. 329.

seemed opposed to those of every other class. Economic theory became class theory, useful capital was mobile instead of fixed in land, and the idea of progress suggested that the system of production and distribution might change from one epoch to the next.

It is something more than a coincidence that the Waverley Novels should take their beginning in the same year with which textbooks of British history bring the eighteenth century to a close. In 1814 Scott himself was casting about for some new source of wealth. He did not, after all, inherit Abbotsford, but purchased it with his success. But no hero in the Waverley Novels earns such a fortune. The romance of Scott projects a strictly passive ideal of inherited property in land. The discrepancy is not so disturbing when we remember that the landowners of history did not suffer a real defeat until the repeal of the Corn Laws in 1846, and that long after that, British entrepreneurs displayed a fondness for converting the profits of free trade into fine estates. In fiction the superiority of property in land was celebrated at least until the last decade of the nineteenth century. The discrepancy between fact and fiction is never illogical in any case: it is either wishful or moral or both.

12. The Romance of Property

If Paley and Blackstone are sensitive to the apparent paradoxes of property and the force with which it "strikes the imagination, and engages the affections of mankind," then one may demand of a writer of fiction an equally sensitive regard for the subject. In his *History of Fiction*, which also belongs to the year 1814, John Dunlop levies a single criticism against *Tom Jones*, a book he otherwise very much admires: his criticism is addressed not to the morality of Jones, but to the insecurity of his property.

> As a story, Tom Jones seems to have only one defect, and it might have been so easily remedied, that it is to be regretted that it should have been neglected by the author. Jones, after all, proves illegitimate, when there would have been no difficulty for the author to have supposed that his mother had been privately married to the young clergyman. This would have had the effect, not only of removing the stain from the birth of the hero, but, in the idea of the reader, would have given him better security for the property of his uncle Allworthy.[60]

Much as civil society secures the property of those who have it, authors should secure the property of heroes. If society is indeed the

---

[60] *A History of Fiction* (3 vols. London, 1814), 3: 378.

creation of property—"in order to ensure that property," writes Blackstone, "recourse was had to civil society"—then so is romance. In
order to inherit that property, recourse was had to fiction. Dunlop
takes quite seriously the issue of property at the end of *Tom Jones*. He
appeals to the close legal bearing of marriage on property, and proposes a very practical use of legitimacy. When Glossin tries to contend, at the end of *Guy Mannering*, that the hero is illegitimate, the
author confounds him by producing an actual bastard (Ch. 56). One
may infer that Scott, for these purposes, was a more careful romancer
than Fielding. When Colonel Mannering advises his daughter that
property "is held in absolute indifference nowhere except in a novel"
(Ch. 51), he speaks only a half-truth. For no matter how indifferent
the hero may be, and the more indifferent the better, he always inherits an estate.

The problem of "assigning to every thing capable of ownership a
legal and determinate owner"[61] becomes acute every time one generation passes into the next. In romance, two generations are as important as the two sexes. Rather than sentiment or the Oedipus complex,
it is property that is probably responsible for so many fathers and
daughters, fathers and sons, guardians, and uncles in romance. As
Jane Austen pointed out in the opening pages of *Northanger Abbey*,
mothers almost never survive the birth of heroes and heroines. Fathers and guardians, on the other hand, have to be met with on the
same terms as brides. Even in real life the succession to property is
much more dramatic than the mere possession. The only social purpose of legal succession is the maintenance of order—lest something
capable of ownership should suddenly lack an owner. This end is distant from the popular idea of the original justification of property—
to guarantee an individual the fruits of his labor. Legal succession requires of society the utmost exercise of reason and long-range interest. At the same time, all but the legal heir are subject to understandable sighs—or fits—of envy. From the view that subsumes all rights to
property in the idea of prescription—a view which suggests that property *has* no origin—succession is less of a right than a mystic rite. The
hero of prescription, the passive hero of the Waverley Novels, can afford to be indifferent to gain because the ritual of romance assures
him his inheritance in any case. He ought to be indifferent because
he has surrendered his prerogatives to society. In romance, at least,
society will fulfill its part of the contract.

The marriage of the hero is closely related to his succession to
property—the two events are commonly referred to in the same paragraph—and the difference between blonde and brunette heroines is

---

[61] Blackstone, *Commentaries*, 2: 15.

instructive on this point. In *The Pirate* the pleasures of Minna Troil are solitary, and she responds most enthusiastically to nature. She aspires to "more important objects" than the everyday realities that surround her. Brenda Troil is more sociable, and, of the two sisters, the people of Burgh Westra admire chiefly Brenda. She is less intellectual, but more rational (Ch. 3). Brenda does not confuse her lover with a Viking sea-king. When the occasion demands—and marriage is such an occasion—the blonde sister can be quite dispassionate. Because she is a part of society and accepts the existing state of things, the blonde heroine—and her consort—may be trusted with real property. The preference of property for fair hair does not prevent the dark heroine from possessing riches. On the contrary, we imagine Rebecca to be fabulously wealthy. But the wealth of the brunette is in conveyables. Her possessions are easily transferred as gifts, and one of the discreet pleasures of a passive hero is to receive some of this bounty. The blonde girl shares his good fortune. At the end of *Ivanhoe* Rebecca delivers a sizable gift to Rowena (Ch. 44). In *The Heart of Mid-Lothian* cash gifts from Effie enable the Butlers to purchase a "little estate" (Ch. 49). In *The Fortunes of Nigel* Hermione, as dowager Lady Dalgarno, bestows her fortune on Margaret and her estate on Nigel (Ch. 37). Even Minna Troil performs a similar favor: by remaining single she leaves the estate of Magnus Troil undivided between the sisters. (Through most of *The Pirate* slander implies that Mordaunt delays his choice between Minna and Brenda until the question of the estate shall be settled.) The dark heroine has no use for wealth and may freely give it away.

The proper hero and heroine are not individual persons but representatives of civil society: Scott carefully protects them from too close an association with "personal" property and heartily endows them with real estate. He is not so impractical as to forget the existence of fluid kinds of wealth, but he separates such wealth from his protagonists by one or two generations or a deed of outright gift. Burke makes a similar and equally "romantic" distinction about wealth:

> It is the natural operation of things, where there exists a crown, a court, splendid orders of knighthood, and an hereditary nobility,—where there exists a fixed, permanent, landed gentry, continued in greatness and opulence by the law of primogeniture, and by a protection given to family settlements,—where there exists a standing army and navy,—where there exists a Church establishment . . . —in a country where such things exist, wealth, new in its acquisition, and precarious in its duration, can never rank first, or even near the first.[62]

---

[62] *Thoughts on French Affairs*, in *Works*, 4: 327.

Such wealth, in fact, is not only secondary but somewhat dangerous. Because it is new, it is more easily envied; and because it is precarious, more tempting. If the foundation of property is simply the law of the land and the present distribution of goods, then the idea of fluid capital and even the possibility of earning more of it are vaguely uncomfortable sensations.

Money that is coming from somewhere or going somewhere inevitably raises the question of selfish interest. The transactions of getting and spending advertise one's motives—whether good or bad; but a passive income from land or an inheritance infers no motive whatever. Scott ruled against any "calculating prudence" in fiction in his review of *Emma*.[63] At the end of the eighteenth century the Christian idea of unselfishness was combined with the prescriptive idea of property as readily as the Christian idea of stewardship had joined with the feudal idea of dominion. In fiction one can easily receive things without wanting them. Near the end of *Old Mortality* Burley demands to know if the hero still hopes to marry Edith Bellenden:

> "Dost thou still hope to possess the fair-haired girl, with her wide and rich inheritance?"
>
> "I have no such hope," answered Morton calmly. [Ch. 43]

Morton answers calmly, but since this is the next to the last chapter of the romance, his resignation is quickly rewarded. In *Kenilworth* and in *St. Ronan's Well*, where the heroes must forgo the happiness of marriage, they still accede to the responsibilities of property. In *Kenilworth* Tressilian inherits the estate of Sir Hugh Robsart (Ch. 41) even though the unfortunate Amy Robsart has married Leicester.

When realty is deliberately confused with reality, the increment or loss of property is difficult to comprehend ideally without recourse to plain good fortune or knavish conspiracy. In the Waverley Novels, just as property is ultimately restored or bequeathed but not earned, so in the course of the story it may be stolen but not sold. Hostility to the hero is largely directed against his property. This animus pervades *Peveril of the Peak*, for example, where the villains employ the fanaticism of the Popish Plot to usurp the Derbyshire property of the Peverils. They succeed so far as to secure both Peverils in the Tower of London. The Duke of Ormonde, one of the friends of justice who typically speak out for the beleaguered heroes of romance, pleads their cause to Charles II:

> Here is valiant old Sir Geoffrey Peveril of the Peak. . . . Here is his son, of whom I have heard the highest accounts, as a gallant of spirit, accom-

---

[63] *Quarterly Review* 14 (1815): 200.

plishments, and courage—Here is the unfortunate House of Derby—for pity's sake, interfere in behalf of these victims, whom the folds of this hydra-plot have entangled, in order to crush them to death—rebuke the fiends that are seeking to devour their lives, and disappoint the harpies that are gaping for their property. [Ch. 40]

As the opponents of property, fiends and harpies have at least a figurative existence. Roughly, there are two sorts of villain in the Waverley Novels: an agent who seems to be an elementary force of violence and evil, and a scheming, craven, self-aggrandizing villain. Sometimes both kinds can be effectively used in the same romance. A typical pair are Glossin and Hatteraick in *Guy Mannering*, whom Adolphus compared with Wycliffe and Risingham in *Rokeby*.[64] The scheming, craven villain is the real target. His sexual ambitions may underscore his threat to property. He is sometimes intimidated not only by justice, but also by the more inhuman evil of a fellow-conspirator.

The passive hero entrusts his rights of person and property entirely to the laws of society. The scheming villain accepts this premise and then attempts to manipulate the law falsely. He is no more violent than the hero—simply selfish instead of unselfish. The true complement for a passive hero is a knavish, ineffectual villain. When Glossin meets the heir of Ellangowan on the shore, he quakes inwardly:

Indeed his appearance and demeanour during all this conversation seemed to diminish even his strength and stature; so that he appeared to wither into the shadow of himself, now advancing one foot, now the other, now stooping and wriggling his shoulders, now fumbling with the buttons of his waistcoat, now clasping his hands together,—in short, he was the picture of a mean-spirited shuffling rascal in the very agonies of detection. [Ch. 41]

In this fashion Scott reduces the opponents of property to rascals; and the rascal, like the passive hero, enjoys a longer future in Victorian fiction than romantic heroes or effective devils. Dirk Hatteraick, who is not bent on supplanting the lost heir of Ellangowan, comes off much more lightly.

The relations of property and villainy are perfectly obvious. But the premium on *having* and the prejudice against *getting* have other extensions in the Waverley Novels. It is as if the romance of property were suspicious of any kind of force or energy. The bias against conveyable goods extends even to the sentiment of love. To love something means to want it. Only dark and subsequently unhappy heroines use the verb "love." Thus Effie in *The Heart of Mid-Lothian* says, "I love

---

[64] [John Leycester Adolphus], *Letters to Richard Heber* (Boston, 1822), p. 150.

Robertson" (Ch. 20); and Fenella in *Peveril of the Peak*, "I will love him till the latest breath of my life" (Ch. 47). The proper heroine never uses this word. In *The Pirate*, when Minna Troil says, "I love Clement Cleveland," her sister's reaction is immediate and profound: "Do not say so . . . do not say so, I implore you!" (Ch. 20). The proper hero and heroine never *love* each other. They do not "get" married, as we say; they will *be* married. The words "affection" and "mutual inclination" are used for a sexual relation destined for a happy conclusion in marriage. Such words express the bare minimum of motion or exchange that the prescriptive doctrine of property and heroic unselfishness can tolerate. The prescriptive doctrine accompanies the contemporary elevation of prudence and rational restraint as the highest form of morality. "Fortunately" for Reuben Butler and Jeanie Deans in *The Heart of Mid-Lothian*, "their passion was of no ardent or enthusiastic cast" (Ch. 9). At the end of *Anne of Geierstein* one reads that "the high blood, and moderate fortunes, of Anne of Geierstein and Arthur de Vere, joined to their mutual inclination, made their marriage in every respect rational" (Ch. 36).

The connection of property with the suppression of passion may seem exaggerated. But in Scott's lifetime property came to symbolize more than itself. In some passages of Burke it stands for the very existence of things, a static principle, a motionless power in the midst of things, opposed to dangerous and unpredictable energies of all kinds. "We have not considered as we ought *the dreadful energy* of a state in which property has nothing to do with the government."[65] In a curious phrase Blackstone even *defines* force as that which opposes property: "the law always couples the idea of force with that of intrusion upon the property of another."[66] These principles are so large and abstract that they become merely two: an idea of force and an idea of resistance. Burke also speaks of force as "ability" and argues from the superior energy of ability to the necessity of "great masses" of property, which alone can have sufficient "defensive power." He appeals to the same generalized conflict of force and resistance. "Nothing is a due and adequate representation of a state, that does not represent its ability, as well as its property. But as ability is a vigorous and active principle, and as property is sluggish, inert, and timid, it can never be safe from the invasions of ability, unless it be, out of all proportion, predominant in the representation."[67] Property, conceived as "sluggish, inert, and timid," and entirely defensive in its power, is the

---

[65] *Letters on a Regicide Peace*, in *Works*, 5: 376–77 (italics added).

[66] *Commentaries*, 3: 211.

[67] *Reflections on the Revolution in France*, in *Works*, 3: 297–98.

best key we have to the inactivity of the hero in the Waverley Novels and so much subsequent fiction. In the language of Erskine's *Institute*, "property . . . implies a prohibition"; it does not imply action.

The conception that "necessity begat property" and that property begat society engenders a very rigid ideal of behavior. Some activities, hunting and fishing and international war, are allowable; but forces that threaten to trespass or even to blur the lines of property are firmly and consistently put down. By the definition of property, such forces are pitted against necessity, reality, the way things are. Even when such forces are wholly innocent, founded in false historical principles, or generous impulse, they must be gingerly put to one side or carefully localized. The system of exile for romantic principals directly relates to the primary respect for property in the Waverley Novels. But the mere discontent of romantic heroes and heroines, whatever form it should take, is enough to trouble the ideal order of things, which is the achieved, existing order. There is the feeling that a single infraction of that order will destroy the whole. In politics this may be called the floodgate philosophy: allow so much as a drop of revolutionary poison to seep through the gate, and the waters will overflow the land. It is a common idea where property is concerned. "If prescription be once shaken," writes Burke, "no species of property is secure."[68] The power of existing relations is so purely defensive that the slightest concession, the slightest weakening of resistance will invite a disproportionate and disastrous surge of violence.

> If the mode of election [to Parliament] be altered, and the scale of it extended, *men of property*, interested *by that property* in the real welfare and stability of the nation, would not be chosen; but *cunning, low-minded men, who had nothing to lose*. Actuated by the lust of *power* and *gain*, under the mask of *Equality*, they would give the watchword to their Friends without doors—declare the King and Lords useless . . . and fabricate what *they would call a Republic*, but, in other words, *a violent usurpation of all the lands and property of the kingdom* . . . [69]

This attitude is seldom confined to political issues. Public morality decries the same possibility of being overwhelmed by unchecked sin; and even an individual may be imagined to live in risk of inundation from his baser passions. There is a natural tendency to externalize this risk, and that may explain why women, in particular, are re-

---

[68] Ibid., p. 433.

[69] No. 10 in *Liberty and Property Preserved against Republicans and Levellers, a Collection of Tracts*, 1793, reprinted in Alfred Cobban, ed., *The Debate on the French Revolution, 1789–1800* (London, 1950), pp. 401–2.

garded by this philosophy as peculiarly sensitive to the accelerating effects of evil. The logic of the anonymous political tract may be compared with a passage on literature and morals, this time by Scott, in his discussion of the heroines of Robert Bage:

> It is true, we can easily conceive that a female like Miss Ross, in *Barham Downs*, may fall under the arts of a seducer, under circumstances so peculiar as to excite great compassion; nor are we so rigid as to say, that such a person may not be restored to society, when her subsequent conduct shall have effaced recollection of her error. But she must return thither as a humble penitent, and has no title to sue out her pardon as a matter of right, and assume a place among the virtuous of her sex as if she had never fallen from her proper sphere. Her disgrace must not be considered as a trivial stain, which may be communicated by a husband as an exceeding good jest to his friend and correspondent; there must be, not penitence and reformation alone, but humiliation and abasement, in the recollection of her errors. This the laws of society demand even from the unfortunate; and to compromise farther, would open the door to the most unbounded licentiousness.[70]

Here civil society rests on the influence of women, and in the same paragraph Scott decries those who would "insinuate a doubt" of that influence. But the main argument is that society cannot condone a moral transgression without opening the door "to the most unbounded licentiousness." An act of transgression is as final or absolute as the lines of morality, which are fixed by prescription. Though Scott writes that the transgressor may "be restored to society," his further remarks qualify her readmission to the point of denying it altogether. Because of the floodgate principle the seduced female can be tolerated only on the condition of her "humiliation and abasement."

In fiction Scott administers this law in even stricter fashion. There transgression involves exile or early death or both; and, as the several dark heroines show, wayward thoughts are sufficient transgression. It is clearly not possible for those who willingly participate in extralegal thought or act to return to society. The career of those who do engage in such activities is pointedly episodic, and we hear of their perishing on the Continent, in America, or at sea, as we close the pages of the book. There can be little difficulty in understanding the passivity of those who are exposed to this episode and yet hope to return. For the proper hero and heroine, even where there is no question of a journey to the Highlands, the action of the romance must consist of a carefully guarded excursion to see how the other half perishes. In

---

[70] *Miscellaneous Prose Works*, 3: 548.

this respect the Waverley Novels impose a sweeping interpretation on time itself. Property not only equates with reality: it signifies futurity. The hero and heroine live happily ever after, and their heirs for ever and ever. The romantic figures and the villains seem to exhaust themselves—the former burn out, as it were, and the latter are snuffed out. Sometimes, as in *The Heart of Mid-Lothian* (Ch. 51), Scott purposively contrasts the hero's faith in immortality with the dark hero's mortalism. Property perpetuates itself, but the forces that jeopardize or oppose property, that cannot conform to reality, have only a finite existence. This simple contrast confers the most extravagant of all rewards on the respecters of property, the proponents of reason and restraint, and the defenders of "necessity."

V

THE HEART OF MID-LOTHIAN

"The case of Effie (or Euphemia) Deans," resumed Saddletree, "is one of those cases of murder presumptive, that
is, a murder of the law's inferring or construction, being derived from certain *indicia* or grounds of suspicion."

"So that," said the good woman, "unless poor Effie has
communicated her situation, she'll be hanged by the neck,
if the bairn was still-born, or if it be alive at this moment?"

"Assuredly," said Saddletree . . . "The crime is rather a favourite of the law, this species of murder being one of its
own creation."

"Then, if the law makes murders," said Mrs. Saddletree,
"the law should be hanged for them; or if they wad hang a
lawyer instead, the country wad find nae faut."

—*The Heart of Mid-Lothian*

13. The Trial of Jeanie Deans

OF ALL THE Waverley Novels *The Heart of Mid-Lothian* enacts
the most comprehensive study of moral themes. The wayward Effie Deans is accused of child murder: under a particular and severe statute of the time, the state does not have to prove
that she has committed this crime; her concealment of pregnancy
and the fact that she cannot produce the living child are presumptive
evidence, and the penalty is death. Both Effie and her seducer beg
Jeanie Deans to testify that Effie did confess her pregnancy to her sister. She did nothing of the sort. But if Effie had told anyone of her
condition, that would destroy the case for murder under this particular law. Jeanie Deans is convinced that her sister is actually innocent
of murder, whatever the law may presume. This emotional claim conflicts directly with the moral requirement that she testify to the truth;
and thus the trial becomes the trial of Jeanie Deans, not of Effie.
When passion is weighed against prudence in the Waverley Novels,
the reader can entertain little doubt of the outcome. But in *The Heart
of Mid-Lothian* Scott contrived to weigh selfless compassion against a
very nice question of rational principle, and the reader joins in
Jeanie's moral dilemma.

The story challenges Scott's imagination. Can the determined separation of morality from immorality survive such a close confrontation? The solution to the dilemma, fortunately, was given in the source—the story of Helen Walker, as communicated to Scott by Helen Goldie and recorded in the 1830 introduction to *The Heart of Mid-Lothian*. It is true that the deaths of the original heroine and of Mrs. Goldie herself made the tale impossible to verify and effectively insulate it from the reader. The significant elements are reproduced in Scott's epitaph for Helen Walker's tombstone, erected in 1831: "Refusing the slightest departure from veracity, even to save the life of a sister, she nevertheless showed her kindness and fortitude, in rescuing her from the severity of the law, at the expense of personal exertions which the time rendered as difficult as the motive was laudable. Respect the grave of poverty when combined with love of truth and dear affection."[1] The prototype for Jeanie Deans represents both principle and emotion, "love of truth and dear affection," side by side, in simple conjunction. The word "nevertheless" ensures their distinction from one another. The word "love," however, is applied to the abstraction, and the word "affection" to the actual emotion.

Throughout the romance Scott stresses Jeanie's "love of and veneration for truth" (Ch. 27). She is also extremely neat and clean, and plain looking—qualities associated with truth and honesty in the lower ranks. The scrupulousness of her entire person, as it were, reflects her clear and orderly perception of the moral issue before her. This perception derives strength from her religion, which has more bearing on Jeanie's conduct than is evident in the more privileged heroines of the Waverley Novels. But her moral perception is also fiercely rational, fully committed to human as well as divine law. Her conviction of her sister's innocence cannot sway her from this rational devotion to law.

> "It is not man I fear," said Jeanie, looking upward; "the God, whose name I must call on to witness the truth of what I say, he will know the falsehood."
>
> "And he will know the motive," said the stranger [George Staunton], eagerly; "he will know that you are doing this—not for lucre of gain, but to save the life of the innocent, and prevent the commission of a worse crime than that which the law seeks to avenge."
>
> "He has given us a law," said Jeanie, "for the lamp of our path; if we stray from it we err against knowledge—I may not do evil, even that good may come of it." [Ch. 15]

---

[1] Quoted in the Centenary Edition of the novel as Note B, p. 540.

Jeanie takes into court this conviction that she must not—indeed, that one cannot—"err against knowledge." At the trial (Chs. 22 and 23) her unshakeable commitment to the letter of the law stands in sharp contrast to the emotion of the scene—to her own emotion, to the emotion of the justice, of the prisoner, and of all present—and Scott achieves the highest use of his unresolved dualism. Jeanie's testimony represents the high moment in which passion conflicts with the rules, and is parallel in this respect to the moment of Effie's yielding to seduction (which lies outside the action of the book): the dark heroine surrenders the rule to passion; but Jeanie defers to the rule.

Effie's position on testifying is given in the course of her judicial declaration: "she declares, she will tell the truth, if it should be the undoing of her, so long as she is not asked to tell on other folk" (Ch. 23). The reservation is important: Effie is not willing to betray her seducer, and she places that motive ahead of the love of truth. The proper heroine cannot make a similar reservation. If asked outright, she must tell the truth, regardless of personal loyalties. We know that in real life people sometimes find themselves in precisely this situation. The judgment of the Waverley Novels is that persons who refuse to tell the truth from such a motive may be generous and even noble, but they are also incurable romantics. At the same time the consequences of full and truthful testimony in such cases, and in *The Heart of Mid-Lothian* in particular, are very distressing. The only course open to those whose loyalty extends first to society is to change the law at its source, by legislation, or to alter its final consequences, through a commutation of the sentence. Through the glass of prescription and in the age of "legislative quiescence," changing a law is an unlikely alternative. Therefore Jeanie Deans sets out for London to secure a pardon from the Queen for her sister. The energy and compassion that had to be overcome in the witness stand find an outlet—to use the words of the epitaph for Helen Walker—in "the expense of personal exertions" of the journey.

Although Scott protests that Jeanie Deans "was no heroine of romance" (Ch. 26), he contends that "there was something of romance in Jeanie's venturous resolution" to walk to London (Ch. 27). In what sense is this journey romantic? In the first place, it is generous as well as venturous. Jeanie's emotion prompts her to undertake this pilgrimage, and to save her sister she relies on moving the compassion of Queen Caroline. In this she succeeds. "Tear followed tear down Jeanie's cheeks, as, her features glowing and quivering with emotion, she pleaded her sister's cause with a pathos which was at once simple and solemn" (Ch. 37). In the second place, her recourse lies essentially outside the law, though technically within it. Sovereigns, presidents, and governors, home secretaries and certain attorneys general have powers to intervene between the judicial process and its final consequences. In them Scott concedes the possibility of a morality that is natural rather than artificial, and individual rather than social and legal. The entire society acknowledges a degree of freedom in such acts of the sovereign. (In *The Heart of Mid-Lothian* the people object strenuously to the Queen's exercise of this freedom on behalf of Captain Porteous, but they cannot countermand it except by violent means.) Qualitatively, however, the Queen's powers are similar to those of the romantic agents in the Waverley Novels who take it upon themselves to open private letters or throw rascals into a lake. Thus in *Redgauntlet* the Pretender to the throne merely acts as if he exercised the sovereign power: "Trouble not yourself to account for my conduct. . . . I have a warrant for what I do, and fear no responsibility" (Ch. 16).

The law itself makes allowance for this recourse to higher authority, as if it were wary of just such a contingency as occurs in *The Heart of Mid-Lothian*. There is always the worry that even if we do not "err against knowledge," we might err against fact—the fact in this case of Effie's innocence. Feelings, so far as the law is concerned, do not really come into it. But feelings serve to warn the human animal that the facts may be escaping him. The counsel for Effie's defense closes his argument on the strength of her own "piteous cry": "Nature herself bears testimony in favour of the tenderness and acuteness of the prisoner's parental feelings" (Ch. 22). The law is willing to respect the cry of nature at least so far as to consult the intuitive compassion of one human being who *is* sovereign—the Queen.

Dorothy van Ghent discerns in the trial of Jeanie Deans, as we may call it, the issue between "'verbal' truth and other kinds of truth."[2] In other words, Jeanie Deans has to weigh the truth of her own testimony against the truth of Effie's innocence which that testimony will obscure. She is asked to evaluate two different truths, and the consequences of surrendering the first seem as nothing compared with abandoning hope of the second. *The Heart of Mid-Lothian* disappoints Mrs. van Ghent, who detects a moral complexity in the issue with which Jeanie, for all her fondness for her sister, does not really come to terms. The heroine falls back on her moral training and in effect refuses to decide between two kinds of truth. In the romance of Scott, however, no one but certain romantic agents presumes to take

[2] *The English Novel: Form and Function* (New York, 1956), pp. 113–24.

such a decision into his own hands. In *The Heart of Mid-Lothian* two such agents urge Jeanie to place the factual innocence of Effie Deans ahead of the truth of her own testimony. She returns their argument with an objection that clears aside every consideration but the relation of her testimony to the law by which her sister stands condemned: "I shall be man-sworn [perjured] in the very thing in which my testimony is wanted, for it is the concealment for which poor Effie is blamed, and you would make me tell a falsehood anent it" (Ch. 15). She goes to the trial and delivers her negative but honest testimony. The moral structure of the Waverley Novels grants her no alternative. To do otherwise would imply a qualified acceptance of the law of the land. Scott's justice summarizes the issue to the jury: "He and the jury were sworn to judge according to the laws as they stood, not to criticise, or evade, or even to justify them" (Ch. 23). All forces in the Waverley Novels are brought up sharply against the laws as they stand.

Though Scott approaches moral complexity in *The Heart of Mid-Lothian*, the dualism of the Waverley Novels cannot be resolved on the moral level. One may agree with Mrs. van Ghent that the real crime in the story is Effie's "illicit sexual indulgence," and that crime cannot be compromised: "sex must be punished, and that is all there is to it."[3] But the romances of Scott do discriminate, more subtly, between "verbal," articulated, public, and codified morality and other forces that may or may not assert a claim to morality. The point is, that Scott does not attempt to negotiate between two such commitments, but efficiently separates them. When Jeanie contends that she "may not do evil, even that good may come of it," she touches an article of faith in our civilization. She also voices the conviction that the structure of morality will crumble if she crosses the border with anything more than heartfelt sympathy. She would willingly give her life to find another way to save her sister, but not willingly compromise the law. The moral pattern of the Waverley Novels takes the shape of an excursion, not an effort to resolve moral conflicts that Scott does not believe in resolving.

Given this precondition, *The Heart of Mid-Lothian* is a moral tour de force. The reader enjoys the unusual spectacle of Scott welcoming on every side additional issues of right and wrong. Once the moral clairvoyance of Jeanie is established, Scott willingly casts new problems in her path. She must evaluate Staunton's proposal to trade his life for Effie's (Ch. 34), and she is required to discriminate between

---

[3] Ibid., p. 121.

"common murder" and the political murder of Porteous (Chs. 34 and 38). She ponders the correct relation between her fallen sister and herself, and whether the money offered by Effie should be declined (Chs. 44 and 48). In fact, Jeanie argues these issues with a freedom that nearly jeopardizes her status as a proper heroine. Early in the story she escapes from Ratcliffe at Muschat's Cairn by means of a ruse (Ch. 18), and that alone suggests a certain improper agility. Her independence and "address" must be attributed to her lower-class origins.

Though Mrs. van Ghent condemns its "disorganization" for obscuring the moral issue, *The Heart of Mid-Lothian* is one of the most artful of Scott's romances. He ingeniously parodies the scruples of Jeanie with those of her father, who believes that any testimony in a court of justice might be construed as an "act of immediate acknowledgment or submission to the present government," which is not "of the true Presbyterian complexion" (Chs. 18 and 19). At the expense of David Deans, Scott achieves not only humor but a closer and more dignified account of Jeanie's reasonable scruple against false testimony. The moral act of Jeanie Deans does not remain in isolation, but rather excites an argumentative tendency throughout the romance. David Deans also disputes whether "in conscience" Reuben Butler ought to accept a living in the Church of Scotland from the Duke of Argyll (Ch. 43). From a very different position Captain Knockdunder assails the question of whether a minister should be elected by the parishioners or appointed by the landlord.

> "Nevertheless," said Mr. Butler, "if any of the parishioners have any scruples, which sometimes happen in the mind of sincere professors, I should be happy of an opportunity of trying to remove"—
>
> "Never fash your peard about it, man," interrupted Duncan Knockdunder—"Leave it a' to me.—Scruple! deil ane o' them has been bred up to scruple onything that they're bidden to do. And if sic a thing suld happen as ye speak o', ye sall see the sincere professor, as ye ca' him, towed at the stern of my boat for a few furlongs. I'll try if the water of the Haly Loch winna wash off scruples as weel as fleas—Cot tam!"—[Ch. 44]

In aesthetic terms, scruples are the unifying motif of this romance. In the following chapter Butler raises with Knockdunder the question of smuggling, and he later argues the moral ill effects of smuggling with George Staunton. "I do not know anything that more effectually depraves and ruins [my people's] moral and religious principles" (Ch. 51). If Butler condoned smuggling, he would then not be able to hold the bulwarks of morality against the sea.

14. Society as an Abstraction

In terms of history, the Waverley Novels endorse stability, the achieved compromise of the past, and the political realities of the present. The passions of dark heroines or romantic heroes are incompatible, or "ill-assorted," with everyday social reality. The very basis of property, or realty, is prescription, the present and reliable ownership of things. The fixed and sufficient laws of morality are the laws as they stand. Even the success of a mountaineering adventure depends upon "the measure of sound sense and reality." In short, the Waverley Novels celebrate "reality" or "being realistic." The nature of this reality must be carefully distinguished from concrete reality.

The appreciation of concrete reality, or the sense of solid and individual objects and persons, is the prerogative of dark heroes and heroines in the Waverley Novels. The embracing and stabbing of human flesh is carried out to the other side of "that ideal boundary." When Minna Troil swears, "I love Clement Cleveland," or the deft Saladin severs the head from the trunk of Conrade, we feel, in one sense, that we are coming to grips with reality. The activities of the proper heroes and heroines, which the Waverley Novels permanently sanction, do not give us this sensation. Furthermore, I have argued that most fiction in this period was not primarily intended to convey a sensation of concrete reality. Eighteenth-century fiction pretended to a knowledge of things and a loyalty to facts. Romantic theory stresses the projection of emotions or ideals.

The reality celebrated by the Waverley Novels is an abstraction, a projected reality. This reality consists not of things but of relations. Reality is the complex structure of rights and restrictions, custom and law, right and wrong that society insists upon; it governs all getting and holding, owning and forfeiting, wedding and dying; it comprises the institutions of marriage, family, property, the courts, and the state. The chief representative of reality is therefore the law, which comprehends, or seeks to comprehend, all these relations and more. Such relations stand at considerable distance from concrete fact. According to the *Institute* of John Erskine, "Things or subjects fall no otherwise under the consideration of law, than as persons may have a right to them."[4] Unattached things have a secondary interest in the Waverley Novels.

Scott did not greatly contribute to the "protest on behalf of value"

---

[4] *An Institute of the Law of Scotland* (2 vols. Edinburgh, 1812), Bk. II, Title 1.

that Alfred North Whitehead discovered in the romantic movement—
the perception of a concrete, unified, thing-in-itself.[5] His dark heroes
and heroines perhaps do react to nature in this way. Scott's reality is
a construction of society. He did not invent his kind of reality, any
more than he invented political conservatism. He argues, outside the
Waverley Novels, that men of property must "use their power."[6] That
power is not mere physical power but legal power, in essence abstract
and derived from an endless series of social promises and commitments. This reality is indeed far removed from the concrete—especially removed from the passions of the individual human being. In
that distance the proponents of reality saw its strength. To the same
degree of abstraction William Blake and other protesters on behalf of
the concrete—including, to an extent, our dark heroines—attributed
the weakness of science and society.

We are now in a position to understand the unique character of
The Heart of Mid-Lothian. In this romance the gap between concrete
fact and the reality imposed by law is explicit and critical. The child-
murder statute of 1690 furnished Scott with a law that presumed to as-
cribe real existence to a concrete event—namely, the act of murder.
(A statute from the criminal code thereby took the same logical form
as a physical law of science.) According to the counsel for the crown
in *The Heart of Mid-Lothian*, "It was the very purpose of the statute to
substitute a certain chain of presumptive evidence in place of a proba-
tion" (Ch. 23). The counsel for the defense, on the other hand, can
reply that "he was so far from acknowledging the alleged probability
of the child's violent death, that he could not even allow that there
was evidence of its having ever lived." Clearly a legal construction of
reality is pitted directly against a question of fact. The counsel for the
crown summarizes the application of the statute as follows:

> It was *not necessary* . . . for him to bring positive proof that the panel [the
> accused] was accessory to the murder, nay, nor even to prove that the
> child was murdered at all. It was sufficient to support the indictment,
> that it [the child] could not be found. According to the stern, but *neces-
> sary* severity of this statute, she who should conceal her pregnancy, who
> should omit to call that assistance which is most *necessary* on such occa-
> sions, was held already to have meditated the death of her offspring, as
> an event most likely to be the consequence of her culpable and cruel
> concealment. And if, under such circumstances, she could not alterna-

---

[5] *Science and the Modern World* (New York, 1925), ch. 5.
[6] *Letters*, 6: 31.

tively show by proof that the infant had died a natural death, or produce it still in life, she must, under the *construction* of the law, be held to
have murdered it, and suffer death accordingly. [Ch. 22; my italics]

In order that the death of the offender should be based, at least, on a
fictitious event, society has in effect legislated a fact. The successive
uses of the word "necessary" in this argument should be noted: first,
what the law prescribes as necessary; second, what is presumed to be
moral necessity; and third, a use of the word suggesting physical necessity. Necessity is par excellence the relation of things, not things or
events in themselves. Necessity is the constraining relation of things
and of human commitments. The word most unambiguously defines
the reality celebrated by the Waverley Novels. Necessity begat property, according to Blackstone; and (apropos the Blakean protest) philosophers used the same word to signify the physical relation of cause
and effect. In the prescriptive doctrine of Burke, necessity caused the
Revolution of 1688 and remains the fundamental justification of the
constitution—"*necessity*, in the strictest moral sense in which necessity
can be taken."[7]

The reality confronted by individuals in *The Heart of Mid-Lothian* is
undisguisedly a "construction" of the law. The reader is furthermore
assured—eventually by the appearance of the illegitimate child himself—that the law has construed the facts incorrectly in this case. The
facts of the case support Effie's innocence—so far as murder is concerned—but the law condemns her. Neither Jeanie Deans nor Scott
himself goes so far as to condemn the law in return—though Mrs.
Saddletree does. But the gross inability of the law to establish the particular fact of murder causes the unusual moral emphasis of the
romance and forces the extreme test of the heroine's scruples. *The
Heart of Mid-Lothian* reveals that the "reality" defended by the Waverley Novels is an abstract construction. It is a "reality principle," not a
concrete fact; it does not have the weight and solidity of wood or
iron. But it is strong: all the tentative romantic energies, and wicked
impulses as well, are constrained by a vast network of relations, of
pacts and polity, promises and property, which is civil society.

The Heart of Mid-Lothian differs just enough from the other romances to start one speculating on the entire principle of reality imposed by society and celebrated by Scott. The relations summarized
by that principle are not strong simply because they are rational: individuals have a large stake in these relations, which must respond at
some level to human desires and fears. Yet because they are so ab-

---

[7] *Reflections on the Revolution in France*, in *Works*, 3: 254.

stract, the relations which compose reality for Scott are also tenuous. Typical of these, the right to property may depend upon a sequence of legal relations extending far back into time. Such a sequence cannot be grasped in a single insight—the power and wealth that it conveys must seem irrational or sacred, depending upon the point of view. The bonds of society exist at some distance from the concrete reality of flesh and blood. Civil society cannot be seen or touched. Property, the very basis of society, is not "natural" but conventional. In the midst of his discussion of property David Hume draws a daring analogy between justice and superstition—so tenuous and arbitrary can the relation of property be made to appear. "Had I worne this apparel an hour ago, I had merited the severest punishment; but a man, by pronouncing a few magical syllables, has now rendered it fit for my use and service." Hume dissolves his comparison by appealing to the principles of utility and necessity: "But there is this material difference between *superstition* and *justice*, that the former is frivolous, useless, and burdensome; the latter is absolutely requisite to the well-being of mankind and the existence of society."[8] For one group of thinkers in the early nineteenth century "the well-being of mankind" would become "the greatest good for the greatest number"; for a conservative thinker, the appeal to the mere "existence of society" is more congenial.

As soon as one argues too narrowly from necessity the argument itself becomes nervous. Supposing the existence of society does depend upon a certain relation—what happens if the relation is violated? The argument from necessity carries with it a vision of the abyss. The argument that places the greatest faith in the security of society sees the greatest danger of insecurity. The floodgate principle of politics and of morality boasts of the achievements of order and society but trembles before a vision of unchecked violence. What if necessity itself should be overwhelmed? Does a single moral transgression threaten the entire principle of reality? When the universe is divided between a power of force and a power of resistance, the celebration of resistance has its hazards. The idea of property as "sluggish, inert, and timid" is too negative; "the total exclusion of the right of every other individual in the universe," too extreme. Resistance can only be defined negatively; one can conceive a force without resistance more readily than a resistance without a force. The idea of society as a collective resistance to individual passions inspires a political fiction like the social contract, or a literary fiction like the passive hero.

---

[8] *Essays Moral, Political, and Literary*, ed. Green and Grose, 2: 191–93.

15. Jeanie Deans Visits the Sick

Such hypothetical questions are easy to phrase but scarcely tell us anything very precise about the Waverley Novels and their hero. They
suggest, however, more depth and complexity to "reality" than the
rigor with which Scott sets it forth would lead one to suspect. Though
no well person can worry about the security and stability of concrete
objects, one may conceivably worry about a more tenuous structure of
relations which comprise "necessity." The Waverley Novels, as we shall
see, do entertain some such worry. The passive hero is beset by a
number of worries and concerns that are in no sense rational. His inactivity may be accounted for by the constraining force of his morality
and by the passive ideal of civil society; but he is also prey to serious
anxieties. Emotions, we have assumed, are the property of dark heroes; but the proper hero has a distinct emotion of his own. Again
The Heart of Mid-Lothian is helpful, since Reuben Butler is an extreme
case. His anxiety is exaggerated because his role is so subordinate to
that of the heroine—even more so than that of Arthur Philipson in
Anne of Geierstein.

In *The Heart of Mid-Lothian* the hero's mental state grows so intense
that he becomes literally sick. Interestingly enough, the dark hero,
George Staunton, also falls prey to a malady of the mind. In both
cases Scott magnifies the strength of mind of his remarkably active
heroine, Jeanie Deans, by contrast with the sick heroes. On her journey to London Jeanie visits each hero at his bedside.

In an early chapter (Ch. 9) Jeanie and Reuben Butler are contrasted even as children. "Reuben was weak in constitution, and,
though not timid in temper might be safely pronounced anxious,
doubtful, and apprehensive." The denial of his timidity cannot be
taken as seriously as the fact that he is "anxious, doubtful, and apprehensive." Jeanie is his superior not only in physical strength but in
courage. "On other occasions they went together to school, the boy
receiving that encouragement and example from his companion, in
crossing the little brooks which intersected their path, and encounter-
ing cattle, dogs, and other perils, upon their journey, which the male
sex in such cases usually consider it their prerogative to extend to the
weaker." The journeys of childhood thus prefigure the climactic journey of the plot. Scott seems determined to insist that it is Butler, not
Jeanie, who is weaker.

Butler's early part in the story is that of an unwilling spectator of
the Porteous riot. The mob forces him to become their chaplain and

to administer to their victim before he is hanged. They instruct him to "consider all that is passing before you as a dream," and he replies that he wishes it were a dream (Ch. 6). So far as the hero is concerned, the episode *is* no more than a bad dream. It suffices, however, to get him into trouble with the magistrates of Edinburgh, who treat him well but force him to leave the city. He therefore is absent from the trial of Effie. Jeanie visits Butler at the start of her journey to London (Ch. 27). Far from being of assistance to the heroine, he has to be supplied with a few gold pieces by the heroine before she departs. Scott's lengthy analysis of Butler's malady states that the sickness begins with his weak constitution but proceeds by ravages of the mind.

> Butler, whose constitution was naturally feeble, did not soon recover the fatigue of body and distress of mind which he had suffered, in consequence of the tragical events with which our narrative commenced. The painful idea that his character was breathed upon by suspicion, was an aggravation to his distress.
>
> But the most cruel addition was the absolute prohibition laid by the magistrates on his holding any communication with Deans or his family. . . . He felt he must be suffering under the bad opinion of the person who was dearest to him, from an imputation of unkind desertion, the most alien to his nature.
>
> This painful thought, pressing on a frame already injured, brought on a succession of slow and lingering feverish attacks, which greatly impaired his health, and at length rendered him incapable even of the sedentary duties of the school, on which his bread depended. . . .
>
> Such was Butler's situation, scarce able to drag himself to the place where his daily drudgery must gain his daily bread, and racked with a thousand fearful anticipations concerning the fate of those who were dearest to him in the world, when the trial and condemnation of Effie Deans put the copestone upon his mental misery.

Thus anxiety has completely immobilized the passive hero. Scott continues to apply the same emphasis in the pages that follow. The hero receives his visitor with alarm:

> The surprise of Butler was extreme, when Jeanie, who seldom stirred half-a-mile from home, entered his apartment. . . .
>
> "Good God!" he said, starting from his chair, while alarm restored to his cheek the colour of which sickness had deprived it; "some new misfortune must have happened!"
>
> "None, Mr. Reuben, but what you must hae heard of—but oh, ye are

looking ill yoursell!"—for the "hectic of a moment" had not concealed from her affectionate eyes the ravages which lingering disease and anxieety of mind had made in her lover's person.

When Reuben hears, with considerable astonishment, of Jeanie's intention to travel to London, he renews his offer to marry her, in order to go with her and confer his protection. But this interchange, also, serves only to contrast Jeanie's strength with Reuben's helplessness.

> "You are kind and good, Reuben, and wad take me wi' a' my shame [the shame of her sister's criminal reputation], I doubtna. But ye canna but own that this is no time to marry or be given in marriage. Na, if that suld ever be, it maun be in another and a better season.—And, dear Reuben, ye speak of protecting me on my journey—Alas! who will protect and take care of you?—your very limbs tremble with standing for ten minutes on the floor; how could you undertake a journey as far as Lunnon?"
>
> "But I am strong—I am well," continued Butler, sinking in his seat totally exhausted, "at least I shall be quite well tomorrow."

Butler's general anxiety seems, if anything, aggravated by his matrimonial hopes and fears. It has clearly destroyed his health.

Jeanie also encounters George Staunton on her journey to London. The meeting itself is a sheer coincidence—but not, of course, a coincidence of the design of *The Heart of Mid-Lothian*. Jeanie has come under the charge of the Rector of Willingham, who happens to be Staunton's father. While she awaits her interview with the Rector, the younger Staunton causes her to be brought to his bedside. He reveals his identity as the "Robertson" of Edinburgh and delivers a long confession of his past (Ch. 33). He now labors under "the utmost agony of mind." He relates how he has ruined at least two women and made his father wretched—how he at last found pleasure in attacking property itself. ("Hitherto I had observed a certain line in my criminality, and stood free of assaults upon personal property, but now I felt a wild pleasure in disgracing myself as much as possible.") He feels his guilt for the ruin and madness of Madge Wildfire like "stabs of a poniard" and as a "tearing with hot pincers, and scalding the raw wound with burning sulphur." His self-condemnation for the seduction of Effie Deans, the reader is given to understand, would have to be presented in even stronger terms. But here he lies helpless, "seemingly exhausted," and as powerless as his passive counterpart.

Staunton has been afflicted not by something physical but by guilt:

he has fallen from his horse by a mischance that is moral. He had resolved to offer his life in London in exchange for Effie's pardon,
when he was stopped, as he sees it, by heaven itself. "Heaven is just,
however, and would not honour me with making this voluntary atone-
ment for the injury I have done your sister. I had not rode ten miles,
when my horse, the best and most sure-footed animal in this country,
fell with me on a level piece of road, as if he had been struck by a
cannon-shot." As in the case of Butler, the affliction has an arbitrary
physical origin, but the suffering is mental. Scott deliberately over-
does the mischance of Staunton's accident: the agony of mind is the
true cause of his illness. His powerlessness is the result of his guilt.
The clear conscience of Jeanie Deans, by contrast, will see her safely
to London without the use of a horse.

An interesting parallel arises, therefore, in the maladies of these
two very opposite kinds of hero, Butler and Staunton. Jeanie inter-
views both invalids in the course of her journey to London. They are
both suffering from mental agony; both are agitated by inner turmoil.
Staunton is sick with guilt; and Butler is sick with anxiety. So much is
clear. The source of Staunton's conflict is evident because conventional: he is torn between his unchecked passion and remorse of conscience. Can the passive hero also be torn between passion and
conscience? Of what can Reuben Butler be said to be guilty? *Between*
individuals and groups in the Waverley Novels the conflict of passion
and morality is a central theme: each side of the conflict has its representatives; an ideal boundary divides them. The parallel sickness of
both heroes in *The Heart of Mid-Lothian* suggests that the same conflict
may engage two sides of a single person. In the face of a series of romances that align him so fixedly on the side of prudence and society,
it is difficult to assert the complexity—or the "guilt"—of the passive
hero. But in Reuben Butler, at least, outward passivity is no proof of
inward quiet. Butler is literally made wretched by anxiety. The com-
motion of his being suggests that an alliance with civil society and
with "reality" leaves something to be desired.

In discussing the moral lines of the Waverley Novels I have virtually
dropped the distinction between the fiction and the moral ideal of
Scott's society. The fiction, so to speak, is that ideal. Our new topics
of discussion, however, will be better appreciated if we keep clearly
in mind that we are dealing with fiction. Toward the end of *Waverley* (Ch. 60) the hero "felt himself entitled to say firmly, though perhaps with a sigh, that the romance of his life was ended, and that its
real history had now commenced." The romance, of course, is not
over. By "romance" Waverley means the romantic episode, which, we
have observed, is characteristically finite. By "history" he signifies an

equally imaginary construction of infinite future time—a part of the reality by which the hero conceives himself to be supported. No one supposes that the money and "society of his own rank" restored to Waverley by Colonel Talbot subsequent to this statement (Ch. 62), and his marriage and inheritance, are not a part of the fiction. Scott firmly subscribed to his idea of society. In his romance the moral edges of society never blur for an instant, unless to accommodate the somewhat freer behavior of the lower ranks. Yet Scott did not suppose that this "reality," let alone the fiction that proclaimed it, was true in the sense that it corresponded to concrete events. The denouement of a typical romance is too good to be true; the rewards of constraining oneself are conventionally exaggerated in fiction—as if we had to invent a fiction to convince us of the transcendent value of our constructions. Hence Scott was frequently, and quite logically, tempted to withhold belief in his own happy ending—by a tag from *The Critic* in *Guy Mannering* (Ch. 50), for example, or by entertaining the demands of Miss Buskbody at the end of *Old Mortality*.

VI

ANXIETY

It is only under the shelter of the civil magistrate that the owner of that valuable property . . . can sleep a single night in security. He is at all times surrounded by unknown enemies, whom, though he never provoked, he can never appease, and from whose injustice he can be protected only by the powerful arm of the civil magistrate continually held up to chastise it.

—Adam Smith, *The Wealth of Nations*

Man himself is no longer in a condition of external tension with the external substance of private property; he has himself become the tension-ridden being of private property.
—Marx, *Economic and Philosophical Manuscripts,*
trans. T. B. Bottomore

16. Authority

THE WAVERLEY NOVELS convey a public wish-dream. The very persons who stand for "the measure of sound sense and reality" are rewarded by a highly wishful and fanciful future of unending happiness. The social and political reality celebrated in the novels always triumphs over attempts to disrupt the existing way of things. After duly respecting the law and expressing his obligation to society, the hero discovers his fortunes to be restored and his marriage assured. *The Heart of Mid-Lothian*—appropriately—is the only one of the Waverley Novels to end with an explicit moral:

> This tale will not be told in vain, if it shall be found to illustrate the great truth, that guilt, though it may attain *temporal* splendour, can never confer *real* happiness; that the evil consequences of our crimes long survive their commission, and, like the ghosts of the murdered, for ever haunt the steps of the malefactor; and that the paths of virtue, though seldom those of worldly greatness, are always those of *pleasantness and peace.* [My italics]

"Real happiness," the reward conferred by reason and law, paradoxically consists of a soothing, dreamlike "pleasantness and peace"; and real happiness, by contrast with "temporal splendour," is eternal.

Scott did not write the Waverley Novels according to plan, however. "I have generally written to the middle of one of these novels, without having the least idea how it was to [end]."[1] The ending was dictated by the romance itself—the romance of property, the myth that property (real happiness) automatically devolves upon those who respect the existing arrangement of things. The over-all plot of each romance was fixed by this ideal. "I never could lay down a plan—or, having laid it down, I never could adhere to it. . . . I only tried to make that which I was actually writing diverting and interesting, leaving the rest to fate."[2]

Though the total action of the romance may be construed as a wish-dream, the prolific "diverting and interesting" incidents cannot be accounted for so directly. The incidents affecting the hero are usually fearsome or unpleasant. Scott characteristically emphasizes the commitment of his hero to social regularity by subjecting him to various scenes of embarrassment and frustration. These discomforting incidents are more like fragments of a nightmare than logical constructions of a hopeful daydream. Scott himself frequently compares the hero's bewildered experience of a romantic world to a bad dream. This is especially true of *Waverley*.[3] "It seemed like a dream to Waverley that these deeds of violence should be familiar to men's minds, and currently talked of, as falling within the common order of things, and happening daily in the immediate vicinity, without his having crossed the seas, and while he was yet in the otherwise well-ordered island of Great Britain" (Ch. 15). When Waverley temporarily commits himself to the romantic episode of this novel, dresses himself in Highland garb, and prepares to do battle in the cause of Prince Charles, the irrational aspect of his situation strikes him with new force: "It was at that instant, that, looking around him, he saw the wild dress and appearance of his Highland associates, heard their whispers in uncouth and unknown language, looked upon his own dress, so unlike that which he had worn from his infancy, and wished to awake from what seemed at the moment a dream, strange, horrible, and unnatural" (Ch. 46). Without being specifically compared to dreams, there are plenty of incidents in the Waverley Novels that are—depending upon the point of view—absurd, "diverting," or nightmarish. At one point, for example, Waverley is caught between a ferocious smithy and his nagging wife: he is suddenly accused of trea-

[1] *Journal*, Feb. 24, 1828.

[2] Ibid., Feb. 12, 1826.

[3] Cf. S. Stewart Gordon, "*Waverley* and the 'Unified Design,'" *A Journal of English Literary History* 18 (1951): 116.

son and surrounded by a mob, and rushed at by the smithy with a red-hot iron; and finally fires his pocket pistol in a futile effort of self-defense (Ch. 30).

Scott fully exploits the affinities of romancing and dreaming. Written documents are the particular symbols of the structure of reality, and are frequently subject to loss or discovery in dreams. Deeds, warrants, letters, and credentials of all sorts are also subject to the vicissitudes of romance. In dreams the identity of persons is often blurred, exchanged, or misplaced; and disguises and missing persons are the very stuff of romance. At a picnic in *The Antiquary* (Ch. 19) a newcomer, Captain M'Intyre, jockeys his way to the side of Isabella Wardour, much to the displeasure of Lovel. The two men are already disposed to quarrel when Oldbuck refers obliquely to the hero's military experience.

> "I am speaking to a military man, then?" said M'Intyre; "may I inquire to what regiment Mr. Lovel belongs?"—Mr. Lovel gave him the number of the regiment. "It happens strangely that we should never have met before, Mr. Lovel. I know your regiment very well, and have served along with them at different times."
>
> A blush crossed Lovel's countenance. "I have not lately been with my regiment," he replied; "I served the last campaign upon the staff of General Sir——— ———."
>
> "Indeed! that is more wonderful than the other circumstance!—for although I did not serve with General Sir——— ———, yet I had an opportunity of knowing the names of the officers who held situations in his family, and I cannot recollect that of Lovel."
>
> At this observation Lovel again blushed so deeply as to attract the attention of the whole company, while a scornful laugh seemed to indicate Captain M'Intyre's triumph.

Lovel then responds with an extraordinary action. He takes out his pocketbook and displays a letter of commendation from General Sir——— ———: but, as M'Intyre "drily observed," the letter bears no address. Lovel's unaccountable paralysis, his powerlessness to vouchsafe his name and rank, and the futile assertion of his identity by means of an incomplete document, with its effect of redoubling the hero's embarrassment, are like the events of an unpleasant dream. The hero has lost his credentials, so to speak. The identity in question is a matter of his name and rank—his individual claim to the structured reality of the Waverley Novels. His physical presence is of no account: so far as this military crisis is concerned, he might as well have no bodily substance whatever.

Such incidents are elaborate testimonies to Scott's imagination.

The question of why a hero should be subjected to such attacks of distress and embarrassment has never been satisfactorily answered. Possibly the pleasure of such scenes consists simply in the hero's capacity to survive them. Disagreeable situations, from mild discomfort to peril of life and death, obviously render the denouement of a romance more agreeable by contrast. The troubles of heroes precede their triumphs. In *The Antiquary* Lovel turns out to be *Major* Neville—one military rank superior to that of the discourteous M'Intyre.

Schopenhauer contended that the perils and discomforts of the hero simply heightened his final happiness. The philosopher's allusion to *Old Mortality* was topical in 1819:

> Great and lively joy can only be conceived as the consequences of great misery, which has preceded it; for nothing can be added to a state of permanent satisfaction but some amusement, or the satisfaction of vanity. Hence all poets are obliged to bring their heroes into anxious and painful situations, so that they may be able to free them from them. Dramas and Epics accordingly always describe only fighting, suffering, tormented men; and every romance is a raree show in which we observe the spasms and convulsions of the agonized human heart. Walter Scott has naïvely expressed this aesthetic necessity in the conclusion to his novel, "Old Mortality."[4]

(In the conclusion Miss Buskbody insists on hearing about the marriage of Edith and Morton and so forth: "Let us see a glimpse of sunshine in the last chapter; it is quite essential.") Schopenhauer's comment nicely applies to a romance that rewards the hero's perseverance with "permanent satisfaction." The asserted stability of civilization and reason would scarcely interest the reader without a studied play on the anxieties that qualify and precede the hero's happiness. According to Robert Louis Stevenson, on the other hand, the perils and anxieties of the hero invite the reader's interest on their own account. The hero experiences discomfort because the reader perversely enjoys the thought of himself in a similar situation.

> Something happens, as we desire to have it happen to ourselves; some situation, that we have long dallied with in fancy, is realised in the story with enticing and appropriate details. . . . It is not only pleasurable things that we imagine in our daydreams; there are lights in which we are willing to contemplate even the idea of our own death; ways in which it seems as if it would amuse us to be cheated, wounded, or calumniated.[5]

[4] *The World as Will and Idea*, ed. R. B. Haldane and J. Kemp (3 vols. London, 1886), Bk. IV, ch. 46.

[5] "A Gossip on Romance," *Longman's Magazine* 1 (1882): 77.

Although emotions recognized as such are the prerogative of dark heroes and heroines in the Waverley Novels, it now appears that the passive hero lives an affective life of his own. Scott peoples the world of his hero with agents good and bad whose kindness or malevolence is exaggerated. Everywhere the hero goes he attracts swift friendship and even more unaccountable enmity. The passive hero (or the reader who associates with him) evidently enjoys this unreal enmity and friendship, and pretends that personal value accrues from it. In *Guy Mannering* "The strangeness of [Bertram's] destiny, and the mysteries which appeared to thicken around him, while he seemed alike to be persecuted and protected by secret enemies and friends, arising out of a class of people with whom he had no previous connection, for some time occupied his thoughts" (Ch. 45).

In the world of the Waverley Novels the passive hero is often an *un*popular person. In *Rob Roy* he attracts the "grins and whispers" of his cousins (Ch. 7). In *St. Ronan's Well* he inexplicably provokes the enmity of the entire company of the Fox Hotel (Ch. 8). There are, in short, insufferable persons, or misguided fools, who hate him. The handsome Damian de Lacy of *The Betrothed* is supposed to be hugely popular with the people: he strikes one as uncommonly fortunate until he is falsely "accused of instigating and heading this insurrection, and of deserting his duty in the field, and abandoning a noble comrade to the swords of the brutal peasants" (Ch. 28). Probably in real life the discomfort of being slandered outweighs the pleasure of being vindicated; but in romance, where nothing is real except as we wish it so, both to be liked and to be disliked are interesting.

The perverse pleasure of being acted upon rises to a critical pitch in the presence of persons of authority. Real power in the Waverley Novels can only be existing power, which operates vertically and downward in the given scheme of things, and opposes forces that attempt to cut crosswise against its directives. If necessity begat property, necessity imposes its authority over the earth. And if reason governs passion, it forces passion down. The psychological implications of this vector of authority are not less important than its political implications. The journey of Jeanie Deans to London dramatizes a characteristic response of the hero in the Waverley Novels. In order to get something done, an inactive hero taps the vertical power of the system by approaching one of the agents of its authority.

This recourse of the hero becomes automatic: he does not stop to think what can be done but turns directly to the nearest authority. From the case of Waverley winning the release of Colonel Talbot from Prince Charles, to the case of Adam Hartley appealing to Hyder Ali to save Menie Gray in *The Surgeon's Daughter*, experience confirms the effectiveness of the recourse to authority. A behaviorist would say that the success of the practice generates the habit. A Freudian psychologist would conclude that the hero constantly appeals to a father-figure for assistance. But since we deal here with a fictional, constructed world, what the hero's experience truly confirms is the justice of the projected scheme of things.

By the same token, when his own well-being is threatened, the hero automatically examines his relation to authority at the given moment. He does not usually seek redress from the courts. Recourse to a legal action is often implicit in the hero's thoughts; but in the formal trials of the Waverley Novels he is generally the accused rather than the plaintiff. When he does appeal to justice, he is likely to find himself in the frustrating situation of Darsie Latimer before Justice Foxley in *Redgauntlet* (Ch. 6)—a situation bearing as close a resemblance to a scene from Kafka as to the Edinburgh Court of Sessions. Psychologically, his implicit appeal to justice is not very distinguishable from a simple appeal to authority. Courts of law do not ideally give or take away anything in any case; they can only restore things according to the order imposed by necessity and overseen by authority. Legal action remains merely a provisional recourse for the hero because it is less emotionally gratifying than a direct answer from authority. In romance as in life one longs for more immediate redress of wrongs than is available from the courts, and a mode of protection that is closer at hand. Since the hero is himself the representative of civil society, there can be little uncertainty of right and wrong in his case, and he requires little more than a policeman to set things right again. Because of his "rank in life" he goes directly to the chief of police, who is more likely to be a duke with a number of troops at his command than a legal magistrate.

This searching about for the police does not tell us much more than we already know of the passive hero—his submission of his individual interests to the accepted morality and order of society—except for the sheer intensity of his respect for authority. When the hero of *Guy Mannering* is threatened with arrest, for example, he protests his deference to authority three times in a single sentence: "Observe . . . that I have no purpose to resist legal authority; satisfy me that you have a magistrate's warrant, and are authorized to make this arrest, and I will obey it quietly; but let no man who loves his life venture to approach me, till I am satisfied for what crime, and by whose authority, I am apprehended" (Ch. 41). The hero's appeal to an authority is instinctive, and he can neither deny nor delay his instinct without debating with himself at great length. When Harry Bertram discovers that the purse that Meg Merrilies has handed him appears to be full of stolen property, he is deeply embarrassed. "His first thought was to

inquire after the nearest justice of peace, and to place in his hands
the treasure of which he had thus unexpectedly become the deposi-
tary, telling, at the same time, his own remarkable story" (Ch. 28). His
second thought is that this action might jeopardize the gypsy woman.

> Besides, he was a stranger, and, for a time at least, unprovided with
> means of establishing his own character and credit to the satisfaction of
> a stupid or obstinate country magistrate. "I will think over the matter
> more maturely," he said: "perhaps there may be a regiment quartered at
> the country-town, in which case my knowledge of the service, and ac-
> quaintance with many officers of the army, cannot fail to establish my
> situation and character by evidence which a civil judge could not suffi-
> ciently estimate. And then I shall have the commanding-officer's assis-
> tance in managing matters so as to screen this unhappy mad
> woman. . . ."

This debate and soliloquy are a page in length. Scott's problem is to
place some stolen goods in the possession of his hero and not allow
him to get rid of them immediately: in the following chapters the
reader must be apprehensive lest the hero be incriminated by his possession of the purse. Scott would argue in his review of Tales of My
Landlord that a passive hero could be easily moved by his author
from one scene to another; but he cannot be moved very easily when
the dictates of his public morality urge him to surrender himself to
the nearest magistrate. Bertram, incidentally, is given no further opportunity to consult either magistrate or commanding officer before
he is arrested thirteen chapters later, with the stolen goods, as the
reader feared, still in his charge.

17. The Emotion of the Hero

Anxiety, the characteristic emotion of the passive hero, was not invented in the twentieth century. The word signifies an irrational fear,
a fear without a visible object, or a fear out of proportion to its
known object—and the general uneasiness of mind accompanying
such fear. Scott repeatedly uses the word in this sense, and also such
near synonyms as "apprehension" and "vexation." The words "anxiety" and "anxious," alluding to the hero's state of mind, occur three
times in one chapter of *The Pirate* (Ch. 12) and at least four times in
as many chapters in *Rob Roy* (Chs. 1, 16, 20, 21) and *The Heart of Mid-
Lothian* (Chs. 9, 11, 13, 27). In the portraits of Reuben Butler and
Arthur Philipson, Scott unmistakably intended to stress anxiety as a
character trait. In *The Heart of Mid-Lothian* it appears as a generalized

quantity or force that must be coped with—"his mind harassed with anxiety, and with painful doubts and recollections" (Ch. 11). In *Rob Roy* Scott conceives of the craven Morris as an exaggerated instance of irrational fear, and once refers directly to the power and enormity of anxiety. The assertion is part of his narrator-hero's boast of courage: "[Morris's] conduct only inspired me with contempt, and confirmed me in an opinion which I had already entertained, that of all the propensities which teach mankind to torment themselves, that of causeless fear is the most irritating, busy, painful, and pitiable" (Ch. 3). The reader soon observes, however, that Frank Osbaldistone is himself a victim of anxiety, and that he later does acknowledge a share in the foibles of the human race. "I suppose that all men, in situations of peculiar doubt and difficulty, when they have exercised their reason to little purpose, are apt, in a sort of despair, to abandon the reins to their imagination, and be guided altogether by chance, or by those whimsical impressions which take possession of the mind, and to which we give way as if to involuntary impulses" (Ch. 21). He is describing a mental state similar to that of Arthur Philipson when poised above the abyss. The talk of exercising reason "to little purpose" strikes an almost subversive note: Frank seems to have come to the edge of his moral world. He confines his admission to "whimsical impressions," however, merely comparing these to "involuntary impulses."

Notwithstanding the degree of courage with which his passive heroes are potentially endowed, Scott elsewhere acknowledges the possible generalized effect of anxiety. Vague threats, on the whole, seem more damaging to a firm state of mind than are certain dangers. In *The Fortunes of Nigel* the hero finds himself surrounded by the strange world of Whitefriars and prey to the "dark hints" of Martha Trapbois: "The bravest man, placed in a situation in which he is surrounded by suspicious persons, and removed from all counsel and assistance, except those afforded by a valiant heart and a strong arm, experiences a sinking of the heart, a consciousness of abandonment, which for a moment chills his blood, and depresses his natural gallantry of disposition" (Ch. 23).

The passive hero suffers from a considerable range of anxieties, from a mild self-consciousness of the way he is dressed to a fear of seeming mad. Dress figures in *Waverley* as a symbol of romantic adventure that may be put on or off—thus confirming the excursion by which the hero can experience the world of romantic action without actually performing any. Waverley carefully dresses himself for the battle of Prestonpans, adjusting his Highland target on his shoulder: "How does it look?" (Ch. 44). After "the romance" of his life is over and "its real history" begun, he requests farmer Jopson "carefully to preserve for him his Highland garb and accoutrements" (Ch. 62). But at the high point of his adventure, as we have seen, a glance at this strange dress overcomes Waverley with nightmarish anxiety (Ch. 46). Throughout *The Heart of Mid-Lothian* the cleanliness of Jeanie Deans and the thoroughness of her housekeeping certify her character to friend and stranger alike; and part of the happy ending of this moralistic romance consists of a trunk from the Duke of Argyll and his daughters "full of wearing apparel of the best quality, suited to Jeanie's rank in life" (Ch. 45). But during the most anxious moments of her journey to London (Chs. 31 and 32), Jeanie is acutely conscious of the "disorderly appearance of her own dress" and the false impression it must make on all who observe her.

It is never clear precisely why Darsie Latimer should be subjected to female dress in the last portion of *Redgauntlet*. Though he submits passively to this disguise, presumably the experience vexes more than it pleases him. Dress, like one's rank in life, is a source of personal identity, and the thought of losing or having to conceal his rank is a cause of anxiety for the hero. Nigel experiences "mental sufferings" at the thought of disguising himself in Whitefriars (Ch. 17). In *Kenilworth*, when Tressilian's suffering mounts to its highest pitch (Ch. 30), one of his chief embarrassments is his "dishabille," and everyone sees that his riding suit, "however handsome it might be," is out of place in the presence of the Queen and courtiers. Scott seems to have checked himself at this point, for he adds in an admitted "digression" that a concern for clothes "may seem something at variance with the gravity of Tressilian's character." He answers that "even the doomed criminal who goes to certain execution, shows an anxiety to array his person to the best advantage."

The passive hero is thoroughly self-conscious about his outward appearance. As a person who is acted upon rather than acting, he feels that he is being watched by everyone in sight. In *Peveril of the Peak* Julian has the privilege of striding through London with a beauty on each arm, but a passive hero cannot altogether enjoy this kind of prominence. "Julian's embarrassment in passing Charing Cross and Northumberland House was so great as to excite the attention of the passengers" (Ch. 32). In *The Fair Maid of Perth* Henry Wynd hurriedly escorts Louise the glee-maiden (a potential dark heroine who has placed herself in his protection) through the back ways of Perth, in vigilant dread that someone will see them and draw the wrong inference (Ch. 12). Such fears seem groundless: Henry and Julian could make their explanations if necessary. But romance, as it were, justifies the anxiety, by enlarging upon it until it seems to have a real object.

"Many passengers looked at them with wonder, and some with smiles; but Julian remarked that there were two who never lost sight of them, and to whom his situation, and the demeanour of his companions, seemed to afford matter of undisguised merriment." These two cox-combs proceed to jostle and insult him, and turn out to be "men of the Duke of Buckingham's." And before Henry Wynd can reach home with Louise, he runs straight into the Pottingar, "a malignant tale bearer . . . by no means well disposed" to the hero. The hero of the Waverley Novels is perhaps particularly anxious for appearances where women are concerned. In *Rob Roy* Scott contrasts Frank's re-gard for appearances against the dark heroine's disregard for the same. He is "flattered with the interest so lovely a creature seemed to take in my fate, yet vexed at the ridiculous appearance I should make, by carrying a girl of eighteen along with me as an advocate, and seriously concerned for the misconstruction to which her motives might be exposed" (Ch. 7).

Persons are especially liable to observation on Sundays. A worri-some embarrassment on the Sabbath occurs, for example, in *The Heart of Mid-Lothian*. After she has fallen into the hands of Meg Murdockson in Lincolnshire, Jeanie Deans is led by the mad Madge Wildfire into the parish of Willingham on a Sunday morning (Ch. 31). "Jeanie sighed heavily, to think it should be her lot on the Lord's day, and during kirk time too, to parade the street of an inhabited vil-lage with so very grotesque a comrade." Madge proposes to enter the church itself, and when Jeanie resists, Madge snatches away her bon-net and pulls her hair. In what follows, Jeanie Deans—the one hero-ine in Scott convincingly motivated by religious principles—has the dread experience of disrupting a church service. The congregation stare at her, and she is burningly aware of her missing bonnet and disheveled hair. She even doubts the propriety of being present at an Anglican service in any case. But Jeanie masters her doubts and em-barrassment with an effort, and resolves to dissociate herself as far as possible from Madge Wildfire: "withdrawing herself from Madge as far as the pew permitted, she endeavoured to evince, by serious and composed attention to what was passing, that her mind was composed to devotion." Scott deserves more credit for psychological observation than is generally accorded him.

Fear of madness receives muted treatment in the Waverley Novels. The actual mad people are minor characters like Madge Wildfire, or Habakkuk Mucklewrath in *Old Mortality*; and there are hints of insan-ity about such romantic villains as Staunton and Burley. Of principal characters only Lucy Ashton is actually driven mad. With his obses-sion for appearances, the hero instead fears that he may be *thought* mad; and villains sometimes plot to make him appear so. In *St. Ronan's Well* Bulmer insinuates that his brother Tyrrel has "a train of something irregular in his mind,—a vein, in short, of madness . . . rendering the poor young man a dupe to vain imaginations of his own dignity and grandeur . . . and inspiring the deepest aversion against his nearest relatives and against myself in particular" (Ch. 25). In *Redgauntlet* Darsie Latimer fears that his captors may try to make out that he is mad: "My demeanour was probably insane enough, while I was agitated at once by the frenzy incident to the fever, and the anxiety arising from my extraordinary situation. But is it possible they can now establish any cause of confining me, arising out of the state of my mind?" (Ch. 5). Darsie's legal training suggests that someone may try to commit him to an asylum.

Heroes are susceptible enough to attacks of anxiety that they may at least appear to be mad. Determined to conceal his marriage from Queen Elizabeth, Leicester has Varney present "attestations" (as if it were a court of law) that Amy Robsart, who has been ordered to be presented at Kenilworth as Varney's wife, is too ill to travel. But the hero, Tressilian, has just seen Amy in a room of the same castle. Forgetting his promise to Amy to say nothing, he blurts out that "these certificates speak not the truth," and there follows a peculiarly tormenting scene of *Kenilworth* (Ch. 31). Tressilian already suffers under considerable embarrassment, the Queen having called him "that slovenly fellow" and mocked him in other ways. No sooner has he hastily impugned Leicester's documents than he remembers his promise to Amy, stops speaking, and adds "indecision and irresolution" to his unfavorable appearance. "He turned the papers over and over, as if he had been an idiot, incapable of comprehending their contents." The villains meanwhile bring forward a series of prejudiced witnesses to support the written attestations. When the Queen gives Tressilian another chance to explain himself, he reflects that Amy and Leicester may yet be reconciled, and he is again overcome with "extreme embarrassment of look, voice, and manner." The Queen, courtiers, and even the friends of the hero conclude that he is mad. The latter drag him from the presence chamber, and lock him up. Tressilian's "gallant and disinterested efforts to save a female who had treated him with ingratitude, thus terminated for the present, in the displeasure of his Sovereign, and the conviction of his friends, that he was little better than a madman."

The chief anxiety of the passive hero is the fear of being misunderstood, or of being implicated in any of the romantic or extralegal events of the Waverley Novels. This anxiety provides the tension of the excursion beyond the ideal boundary, and responds to the risk involved in all such journeys. The hero is by definition safe from irrevocable involvement in the extralegal world, but cannot escape the risk of guilt by association. Precisely because the hero is aligned with society and the law, because he is ultimately rewarded for maintaining his firm stand, and because nothing serious or permanent can happen to him, the plot in the Waverley Novels depends upon anxiety for its emotional currency. It is sufficient in the long run to be innocent; but it is better still to be nowhere near the scene of the crime. Scott places his hero at the scene, where he hazards all sorts of misconstructions of his innocent intentions. Damaging associations exist even independent of the main action and have a way of multiplying on the hero. The hero of *The Fortunes of Nigel*, in the midst of his other troubles, finds himself charged with the seduction of Dame Christie. Christie himself (the honest ship-chandler) accuses Nigel of this infamy as the latter awaits his fate in the Tower of London; and when Christie has stormed out of the room, "Nigel had full leisure to lament the waywardness of his fate, which seemed never to tire of persecuting him for crimes of which he was innocent, and investing him with the appearances of guilt which his mind abhorred" (Ch. 28). Such gratuitous charges not only justify the hero's complaint but suggest that anxiety is the very stuff from which the romance is constructed.

18. Prudence

We are accustomed to associate anxiety with repression—the mechanism, whether social or individual, by which desire is checked and prevented from operating on the surface of the mind. The notion of morality as essentially a form of repression enjoyed a considerable popularity in the early nineteenth century. In the period in which the Waverley Novels were written, morality was typically construed in terms of prudence, restraint, suppression, precaution, reason, principle, and "masculine" self-denial; such expressions could be used more or less interchangeably. The spirit of this morality can be detected in popular conceptions of society itself: "A state of society is founded on reason, and is precisely the reverse of a savage state, which can admit of no other basis than that of mere animal instinct."[6] The same morality cautions even against one's higher feelings. In a passage in *Old Mortality* Scott indicates that a sense of guilt may accompany any kind of indulgence of feeling: "There are periods of mental agitation

[6] J.S.C. Somers, *A Short Treatise on the Dreadful Tendency of Levelling Principles* (London, 1793), p. 13.

when the firmest of mortals must be ranked with the weakest of his brethren; and when, in paying the general tax of humanity, *his distresses are even aggravated by feeling that he transgresses,* in the indulgence of his grief, the rules of religion and philosophy, by which he endeavours in general to regulate his passions and his actions" (Ch. 39; my italics). The same passage regards the "rules" of religion and philosophy as a sort of restraining mechanism.

In *Rob Roy* "prudence, and the necessity of suppressing my passion" induce Frank Osbaldistone to leave the library at Miss Vernon's command, even though he is outraged by signs of an eavesdropper behind the tapestry (Ch. 16). In *Redgauntlet* Darsie Latimer twice asserts that "my principles and my prudence alike forbid" joining his uncle's romantic conspiracy (Chs. 18 and 19). "Principles," in this context, literally means the restraining mechanism. The poetry of the troubadours, according to a passage in *Anne of Geierstein,* "was too frequently used to soften and seduce the heart, and corrupt the principles" (Ch. 29). In nonfiction Scott is even more explicit. "There never did, and never will exist, anything permanently noble and excellent in character, which was a stranger to the exercise of resolute self-denial."[7] We have already observed the passage in which he declares that the individual morality of Bage's "philosophical heroes" can serve only as "a perpetual apology for evading the practice of abstinence"[8]—a phrase that inverts and elevates self-denial to a positive function.

A significant conclusion may be rescued from the strange paragraph in the introduction to *Ivanhoe* in which Scott conjures away the reputation of Rebecca. In spite of himself, as it were, Scott asserts both Rebecca's "rashly-formed or ill-assorted passion" for Ivanhoe, and her "sacrifice of passion to principle." Both conditions are possible in a temporal sequence: Rebecca experiences the passion and then suppresses it. She receives credit for suppressing passion, but this credit does not cancel the misfortune—and the opprobrium, since we are speaking of moral credit—of rashly conceiving the passion in the first place. In other words, Rebecca should have repressed her passion for Ivanhoe so successfully that she would not have become conscious of it herself. A blonde heroine would be able to do this. Ideally a proper heroine is not conscious of love for a hero until he has asked her to marry him.

This rule pushes the conflict of passion and principle well back to the very edge of consciousness. In a woman, at least, principle suffers a defeat if the passion so much as makes itself known. She is then in

[7] *Miscellaneous Prose Works,* 3: 348.
[8] Ibid., 3: 554.

the position of Rebecca; and she will wish to be exiled. At a higher level, and in a subsequent moment, Rebecca does sacrifice her passion to principle in time to escape the social consequences—though not in time to escape entirely the moral opprobrium, for we tend to blame people for what they do to themselves as well as what they do to others. But it is Rebecca who has been injured. From Wilfred of Ivanhoe's point of view—and ultimately for the reader—Rebecca's passion is agreeable enough. To be loved by a beautiful woman in exotic plumage is a pleasant sensation. Oddly enough, because Ivanhoe's social consciousness warns him of trouble, and because he possesses a handsome alternative in Rowena, it is also agreeable that Rebecca overcomes her passion.

Scott was aware that the necessary degree of repression could be administered too late—the explanation of Roland Graeme's trouble in *The Abbot*—and that it could be administered too suddenly. In *The Heart of Mid-Lothian* he attributes the asocial behavior of George Staunton to a pampered childhood, interrupted by abrupt discipline. The notion of morality as repression colors the narrative much as it does in our post- Freudian interpretations of childhood:

> He passed the first part of his early youth under the charge of a doting mother, and in the society of negro slaves, whose study it was to gratify his every caprice. . . . Indeed, what Mr. Staunton did do toward counteracting the baneful effects of his wife's system, only tended to render it more pernicious; for every restraint imposed on the boy in his father's presence, was compensated by treble licence during his absence. So that George Staunton acquired, even in childhood, the habit of regarding his father as a rigid censor, from whose severity he was desirous of emancipating himself as soon and absolutely as possible. [Ch. 34]

The real difficulty, however, stems from the "beautiful and wilful" Mrs. Staunton and the Negro slaves. The basic difference between this view of 1817 and the view of our own era, is that, today, in theory, we broadly condemn repression. Scott took it for granted that repressed individuals made better members of society and led happier lives. The contrast of rude and civilized peoples confirmed the impression that unrepressed individuals could not *be* members of society.

The idea of a struggle between the passions and the higher faculties of man is a very old one. The emphasis on suppressing the passions seems to have increased, however, toward the end of the eighteenth century. In the course of that century, pursuant to the formal exegesis of Francis Hutcheson, David Hume, and Adam Smith, reason was gradually conceived to have no actual motive force in itself. This does not mean that reason ceased to have a moral function, nor, indeed, a high moral connotation. But reason in itself could not, in theory, cause or inspire a desirable course of action. To the rational faculties fell the task of selecting ends appropriate to long-range and stable desires, determining how such desires might be eventually satisfied, and clarifying for the individual the sharp conflict between immediate satisfaction and more lasting gains. "Prudence," therefore, was the name for reason functioning in this moral area—not a motive in itself but a vigorous caution that distant ends are as desirable as immediate satisfactions. Prudence also taught that some kinds of indulgence precluded future satisfaction. The highly abstract relations of life—property, marriage, and the entire range of legal contracts—are not enhanced by prudence and principle: prudence makes evident their claim as desirable conditions. If one is prudent—that is, if one is intelligent enough to perceive the benefits of such relations—one will choose, in some sense, to constrain more obvious desires. This relation between the passions and reason implies a more or less constant repression of the former by the latter—and successful repression, too, if the complex relations of society are tenable.

Repression in this sense was a theoretical as well as a practical possibility long before the Id and the Ego and the Superego became household words. When the romantic movement publicized the passions, prudence did not retire from the stage. The mechanics of the system suggest the contrary. An increased respect for passion could only imply the increased necessity for prudence—just as the French Revolution advanced the prestige of property. As soon as it became generally accepted that moral behavior was part of the affective life of individuals, the control of emotion achieved its heightened dignity. "Prudence," according to Burke, "is not only the first in the rank of the virtues political and moral, but she is the director, the regulator, the standard of them all."[9] This is the period, we remember, in which Malthus pitted moral restraint against the ruthless law of population.

Granted that prudence enjoys official status in the Waverley Novels, as elsewhere, the relation of prudence to anxiety is less simple. Prudence is not itself an emotion: not prudence, but the long-range interests that it discloses compete directly with unacceptable passions. Prudence does seem to borrow a certain affective energy from fear. The dark hero and heroine make our passive hero uneasy; and Frank Osbaldistone doubts whether he can visit the Highlands in safety and comfort. The hero of *Peveril of the Peak* becomes "dizzy, and almost sick, with listening to the undisguised brutality" of the villains (Ch.

[9] *An Appeal from the New to the Old Whigs*, in *Works*, 4: 81.

20). The hero may fear direct injury from illicit agencies; or he may fear that they jeopardize the abstract reality that supports his existence. On the whole, however, the hero's anxiety is directed elsewhere. The antics of romantic agents and the machinations of villains, in this scheme of things, are justifiable sources of fear. We are searching for the cause of an unjustifiable fear.

None of the kinds of anxiety that we have observed can be interpreted as fear of the romantic agents in the Waverley Novels, or even of any lurking psychic forces that these may represent. Anxieties about dress and "rank," the feeling of being watched or censured, the thought of interrupting a church service or not seeming prayerful, the possibility of appearing insane, and the anxiety of being erroneously implicated in extralegal or immoral activity are all social anxieties. These apprehensions all face toward society, and the structured reality of the hero's world. The hero, all things considered, gets along surprisingly well with the agents of the other world. The peril they represent to him is chiefly the appearance, in the eyes of his own society, of being allied to the world of unchecked passion.

It comes with a shock to realize that, in a romance which respects above all the existing law and order, he who is constantly threatened with arrest, and frequently imprisoned by the government, is the passive hero of civil society. The villain is never thrust into the Tower to speculate on the cruelty of his fate. In the typical situation of melodrama it is always the villain who serves the warrant. Why is the hero the one to stand trial for his unlikely guilt? And what can the hero be supposed to be guilty of? In *Guy Mannering* the sensation of being in a Scottish jail is discovered to be more frightening than the hero's experiences in India. "Bertram, for the first time in his life, felt himself affected with a disposition to low spirits" (Ch. 45). An uneasy fear of jails runs all through the Waverley Novels. As if to answer the hero's worst expectations, there is frequently someone ready to swear out a warrant for his arrest.

The instinctive anxiety of the hero should have been obvious to us from the beginning. As soon as we realize that the hero casts an anxious eye over his shoulder, not because of the threat of any romantic agent but because of some perilous imminence of his own society, numerous small incidents fall into place. After Jeanie Deans has withstood her ordeal in the church, she awaits in trepidation an interview with the rector (Ch. 32). "It is true, it was difficult to suppose on what pretext a person travelling on her own business, and at her own charge, could be interrupted upon her route"—but Jeanie is nevertheless anxious lest this official check her interests and put a stop to her journey.

Mr. Staunton [the rector] spoke to her with great mildness. He observed, that, although her appearance at church had been uncommon, and in strange, and he must add, discreditable society, and calculated, upon the whole, to disturb the congregation during divine worship, he wished, nevertheless, to hear her own account of herself before taking any steps which his duty might seem to demand. He was a justice of the peace, he informed her, as well as a clergyman.

Jeanie is right to be apprehensive, for this is an ominous "mildness." The figure of authority, to whom she feels she must turn for protection, poses a certain threat—more vague and ill-defined even than the inexplicable threat from Meg Murdockson. When Jeanie tells her story of being kidnapped by Meg and her gang the night before, the rector replies, "Here has been, according to your account, a great violence committed without any adequate motive. Are you aware of the law of this country—that if you lodge this charge, you will be bound over to prosecute this gang?" He thus levies against her an appropriate countercharge of society—namely, that her tale is unreal—and threatens her with some unpleasant implications of the law that is designed to protect her.

The "reality" celebrated by the Waverley Novels is responsible for the hero's anxiety. It is as if he feared the kind of factual error inflicted by the law in *The Heart of Mid-Lothian*. The structure of his reality is so attenuated, so abstract, and yet so powerful that his intentions may be misconstrued. The more he propitiates authority and represses all unacceptable passions, the more he seems to worry. Into the Waverley Novels Scott introduced the kind of anxieties that only very well-behaved persons can entertain for customs officials or traffic signs that they do not intend to disobey. The passive hero is not only inactive but passive in the sense of "suffering." What he suffers, however, and the direction from which he seems to be threatened, are somewhat surprising: his anxiety can be studied further in *Rob Roy*.

VII

ROB ROY

It is the object of the novel-writer, to place before the
reader as full and accurate a representation of the events
which he relates, as can be done by the mere force of an
excited imagination, without the assistance of material objects. His sole appeal is made to the world of fancy and of
ideas, and in this consists his strength and weakness, his
poverty and his wealth. He cannot, like the painter, present a visible and tangible representation of his towns and
his woods, his palaces and his castles . . . He cannot, like
the dramatist, present before our living eyes the heroes
of former days, or the beautiful creations of his own
fancy, embodied in the grace and majesty of Kemble or
of Siddons . . .

—Scott, "Henry Fielding"

19. Francis Osbaldistone

THE ADVENTURES of the hero of *Rob Roy* seem arbitrary in
the extreme. He is merely placed at the scene of action and informed from time to time of impalpable dangers. Even more
than Harry Bertram of *Guy Mannering*, Francis Osbaldistone is "the
mere king of a chess-board, advanced, withdrawn, exposed, protected, at the pleasure of those who play the game over his head."[1]
His father sends him to Northumberland for no other reason than
the possibility that his "presence may be requisite" (Ch. 2); at Osbaldistone Hall it appears that he might better serve his father's interests
in London. "But how can I, in disgrace with my father, and divested
of all control over his affairs, prevent this danger by my mere presence in London?" Diana Vernon answers, "That presence alone will
do much" (Ch. 16). As it happens, Frank goes to Glasgow instead; but
the propositions concerning his *presence* provide the single controlling
principle of the romance. The presence of the hero never accom-
plishes any action, very true, but it sensitively registers the anxiety of
the hero of society.

An experience on the Sabbath in Glasgow may be taken to illus-

---

[1] [Adolphus], *Letters to Richard Heber*, p. 138.

trate the niceness of the hero's state of mind. Amidst the reverent citizens who solemnly pace beside the Clyde in the Sabbath evening, Frank worries that he is somehow conspicuous:

> Insensibly I felt my mode of sauntering by the side of the river, and crossing successively the various persons who were passing homeward, and without tarrying or delay, must expose me to observation at least, if not to censure; and I slunk out of the frequented path, and found a trivial occupation for my mind in marshalling my revolving walk in such a manner as should least render me obnoxious to observation. [Ch. 21]

From the perspective of his lifetime the narrator of *Rob Roy* recognizes the compulsive nature of this little byplay, and characterizes it as "childish manoeuvres." This is not the hero in his role of observer, but the hero anxious lest he be exposed to observation, wary lest anyone regard him with censure. So far as the context is concerned, the emotion is gratuitous: the passage epitomizes the passive hero's vague self-consciousness.

These "childish manoeuvres" in the park are clearly not directed against any romantic or extralegal forces lurking in the shrubbery. The burghers of Glasgow are as law-abiding as Frank himself. In general, in *Rob Roy*, the anxieties of the hero arise *in proximity* to thieves, Highlanders, and Jacobites: but the cause of the anxiety is not the threat of such romantic agents; it is the danger of being associated with them. This is not to say that mystery and uncertainty have no effect on the hero. On the same Sabbath, before a midnight rendezvous with a mysterious stranger, his impatience becomes "nearly ungovernable. I began to question whether I had been imposed upon by the trick of a fool, the raving of a madman, or the studied machinations of a villain, and paced the little quay or pier adjoining the entrance to the bridge, in a state of incredible anxiety and vexation" (Ch. 21). When the stranger arrives, however, Frank is not afraid. In fact, Rob Roy (the stranger) is rather perturbed that the young man does not fear him.

> "And why should I?" replied I. "I again repeat, I fear nought that you can do."
>
> "Nought that I can do?—Be it so. But do you not fear the consequences of being found with one whose very name whispered in this lonely street would make the stones themselves rise up to apprehend him . . . ?"

The stranger assures Frank that he is not an enemy, but his words above indicate the danger—from association—that he poses to the hero nonetheless. When Rob Roy explains that they must visit the

Glasgow prison, Frank, mistaking his intention, becomes much more excited: "'To prison!' I exclaimed—'by what warrant or for what offence? —You shall have my life sooner than my liberty—I defy you, and will not follow you a step farther.'" The prison, it will be observed, represents the coercive power of civilization, not of outlaws.

This threat of prison is purely imaginary—but so is the entire romance. The very first threat to Francis Osbaldistone arises from his proximity to a case of highway robbery. He is implicated in the robbery without even knowing that it has occurred. In fact, because of Rashleigh's sly insinuations, Sir Hildebrand Osbaldistone persists in privately congratulating Frank for hijacking Morris's portmanteau, and the payroll of the Hanoverian government—to which Frank must reply that "it is the most provoking thing on earth, that every person will take it for granted that I am accessory to a crime which I despise and detest, and which would, moreover, deservedly forfeit my life to the laws of my country" (Ch. 11). Soon he finds that Andrew Fairservice, who has promoted himself to the hero's service, has stolen the mare of Thorncliff Osbaldistone: "I . . . considered it as a hard fate, which a second time threw me into collision with a person of such irregular practices" (Ch. 18). Thus the romance gives the hero every reason to be wary of "collision" with the law as well:

> At finding myself so unexpectedly, fortuitously, and, as it were, by stealth, introduced within one of the legal fortresses of Scotland, I could not help recollecting my adventure in Northumberland, and fretting at the strange incidents which again, without any demerits of my own, threatened to place me in a dangerous and disagreeable collision with the laws of a country which I visited only in the capacity of a stranger. [Ch. 21]

Throughout *Rob Roy* the hero labors under some vague threat from the law and its administrators, whether Scottish or English. Even the name Osbaldistone seems to implicate him, since his cousins by that name are all Jacobites. The hero's better half, so to speak, counts on the law and the authorities to remedy his situation. Yet when he threatens to take Rashleigh Osbaldistone before a magistrate, the villain replies that Frank has more reason "to dread the presence of a magistrate" (Ch. 25).

In the course of the adventures in the Highlands (Chs. 27–35) one would expect any uneasiness of the hero to derive entirely from his wild surroundings and their wild inhabitants. But on the whole, Frank is agreeably impressed by the scenery, and though sensible to the dangers of provoking a savage people he seems safe so long as he does not move too suddenly and so long as he makes clear his peaceful intentions. Much more ambiguous is his relation to the soldiers of the crown who are also in the Highlands—his relation to Captain Thornton and to the unnamed duke. Captain Thornton discovers the hero "in written communication with the outlawed robber," and "in immediate correspondence with the enemy" (Ch. 29). Thus the freedom of the Highlands is not extended to the hero, who is pursued forever by the nice anxiety of his relation to his own government. Whenever Frank finds himself among the soldiers, he becomes a kind of prisoner—not precisely a prisoner, because we are not allowed to forget his loyalty and rank in society. "The Captain took the opportunity to make us some slight apology for detaining us. 'If we were loyal and peaceable subjects,' he said, 'we would not regret being stopt for a day, when it was essential to the king's service; if otherwise, he was acting according to his duty'" (Ch. 30). The role of prisoner—or quasi-prisoner—is familiar to Scott's heroes because it typifies the adherence of the hero to authority and also projects his anxiety in that relation. In other words, the role offers the same mixed pleasure as visiting jails in the night.

Frank again mingles with the forces of the government when he conveys the intentions of the Highlanders to revenge the capture of their leader (Ch. 32). The same ambiguous relationship is immediately resumed: "I received an intimation, rather than an invitation, to attend the party; and I perceived, that, though no longer considered as a prisoner, I was yet under some sort of suspicion." At this point in *Rob Roy* the dark hero escapes from the soldiers into the waters of a ford, and the passive hero is lost in the confusion. From the excitement of Rob Roy's escape there arises a threat to Frank himself. For its elaboration of the hero's relation to authority the passage is one of the most interesting in the Waverley Novels:

> Hitherto I had been as it were a mere spectator, though far from an uninterested one, of the singular scene which had passed. But now I heard a voice suddenly exclaim, "Where is the English stranger?—It was he gave Rob Roy the knife to cut the belt." [Untrue.]
>
> "Cleeve the pock-pudding to the chafts!" cried one voice.
>
> "Weize a brace of balls through his harn-pan!" said a second.
>
> "Drive three inches of cauld airn into his brisket!" shouted a third.
>
> And I heard several horses galloping to and fro, with the kind purpose, doubtless, of executing these denunciations. I was immediately awakened to the sense of my situation, and to the certainty that armed men, having no restraint whatever on their irritated and inflamed passions, would probably begin by shooting or cutting me down, and afterwards investigate the justice of the action. Impressed by this belief, I

leaped from my horse, and turning him loose, plunged into a bush of alder trees, where, considering the advancing obscurity of the night, I thought there was little chance of my being discovered. Had I been near enough to the Duke to have invoked his personal protection, I would have done so; but he had already commenced his retreat, and I saw no officer on the left bank of the river, of authority sufficient to have afforded protection, in case of my surrendering myself. I thought that there was no point of honour which could require, in such circumstances, an unnecessary exposure of my life. My first idea, when the tumult began to be appeased, and the clatter of the horses' feet was heard less frequently in the immediate vicinity of my hiding place, was to seek out the Duke's quarters, when all should be quiet, and give myself up to him, as a liege subject, who had nothing to fear from his justice, and a stranger, who had every right to expect protection and hospitality. . . .

After a moment's reflection, I began to consider that Fairservice, who had doubtless crossed the river with the other domestics, according to his forward and impertinent custom of putting himself always among the foremost, could not fail to satisfy the Duke, or the competent authorities, respecting my rank and situation; and that, therefore, my character did not require my immediate appearance, at the risk of being drowned in the river—of being unable to trace the march of the squadron in case of my reaching the other side in safety—or, finally, of being cut down, right or wrong, by some straggler, who might think such a piece of good service a convenient excuse for not sooner rejoining his ranks. I therefore resolved to measure my steps back to the little inn, where I had passed the preceding night. [Ch. 33]

When Rob Roy escapes from the government, and the "passions" of the soldiery escape from "restraint"—where violence is loosed, in short—a hero necessarily studies his relationship to those in authority. What is extraordinary is the extent of the hero's argument with himself and the anxiety he displays. As a storyteller Scott's purpose is simply to remove the hero from the scene, once he has witnessed the thrilling escape, and to return him to the opposite camp, where he can join Rob Roy and pursue the action further. But the hero is not to be moved from his state of semicaptivity with ease. For the space of about two pages (I have omitted an entire paragraph) Frank must worry whether he can depart from the scene without reporting to the duke. Because the soldiers, in the heat of the chase, have mistakenly assumed his complicity, the hero is anxious to submit his "character" or reputation to some "competent authorities" for a fresh clearance. Twice he repeats that he would have adopted the proper procedure if only circumstances had not argued so persuasively against it. In point of fact, Frank did overhear the escape being plotted just before Rob leaped for safety, and therefore is, in a sense, a party to the act. His concluding reflection, however, is that his "rank and situation," his prior membership in Hanoverian civilization, must support him in such exigencies.

20. The Plot

For a century and a half readers have scorned the plot of *Rob Roy* as either unimportant or unintelligible. There are no serious loose ends, however: the action seems inchoate because there are too many sources of interest, no one of which commands the whole. As a vicarious spectator the reader enjoys the encounters with Rob Roy, the stirrings of Jacobite rebellion, the tour of Glasgow and the Highlands, and the fate of the commercial house of Osbaldistone. (Scott *asserts*—in Chapter 26—a connection between the schemes against the house of Osbaldistone and the Highland uprising, but he never convincingly presents this connection to the reader.) In addition there are issues that touch the hero personally: his love for Diana Vernon and its threatened frustration, the question of filial obedience and a vocation for the hero, and the recovery of his rightful estate. The dissipation of all these sources of interest is compounded by mystery—by the deliberate withholding of information in the interest of suspense. And this withholding is itself compounded by the narrative in the first person, which makes it seem unnecessarily arbitrary.

The best reply to the charge that the action of *Rob Roy* is centrifugal is that the passive hero draws it together again, and that the dominant source of interest is his largely unconscious fear of jails. This is not the intended source of unity, however. In this romance Scott seriously attempts to make his hero morally responsible for his troubles: that is, if Frank had been less stubborn and joined his father in business, none of the spectres that now disturb the family would have been raised. "The perverse opposition to my father's will . . . rose up to my conscience as the cause of all this affliction" (Ch. 22). This relation of moral cause and effect is not sufficiently central. If the moral were driven home, Francis Osbaldistone would be one kind of active hero—a hero who did nothing, but whose failure to act brought serious consequences. The moral does not convince us precisely because Frank is a *typical* hero in the Waverley Novels. It is the father who is atypical—a man of business. Though Scott at one point asserts the "romance" of business, the sympathies of the romance itself—the entire projected fiction—are with the son, who is no more inclined to business than any other hero of Scott. Neither the author nor the reader can seriously equate this disinclination of his class to moral irresponsibility. The fascination of business is, of course, provocative:

> In the fluctuations of mercantile speculation, there is something captivating to the adventurer, even independent of the hope of gain. He who embarks on that fickle sea, requires to possess the skill of the pilot and the fortitude of the navigator, and after all may be wrecked and lost, unless the gales of fortune breathe in his favour. This mixture of necessary attention and inevitable hazard,—the frequent and awful uncertainty whether prudence shall overcome fortune, or fortune baffle the schemes of prudence, affords full occupation for the powers, as well as for the feelings of the mind, and trade has all the fascination of gambling without its moral guilt. [Ch. 1]

"Prudence" cast upon the sea does not strike one as the prudence familiar in the Waverley Novels. "*Schemes* of prudence" and "hope of gain" suggest even calculating prudence. In the Waverley Novels, finally, the spirit of romantic adventure is confined to a limited episode—and this turns out to be the case in *Rob Roy* also.

Osbaldistone senior, the London merchant, is the sole champion in the Waverley Novels of the labor theory of property: "Yes, Frank, what I have *is* my own, if labour in getting, and care in augmenting, can make a right of property" (Ch. 2). But the romance as a whole favors merely primogeniture as a theory of property. The elder Osbaldistone has been disinherited in favor of a younger son. This may help to explain why "Scott's picture of Sir Hildebrand and his household is savagely contemptuous."[2] The picture of the younger brother and his family is not "savagely" contemptuous, but it is perhaps less funny than Scott imagines. He has only two choices—to make Sir Hildebrand a villain or a clown. He elects the clown and throws in Rashleigh Osbaldistone for a villain. Some of Rashleigh's evil undoubtedly distributes itself throughout this entire branch of the family. So far as property is concerned, the excursion of this romance spans two generations. When Scott, with light-hearted abandon, kills off all five of the intervening cousins and restores Osbaldistone Hall to Frank (Ch. 37), the excursion is complete. Granted that the thing is done with gusto (and with some disbelief on the author's part), the reader hears no more of the question that loomed so large at the beginning of the story—namely, whether Frank would carry on his father's business. The riches gained in commerce merely assist

[2] Donald Davie, *The Heyday of Sir Walter Scott* (London, 1961), p. 61.

the hero to secure his rightful lands. Never was a right to property more thoroughly reaffirmed: morally, because the property should have been his father's in the first place and because even Sir Hildebrand has preferred the hero to Rashleigh; legally, because the hero has "an authenticated copy" of the will, has purchased "the rights to certain large mortgages," and taken "all necessary measures to secure that possession which sages say makes nine points of the law"; and magically, in the fine recompense of fiction, when Rob Roy slays Rashleigh.

Apart from its topographical contrast, ranging the civil state against the state of nature, the construction of *Rob Roy* is weak. But a wealth of suggestion compensates for this weakness. The hero encounters not merely wickedness but hints of diabolism. Such hints are common in the Waverley Novels, but not always successfully balanced against Scott's demand for rational common sense. In *Rob Roy* the author takes sufficient pains with Rashleigh Osbaldistone to convince the reader, without ever asserting such nonsense outright, that the enemy of the hero is the enemy of mankind. Only once does the narrator directly compare Rashleigh to the devil (Ch. 25). (Scott often exercises much less restraint—in *Guy Mannering*, for example, Dirk Hatteraick pays obeisance to the devil in almost every speech.) But Rashleigh's sexual and political ambitions are unlimited; he has that traditional potency of language and "a voice the most soft, mellow, and rich in its tones that I have ever heard" (Ch. 6); and his countenance changes "almost instantaneously from the expression of one passion to that of the contrary" (Ch. 12). These characteristics are played on throughout the romance. Rashleigh performs scientific experiments and reads "Greek, Latin, and Hebrew" (Ch. 14). Above all, we are to suppose him endowed with an abnormally powerful intellect and means of persuasion—though "better acquainted with men's minds than with the moral principles that ought to regulate them" (Ch. 10).

The library, then, is the center of the hero's experience at Osbaldistone Hall—a somewhat different library from the collection of chivalric romance at Waverley-Honour. The Faustian quality of Rashleigh's pursuits also characterizes the world of his pupil, Diana Vernon, who also has a "powerful mind" (Ch. 13) and passes her days in the library. "Science and history" are her principal studies, but also "poetry and the classics." She knows "Greek and Latin, as well as most of the languages of modern Europe" (Ch. 10). Her accomplishments are exaggerated, perhaps, for a woman of eighteen, but they follow a significant pattern.

As I learned out of doors to ride a horse, and bridle and saddle him in case of necessity, and to clear a five-barred gate, and fire a gun without winking, and all other of those masculine accomplishments that my brute cousins run after, I wanted, like my rational cousin [Rashleigh], to read Greek and Latin within doors, and make my complete approach to the tree of knowledge, which you men-scholars would engross to your-selves, I suppose, for our common mother's share in the great original transgression. [Ch. 10]

The hero's adventures have brought him vicariously, at least, to the taste of forbidden fruit. Diana, like Eve, longs to be something greater than herself; she longs to change her very sex. Not only does the narrator comment again and again on her masculine dress and habits—from "Call me Tom Vernon" (Ch. 6) to "I belong . . . rather to your sex . . . than to my own" (Ch. 13) she herself expresses her intention. At the same time, as a woman, she is unspeakably lovely. It is hard to say which is more enticing, her mysterious dedication to the cloister or her availability as a "man." All of this makes very intriguing the terms of her rejection of Frank's suit: "Any other union [but disinterested friendship] is as far out of our reach as if I were man, or you woman" (Ch. 17).

The beauty of Die Vernon, her forwardness, her preference of Frank to her cousins, are pleasures easily appreciated. She is clearly a dark heroine. For one thing, if there is a sexual threat to a proper heroine in the Waverley Novels, it is the threat of rape: when Rash-leigh presumptuously attempts to *seduce* Miss Vernon, it underscores her wrong sexual precocity. Yet *Rob Roy* contains no Rose Bradwardine or Alice Bridgenorth, and the dark heroine actually marries the hero. The exception proves the rule: if there were no such distinction as that between light and dark heroines, no one would be disturbed by this marriage. As it is, critics have traditionally sensed that the hero and heroine should have parted forever in the Highlands.[3] Scott himself seems to have felt the force of his exception, for he qualifies the denouement of *Rob Roy* in an interesting fashion. On the last page of the romance the reader suddenly learns that Die Vernon is dead when these memoirs are being written. She is last spoken of as "lamented": "You know how long I lamented her; but you do not know—cannot know, how much she deserved her husband's sorrow" (Ch. 39). This is all very much in the past tense; there is no suggestion that any children are born to them; there is none of the sense of

---

[3] E.g. E. A. Baker, *The History of the English Novel* (London, 1942), 6: 159; or Thomas Seccombe, "Rob Roy," in *Scott Centenary Articles* (London, 1932), p. 54.

futurity which a proper hero and heroine ought to enjoy. With the intuitive sense of poetic justice shared by his critics, Scott makes death the last word for Die.

21. Tentative Fiction

All fiction is dissembling. But romance pretends to fact less than the realistic novel does, and in this sense the language of romance falsifies less than the language of realism. Scott's fiction respects fact by restricting its invention to what might be so, to what might happen to the hero. Incidents of the plot do not befall the passive hero so much as threaten him. Because so many threatened events never do come to pass, the entire fiction takes on a tentative aspect. The practice of tentative fiction reflects both the projective theory of fiction and the prestige of fact in the early nineteenth century. Rather than report things, the Waverley Novels conceive possible conditions and events that are frankly projections of the mind of author and reader alike. The resulting diffuseness of the prose may be regarded as the appropriate and felicitous language for romance. In the words of W. P. Ker, "Romance is distinguished from the deeper forms of the imagination in its refusal to make things definite, to bring things to the highest pitch of definiteness and individuality. Romance is diffuse and vague when compared with the intensity of the drama."[4] The surface of Scott's fiction confirms this generalization.

Scott noted in his journal that verse he wrote "twice, and sometimes three times over"[5]—a confession with discouraging implications for students of prose. The second and third volumes of *Waverley*, he claimed, were "begun & finished between the 4th June & the 1st July during which I attended my duty in court and proceeded without loss of time or hindrance of business."[6] Scott wrote, in fact, with such notorious speed and vigor that some (mistaken) critics have supposed that certain of the Waverley Novels must have been composed before 1814.[7] Scott's pace and attitude toward composition helped to produce his particular lack of commitment to pretended fact. A number of unconscious devices also diminish the denotative force of the nar-

---

[4] *On Modern Literature: Lectures and Addresses by W. P. Ker*, ed. Terence Spencer and James Sutherland (Oxford, 1955), p. 109.

[5] *Journal*, Feb. 12, 1826.

[6] *Letters*, 3: 479.

[7] Such theories are ably refuted by Robert D. Mayo, "The Chronology of the Waverley Novels: The Evidence of the Manuscripts," *PMLA* 63 (1948): 939–49.

rative. Scott frequently uses language in such a way as to avoid the implication that anything actually takes place beyond the words themselves. He hesitates to pretend outright that the events of his romance are anything more than imagined events—what might happen rather than what does or did occur.

In the last of the romances, *Castle Dangerous*, Sir Aymer de Valence sets out on a mission from Douglas Castle: "A horseman or two, together with his squire Fabian, accompanied him" (Ch. 9). In the chapter that follows there are some forgivable inconsistencies as to the number of Sir Aymer's retinue. The difficulty begins with the compound subject, "a horseman or two." From the very beginning Scott has no fixed number of horsemen in mind: he does not imagine the scene in complete graphic substance. The invention of the scene is tentative, and fails to confer even fictitious existence on the horsemen. The act of imagining Sir Aymer's retinue is left partly to the reader, as if the event were taking place in the mind's eye, and not occurring (fictitiously) in a moment of historical time. A similar usage may be discovered even in a static description, as in *A Legend of Montrose*:

> As usual at that period, one or two high-ridged narrow buildings, intersecting and crossing each other, formed the *corps de logis*. A projecting bartizan or two, with the addition of small turrets at the angles, much resembling pepper-boxes, had procured for Darnlinvarach the dignified appellation of a castle. It was surrounded by a low courtyard wall, within which were the usual offices. [Ch. 4]

Here Scott applies a historical generalization without attempting to impute the existence of a specific (albeit fictitious) building.

The subject of the Waverley Novels is an abstract "reality," and the prose that deals with relations, rather than things, tends to employ general and abstract terms. In his study of eighteenth-century fiction, Ian Watt declares that "the function of language is much more largely referential in the novel than in other literary forms . . . the genre itself works by exhaustive presentation rather than by elegant concentration."[8] This generalization does not hold for the romance of Scott. Especially in accounting for the fortunes of the hero, Scott's language is not typically referential. The discursive portions of the Waverley Novels are composed in the style of the *Quarterly Review*, studded with relative clauses that bear on distant, and frequently abstract, antecedents. Even where the denotation is specific and the sub-

---

[8] *The Rise of the Novel* (Berkeley and Los Angeles, 1957), p. 30.

ject has several proper names, Scott often prefers a description to a name or pronoun: the hero becomes "the unfortunate young man" or "the unfortunate prisoner."

Scott sometimes reduces the degree of exact denotation in his prose by softening the assertion of his verbs. He may supply the verb "to seem" or an equivalent where the context would as readily support the verb "to be"; or he may substitute the conditional mood of a verb where the indicative would logically complete the sense. The characteristic emotion of the hero is anxiety, and anxiety requires for its object something that may happen, or seems to be the case, rather than what has happened, or is the case. In a passage already cited from *Guy Mannering* (Ch. 45) Scott speaks of "the mysteries which *appeared to* thicken around [Bertram], while he *seemed* alike to be persecuted and protected by secret enemies and friends." (I have supplied the italics in this and the following illustrations.) If one takes the fiction at its face value, mysteries *are* thickening around Bertram, and he *is* persecuted and protected by secret enemies and friends. Similarly, in *Old Mortality*, when Morton has been delivered from the Cameronian fanatics by Claverhouse, "his first occupation was the returning thanks to Heaven for redeeming him from danger, even through the instrumentality of those who *seemed* his most dangerous enemies" (Ch. 34).

This qualification of the predicate may occur even where there can be no question of reflecting the hero's imagination or blurred perception of the facts. In *Guy Mannering* the reader is not literally informed that Hatteraick strangles Glossin, but that the latter's body "bore uncommon marks of violence. . . . So that *it would seem that* his inveterate antagonist had fixed a fatal gripe on the wretch's throat, and never quitted it while life lasted" (Ch. 57). The effect of this language is to withdraw belief in the event and to reduce Hatteraick's poetic justice to a wish. In *The Heart of Mid-Lothian*, similarly, Scott does not assert outright that Staunton is slain by his bastard son but says that he "offered the bravest resistance till he fell, *as there was too much reason to believe*, by the hand of a son, so long sought, and now at length so unhappily met" (Ch. 52). In addition to the qualified ascription of the deed, the doer is not referred to directly (as "his son") but by means of a description ("a son, so long sought, and . . . so unhappily met").

Such techniques of romance have in common the very tentative, or withdrawn, imputation of the existence of fictional events. Scott's language accords with a notorious fact about romance: insofar as the protagonists are concerned, the events never rise to a final crisis. This circumstance is too familiar to require documentation: in *Ivanhoe* the sounding of a bugle outside the walls of Torquilstone Castle forestalls the imminent rape of two heroines and the torture of Isaac of York. The phenomenon is one of plot, but also of style. Ker summarized this quality of romance by writing that, in *Waverley*, "Scott gets very near to the tension of tragedy, but never quite uses it"; and that, "there is the shadowing of tragedy all through *Old Mortality*, but never the tragic inference."[9] The impression of diffuseness, and the withholding of tragic implication, derives from a series of many incidents, as in *Old Mortality*, when Claverhouse rescues the hero:

> Several pistol-shots were fired; the whig who stood next to Morton received a shot as he was rising, stumbled against the prisoner, whom he bore down with his weight, and lay stretched above him a dying man. This accident *probably* saved Morton from the damage he *might otherwise have received* in so close a struggle, where fire-arms were discharged and sword-blows given for upwards of five minutes.
>
> "Is the prisoner safe?" exclaimed the well-known voice of Claverhouse; "look about for him, and dispatch the whig dog who is groaning there." [Ch. 33]

The passive hero is characteristically threatened with violence but seldom physically suffers anything worse than a temporary incarceration. In *Rob Roy*, a romance replete with vague threats and vague rescue, this rule undergoes an interesting inversion. *Rob Roy* is unique among the Waverley Novels (with the exception of a portion of *Redgauntlet*) in that it is narrated in the first person through the voice of the hero. A curious thing happens: Francis Osbaldistone continually threatens to *do* violence to someone. This violence, to be sure, remains as tentative as the violence threatened against the heroes of Scott.

The impertinence of Justice Inglewood's clerk, Joseph Jobson, provokes the first of the narrator-hero's impulses to hit someone. He threatens to "chastise" Jobson if he does not mind his manners to Die Vernon; but "Miss Vernon laid her hand on my arm, and exclaimed, 'Come, Mr. Osbaldistone, I will have no assaults and battery on Mr. Jobson; I am not in sufficient charity with him to permit a single touch of your whip—why, he would live on it for a term at least'" (Ch. 9). An impressive series of violent thoughts is next inspired in the hero by Rashleigh—"I felt I could with pleasure have run Rashleigh Osbaldistone through the body all the time he was speaking" (Ch. 11). In a state of intoxication—I believe the only such case in

---

[9] *On Modern Literature*, pp. 108–9.

the Waverley Novels—Frank actually draws his sword against Rashleigh a short time later; but the two men are held apart by the latter's brothers (Ch. 12). When Die makes known that Rashleigh has at some time attempted to seduce her, the narrator records,

> I was so much struck with the sense of perfidious treachery which these words disclosed, that I rose from my chair hardly knowing what I did, laid my hand on the hilt of my sword, and was *about to* leave the apartment in search of him on whom I *might* discharge my just indignation. Almost breathless, and with eyes and looks in which scorn and indignation had given way to the most lively alarm, Miss Vernon threw herself between me and the door of the apartment. [Ch. 13]

The last tentative encounter with Rashleigh is the duel in the college yards at Glasgow:

> I followed him accordingly, keeping a strict eye on his motions, for I believed him capable of the very worst actions. . . . I was on my guard, and it was well with me that I was so; for Rashleigh's sword was out and at my breast ere I could throw down my cloak, or get my weapon unsheathed, so that I only saved my life by springing a pace or two backwards. He had some advantage in the difference of our weapons; for his sword, as I recollect, was longer than mine. . . . He fought, indeed, more like a fiend than a man. . . . His obvious malignity of purpose never for a moment threw him off his guard. . . . My first resolution . . . was to attempt to disarm my antagonist. . . . By degrees I became exasperated at the rancour with which Rashleigh sought my life, and returned his passes with an inveteracy resembling in some degree his own; so that the combat *had all the appearance of being destined to have a tragic issue.* That issue *had nearly taken place* at my expense. My foot slipped in a full lounge [sic] which I made at my adversary, and I could not so far recover myself as completely to parry the thrust with which my pass was repaid. Yet it took but partial effect, running through my waistcoat, grazing my ribs, and passing through my coat behind. . . . Eager for revenge, I grappled with my enemy, seizing with my left hand the hilt of his sword, and shortening my own *with the purpose of* running him through the body. Our death-grapple was interrupted by a man [Rob Roy] who forcibly threw himself between us. [Ch. 25]

The intervention of the dark hero is nicely timed to prevent the hero from killing as well as being killed. Before even the "purpose" of killing can occur to Frank, his excellent patience is most cruelly provoked by the villain. The duel *almost* becomes decisive at least three times, but each time the crisis proves to be of the tentative variety. Midway through the duel the language betrays the outcome. The inci-

dent has "all the appearance of being destined to have a tragic
issue"—very nearly Ker's exact words for the tentative quality of
Scott's romance.

Andrew Fairservice bears the comic brunt of the narrator's arrested
impulse to strike someone. Certainly in no other romance of Scott
does a retainer of the hero undergo so many potential, though un-
realized, beatings. "I attempted once or twice to get up alongside of
my self-willed guide, with the purpose of knocking him off his horse
with the butt-end of my whip" (Ch. 18). "I meditated for Mr. Fairservice the unpleasant surprise of a broken pate on the first decent
opportunity" (Ch. 21). "However, the tumultuous glee which he felt,
or pretended to feel, at my return, saved Andrew from the broken
head which I had twice destined him" (Ch. 24). In the same chapter
(Ch. 24) the hero threatens Andrew twice more, and again somewhat
later (Ch. 27).

The most expressive instance of such tentative action in *Rob Roy* occurs in the library of Osbaldistone Hall just as the hero has excitedly
pressed Die's hand to his lips in the forwardness of leave-taking. Die
responds to this "unmanly burst of passion," as she calls it, with the
traditional feminine mixture of pleasure and displeasure.

> At these words she broke suddenly off, and said, but in a suppressed
> tone of voice, "Leave me instantly—we will meet here again, but it must
> be for the last time."
>
> My eyes followed the direction of hers as she spoke, and I thought I
> saw the tapestry shake, which covered the door of the secret passage
> from Rashleigh's room to the library. I conceived we were observed, and
> turned an inquiring glance on Miss Vernon.
>
> "It is nothing," said she, faintly; "a rat behind the arras."
>
> "Dead for a ducat," *would have been* my reply, had I dared to give way
> to the feelings which rose indignant at the idea of being subjected to an
> eavesdropper on such an occasion. Prudence, and the necessity of sup-
> pressing my passion, and obeying Diana's reiterated command of "Leave
> me! leave me!" came in time to prevent my rash action. I left the apart-
> ment in a wild whirl and giddiness of mind, which I in vain attempted to
> compose when I returned to my own. [Ch. 16]

Here the tentative "rash action," arrested by prudence and necessity,
is associated with a critical moment in the drama of *Hamlet*. The allusion to that famous scene, however, is expressed in the conditional
mood and confined to a mental state, which is accelerated ("a wild
whirl and giddiness of mind") rather than diminished when the moment for action is past. Ruskin must have had this passage in mind
when he wrote: "Nothing is more notable or sorrowful in Scott's

mind than its incapacity of steady belief in anything. . . . He never can clearly ascertain whether there is anything behind the arras but rats; never draws sword, and thrusts at it for life or death."[10]

The allusion to *Hamlet* is sounded again in *Rob Roy* by Bailie Jarvie, who upbraids the hero for his neglect of his father's business and the subsequent imprisonment of Owen, clerk of the house of Osbaldistone, in the Glasgow jail: "Weel, sir, what say you to your handiwark? Will Hamlet the Dane, or Hamlet's ghost, be good security for Mr. Owen, sir?" (Ch. 23). In a sense, Shakespeare's hero is a prototype of the passive hero: but when the arras moves, Hamlet thrusts home with his rapier. In the play the death of Polonius is fraught with Ker's "tragic inference." The passive hero is merely a tentative Hamlet. In these numerous instances Francis Osbaldistone betrays his impulse to thrash and stab but never draws blood. The hero of *Rob Roy*, in Bailie Jarvie's qualification, is not Hamlet but "Hamlet's ghost."

---

[10] *Modern Painters*, 3: Pt. IV, ch. 16, sec. 31, in *Works*, ed. E. T. Cook and Alexander Wedderburn (London, 1904), 5: 336.

VIII

HONOR

I have but one path, Captain Jekyl—that of truth and honour.

—*St. Ronan's Well*

I like not such grinning honour as Sir Walter hath. Give me life; which if I can save, so; if not, honour comes unlooked for, and there's an end.

—Falstaff, in *I Henry IV*

22. Rank in Life

THE POINT of *Rob Roy* would be gravely mistaken if we imagine Frank Osbaldistone to be a poet. He is a gentleman, whose slight ability in verse is a mere amateur grace. His "principal attention had been dedicated" not to literature alone but "to literature and manly exercises" (Ch. 1). Without understanding that Frank is a gentleman, and that being a gentleman denotes a specific role and rank in life, one can neither sympathize with his dislike of commerce nor appreciate the immediate friendship he inspires in all the "good" people he encounters—Diana Vernon, Bailie Nicol Jarvie, and Rob Roy himself. For such persons respond instinctively to a hero's innate character: "'I protest,' said the Highlander, 'I had some respect for this callant even before I ken'd what was in him; but now I honour him for his contempt of weavers and spinners, and sic-like mechanical persons and their pursuits'" (Ch. 23). Herein lies one secret in the construction of romance from antiromantic themes: the passive hero is as innocent of useful employment as the Highland chief.

If the hero's rank as a gentleman is a necessary assumption in *Rob Roy*, it is the central issue in a story like *Guy Mannering*. The romance of Harry Bertram is that of the missing heir, no longer a prince in rags but a gentleman divided from his estate. Rank and property together govern the main action of the plot, but the mere question of the hero's identity as a gentleman controls all the smaller crises of the story. Bertram cannot even prove his identity as Captain Brown, a British officer. Like Francis Osbaldistone, he is confident that his "rank and character" must protect him. "But an arrest in a strange country, and while he was unprovided with any means of establishing

his rank and character, was at least to be avoided" (Ch. 40). Scott
makes abundantly clear that if Sir Robert Hazelwood had the least suspicion that Brown was a British officer, he would *not* arrest him.
Hazelwood himself, and indeed most of the characters in *Guy Mannering*, are set up by their author as checks and definitions of rank. Sir
Robert is a born gentleman, but fails the test of true modesty and
minimal good sense. He corresponds to Sir Walter Elliot of Jane
Austen's *Persuasion*: but the genial ridicule applied to these baronets
cannot be interpreted in either author as disrespect for rank—the
higher the rank, the higher the obligation for good character. At the
other end of the scale Glossin, the villain of *Guy Mannering*, cheats
and purchases his way to pretended rank, and therefore shivers and
quakes even before the presence of a Sir Robert Hazelwood.

The titular "hero" of *Guy Mannering* is in truth the finest gentleman in the Waverley Novels. Thus the sharpest test of "rank and character" for Harry Bertram is Colonel Mannering, not only as father of
the heroine but as the exemplar of gentlemanly status and sentiments. Mannering is a man of means whose self-respect and compassion are alike tempered with great delicacy. Though he can be moved
to tears, he knows that even an offer of one's services can be misconstrued as an intrusion (Ch. 13). His altruism is supported by a stern
morality. His "commanding tone of rightful anger" silences the bully
(Ch. 13), and his excellent plan to purchase the estate of Ellangowan
himself is foiled only by the "sloth and drunkenness" of a "rascally
messenger" (Ch. 14). Above all, Colonel Mannering possesses that in-
describable but commanding presence of the gentleman—that immediate impact without which so many incidents in the Waverley Novels
would be inexplicable. "His appearance, voice, and manner, produced an instantaneous effect in his favour.... Every point of his
appearance and address bespoke the gentleman" (Ch. 11). Thus the
surface eloquently testifies to the interior. The confrontation of the
Colonel and the younger hero is bound to be momentous in its way.
Scott embroiders the event with great formality of speech:

> "Mr. Brown, I believe?" said Colonel Mannering.
> "Yes, sir," replied the young man, modestly, but with firmness, "the
> same you knew in India; and who ventures to hope, that what you did
> then know of him is not such as should prevent his requesting you
> would favour him with your attestation to his character, as a gentleman
> and man of honour." [Ch. 50]

For all their difference in age and their tentative rivalry, Harry Bertram and Colonel Mannering have remarkably similar backgrounds.
Mannering in his youth has rejected both clerical and commercial positions in favor of the military—though he is sole heir of one uncle's

commercial fortune (Ch. 12). "Brown," as an unknown orphan, "was bred to commerce" in Holland but has joined the army in India. "Brown, whose genius had a strong military tendency, was the first to leave what might have been the road to wealth, and to choose that of fame" (Ch. 18). In his true character of Harry Bertram, therefore, his wealth is purely hereditary. In fiction, as we have seen, Scott permits earned wealth only in earlier generations. The hero has no profession but that of proprietor. Only Henry Wynd, who is not a gentleman, and Reuben Butler, an impoverished minister, are exceptions. One may also wish to except Quentin Durward and Hereward the Saxon, full-time soldiers, but in the end both settle down to large estates. The military experiences of the others are significant but temporary affairs.

This prejudice against gainful employment reflects an ideal of life for the gentleman. But in fiction the hero is free even from the efforts to manage his affairs or to collect rents that beset the gentleman in real life. The fictional ideal is selfless in practice as well as in sentiment. In no case does a hero set out to improve his worldly position. The hero of *Rob Roy* is actually urged to improve himself, but he replies, "I only saw in my father's proposal for my engaging in business, a desire that I should add to those heaps of wealth which he had himself acquired; and imagining myself the best judge of the path to my own happiness, I did not conceive that I should increase that happiness by augmenting a fortune which I believed was already sufficient, for every use, comfort, and elegant enjoyment" (Ch. 1). And in that passage Frank is much more sensible and candid about the use he would make of his fortune than most of Scott's heroes. For two things seem essential for the gentleman: to have wealth and to value it little. The author of a contemporary handbook for gentlemen, *The Broad Stone of Honour* (1823), devotes very few pages to "The Professions of the Order" and none at all to the possibility of gaining wealth:

> It did not appear necessary to enter upon a review of those pursuits which are chiefly directed towards the attainment of wealth, because I had no reason to suppose that there was any motive or influence that could induce you to embrace them. . . . It is not easy for a gentleman to become rich, being neither disposed to receive nor to keep money, but liberal, and esteeming it only as the instrument of generosity. Therefore, wealth is termed fortune, because they are the least rich who are the most deserving of riches.[1]

The truth is that almost any form of activity implies the operation of

---

[1] [Kenelm Digby], *The Broad Stone of Honour: or, Rules for the Gentlemen of England* (2nd ed. London, 1823), pp. 492–94.

some interested passion, and the gentleman is an entirely disinterested person.

> In the crowded streets of a commercial and manufacturing city, or even in the walks of men who are engaged in the drudgery of a learned profession, or in the harassing pursuit of distinction or wealth, or of any end which excites the base passions of the human heart, with what ease and pleasure does the eye recognize a countenance which denotes an exemption from these evils, the "ingenui vultus puer," the true, frank, and courteous gentleman.[2]

But the exemption from such passions and evils requires a store of independent wealth—independent of the living, that is, though clearly dependent on past generations. When the elder Osbaldistone inquires how his son will support himself, the hero confesses "that being bred to no profession, and having no funds of my own, it was obviously impossible for me to subsist without some allowance from my father" (Ch. 2). The relation of the hero to money is a subject in itself: in general, he expends a considerable sum in gratuities in the course of a single romance; he seldom pays or receives fixed sums; and when pressed for cash, he sometimes accepts a loan from an adherent in the lower ranks.

The nature of rank, therefore, follows closely the prescriptive doctrine of property. A gentleman may be ideally defined as one who derives an unearned income from real property—so long as his appearance and demeanor favorably reflect his privileged status. Just as it may be debated whether property or civil government originated first in time, so it may be argued whether rank preceded property or vice versa. It was clear to Scott's generation, however, that property and rank together achieved the order and refinement of civilization.

> The authority derived from wealth, is not only greater than that which arises from mere personal accomplishments, but also more stable and permanent. Extraordinary endowments, either of mind or body, can operate only during the life of the possessor, and are seldom continued for any length of time in the same family. But a man usually transmits his fortune to his posterity, and along with it the means of creating dependence which he enjoyed. Thus the son, who inherits the estate of his father, is enabled to maintain an equal rank, at the same time that he preserves all the influence acquired by the former proprietor, which is daily augmented by the power of habit, and becomes more considerable as it passes from one generation to another.[3]

[2] Ibid., pp. 568–69.
[3] John Millar, *The Origin of the Distinction of Ranks* (4th ed. Edinburgh, 1806), pp. 152–53.

For our purposes, the historical validity of this doctrine is less important than the suggestion that rank and privilege are not admired for their own sake, as "endowments . . . of mind or body," but only as stabilized, virtually immortalized, by property. In real life, then as now, rank unquestionably confers power; as an ideal, however, rank confers merely stability, the ability to maintain one's position in society. In terms of this ideal, any material ambition runs counter to rank. This entire concept of society is supported by the institutions of primogeniture and entail, which provide that rank and property shall not be at the mercy of the individual facts of birth and death. Thus, in the words of a prize essay of 1808, "in England, by a wise and provident regulation, the disproportion between riches and honour has, in great measure, been avoided."[4]

Honor has always been class-conscious—it is the code of behavior of the aristocracy. By the time of the Waverley Novels, however, the aristocracy has been redefined as the gentlemen of England—"the gentlemen of independent estates and fortune" whom Blackstone calls "the most useful as well as considerable body of men in the nation."[5] This independent and decentralized aristocracy was thought to be the bulwark against tyranny on the one hand and mob rule on the other—and that estimation contains some historical truth. The unfortunate history of France seemed to prove the validity of this doctrine: in the judgment of Edmund Burke, "Jacobinism is the revolt of the enterprising talents of a country against its property";[6] and in the less persuasive but graphic account of *The Broad Stone of Honour*, the Jacquerie "wished to exterminate all gentlemen."[7] The class of gentlemen must ideally maintain a high sense of honor. The chivalric summary by the youthful Kenelm Digby exists as a rather fantastic monument to this sentiment; but the mature political philosophy of Burke also demands, in a society of unequals, that gentlemen act with honor. The first and simplest argument for an aristocratic code of honor is that the higher ranks are always in the public view, serving as examples to the lower. But there are two further relations between rank and honor. Honor is self-imposed virtue and therefore requires freedom of action—what Scott would call "free agency." Translating this freedom into the language of property, honor requires "an independence." Lucy Bertram, in *Guy Mannering*, prays that her brother

---

[4] [Charles Edward Grey], *Hereditary Rank, an Essay, Recited in the Theatre, at Oxford, Tuesday, June 28, 1808* [Oxford, 1808], p. 22.

[5] *Commentaries*, 1: 7.

[6] *Letters on a Regicide Peace*, in *Works*, 5: 309.

[7] [Digby], *The Broad Stone of Honour*, p. 371.

may inherit at least "an honourable independence," so that he may protect "the old and destitute dependents of our family" (Ch. 52). The third importance of honor for the higher ranks is that character, when one has means and privileges beyond the common, must be self-governing. Virtue, in this period, means restraint. A theory that order and civilization depend upon a system of unequal rank demands that the superior ranks be restrained by their own sense of honor. "The most stable foundation of legal and rational government," according to Blackstone, "is a due subordination of rank, and a gradual scale of authority." This is also, he acknowledges, a formula for tyranny—"with this difference, however, that the measure of obedience in the one is grounded on the principles of society, and is extended no farther than reason and necessity will warrant: in the other it is limited only by absolute will and pleasure."[8]

23. Self-Sacrifice

Except in the earliest times honor has always had two meanings. The original meaning was fame; but Socratic and Christian teachings, scorning fame, insisted that honor was the love of virtue for its own sake. This confusion of two meanings is represented in controversies over fame and humility that extend from the Renaissance into the eighteenth century, and results in the modern compromise of honor as the reputation *of* virtue. In *The Talisman* Scott explicitly contrasts the two meanings of honor by means of his opposing heroes, Sir Kenneth and Saladin: "Both were courteous; but the courtesy of the Christian seemed to flow from the good-humoured sense of what was due to others; that of the Moslem, from a high feeling of what was to be expected from himself" (Ch. 2). The word "good-humoured" suggests the eighteenth-century doctrine of sympathy rather than medieval Christianity, but the purport of the contrast is clear: the proper hero's courtesy is an interior matter, affecting him from within; the dark hero is courteous from a feeling for his reputation among men. The source of Sir Kenneth's honor is good humor; the source of Saladin's, good opinion. The two kinds of honor, however, have much in common. Well-ordered societies have been founded on either principle, and usually on both. In both cases honor is an individual, self-operating, and self-restraining regard for social norms. Scott indeed sometimes glories in the honor of his romantic figures, but he insists that his passive hero is also honorable. It is a mistake to conceive of

[8] *Commentaries*, 4: 105.

the contrast as that between old-fashioned *honor* and modern *morality*, because that view overlooks the honor of the hero and attributes to him the wrong morality altogether. Thus, in making this contrast, one recent critic suggests that Waverley and Colonel Talbot stand for "reasonableness, public spirit, justice, or 'the greatest happiness of the greatest number.'"[9] Reasonableness, public spirit, justice, or the British Constitution, yes, but not the utilitarian principle. The proper hero stands for a modern principle of honor.

The modern sense of honor (modern in 1814) is strictly defensive—just as the doctrine of private property is defensive. The marked difference between Waverley and Fergus Mac-Ivor lies in the ambition of the latter, including his hankering for Rose Bradwardine's property. The modern sense of honor is entirely without ambition, whether of fame or wealth. It is a contemplation of the fame one already possesses, the fame to which one is entitled. Burke readily associates fame and belongings as things to be defended: "The strong struggle in every individual to preserve possession of what he has found to belong to him, and to distinguish him, is one of the securities against injustice and despotism implanted in our nature. It operates as an instinct to secure property, and to preserve communities in a settled state. What is there to shock in this? Nobility is a graceful ornament to the civil order. It is the Corinthian capital of polished society."[10] By the early nineteenth century the modern concept of honor is a standard implicit, and sometimes explicit, in British political thinking. Honor means self-imposed restraint; orderly government and the preservation of property depend upon the restraint of individuals. Elie Halévy credits Methodism and Evangelicalism with the elevation of self-restraint as a political virtue: in the seventeenth and eighteenth centuries "the English regarded their country as the citadel of freedom at war with a 'Turkish' despotism. No doubt during the first fifteen years of the nineteenth century, they still cherished the same belief; but the word 'liberty' no longer bore for them the sense it had borne for their fathers. They now understood by liberty restraint self-imposed and freely accepted as opposed to restraint forcibly imposed by the Government."[11]

The use of the actual word "honor" for this sentiment can be traced in journalism of the period if not in the philosophers. In a short essay on honor Reginald Heber, the brother of Richard Heber and future bishop of Calcutta, argues that a depreciation of honor

---

[9] Donald Davie, *The Heyday of Sir Walter Scott* (London, 1961), p. 31.
[10] *Reflections on the Revolution in France*, in *Works*, 3: 415–16.
[11] *England in 1815*, p. 451.

"would by an inevitable inference lay the axe to the root of civil government itself."[12] Heber's is one of the more articulate tracts on honor. He defines the concept in the modern way: "A sense of honour, then, is a pleasurable reflection on our own merit, occasioned by the presumption of our claim on the love and reverence of the world." He is fully aware that he is defining a motive distinct from conscience or religion and gives the classical argument for honor: that there is no such thing as self-respect "without reference to the rest of mankind." He speaks of the power of shame, not guilt, and "a high and almost spiritual exaltation, elevated above the region of external pain!" Ambition, moreover, is the opposite of honor: "The pleasure of the one consists in pursuit, the other's in possession." Burke often argues that the interest of property conduces to loyalty as well as freedom; Heber gives the parallel argument that the sense of honor "is at once the parent of loyalty, and the preserver of freedom." And finally, he touches on honor as that instinctive *distaste* for wrong-doing and wrong-doers. "It is decency, it is regard for reputation, and a sense of the rank we hold in society, which fence off the avenues of guilt, and not only resist, but resent the first approaches of pollution."

These precepts, or their operation, are familiar in the Waverley Novels, including the intense feeling of contamination or pollution sometimes aroused by evil acts or persons. When Harry Bertram faces imprisonment in the House of Correction at Portanferry, though he has presumably experienced much worse horrors in oriental prisons, he feels "his heart recoil with inexpressible loathing":

> When he had cast his eye around, on faces on which guilt, and despondence, and low excess, had fixed their stigma—upon the spendthrift, and the swindler, and the thief, the bankrupt debtor, the "moping idiot, and the madman gay," whom a paltry spirit of economy congregated to share this dismal habitation, he felt his heart recoil with inexpressible loathing from enduring the contamination of their society even for a moment. [Ch. 44]

This form of resistance to evil, the instinctive loathing and sense of contamination, outreaches even the hero's legal scrupulosity. The entire credibility of the action in *St. Ronan's Well* hinges on some such point of honor. Why cannot Frank Tyrrel rescue the unfortunate Clara Mowbray by marrying her? We know that in the original version he is supposed to have himself contaminated her, *before* the false marriage to his brother, the villain Bulmer. In the published version all

[12] *A Sense of Honour* (Oxford, 1805), pp. 6ff.

hints of the heroine's sexual transgression were erased.[13] But regardless of who, if anyone, has slept with Clara Mowbray, both the manuscript and the subsequent editions of *St. Ronan's Well* report one much more narrow cause of the hero's estrangement. When Clara Mowbray went through the ceremony of marriage with the villain, she thought she was standing beside the hero. But that makes no difference to Tyrrel: "Were Clara Mowbray as free from her pretended marriage as law could pronounce her, still with me—*me*, at least, of all men in the world—the obstacle must ever remain, that the nuptial benediction has been pronounced over her and the man whom I must for once call *brother*" (Ch. 29). Thus the sense of honor goes much further than either law or religion in respecting the ceremony of marriage—or any of the compacts on which civil society rests.

Late eighteenth-century tracts against dueling display the same redefinition of honor. The private duel is wrong: but to demonstrate this wrong does not require an attack upon honor itself. Rather, the argument runs, dueling is *dis*honorable. "True honor, to ourselves, is the utmost refinement of virtue in the exercise of every duty in life, and the divine attribute of an upright heart."[14] Or, in the definition of another tract, "true honour consists in keeping one's word exactly, in being grateful to benefactors, courageous in unavoidable dangers, in being a kind husband, a dutiful son, a careful father, a faithful friend, an obliging neighbour, an affable companion, an useful citizen, a loyal subject."[15] A gentleman, whether of fiction or real life, ought never to provoke a duel; on the other hand, even pious opponents of dueling conceded that it was difficult for a gentleman to refuse a challenge. On the question of dueling, as in other respects, the modern concept of honor is self-defensive, and limited to self-defense.

Guy Mannering, which is in so many ways a treatise on real and pretended gentlemen, contains a well-known justification of dueling. Scott confines the argument to self-defense, and even so is careful to place it in a letter to Colonel Mannering from his friend Arthur

---

[13] For the evidence of a canceled proof sheet see J. M. Collyer, " 'The Catastrophe' in 'St. Ronan's Well,' " *Atheneum*, Feb. 4, 1893. John Gibson Lockhart constructed yet another version of the story (*Memoirs of Sir Walter Scott*, 5 vols. London, 1914, 4: 141), but the manuscript in the Pierpont Morgan Library, New York, confirms Collyer's evidence. See also Scott, *Journal*, July 28, 1826; and W. P. Ker, *Collected Essays*, ed. Charles Whibley (2 vols. London, 1925), 2: 198–206.

[14] *Strictures on Duelling . . . by a Gentleman Late of the University of Oxford* (London, 1789), p. 13.

[15] *Reflections on Duelling and the Most Effective Means for Preventing It* (Edinburgh, 1790), p. 9.

Mervyn, a character who does not appear in the foreground of the story. The argument rests on the parallel between reputation and property.

> Wise men say, that we resign to civil society our natural rights of self-defence only on condition that the ordinances of law should protect us. Where the price cannot be paid, the resignation becomes void. For instance, no one supposes that I am not entitled to defend my purse and person against a highwayman, as much as if I were a wild Indian who owns neither law nor magistracy. . . . An aggression on my honour seems to me much the same. The insult, however trifling in itself, is one of much deeper consequence to all views in life than any wrong which can be inflicted by a depredator on the highway, and to redress the injured party is much less in the power of public jurisprudence, or rather it is entirely beyond its reach. If any man chooses to rob Arthur Mean of the contents of his purse . . . who will say I am bound to wait for this justice, and submit to being plundered in the first instance, if I have myself the means and spirit to protect my own property? . . . Of the religious views of the matter I shall say nothing, until I find a reverend divine who shall condemn self-defence in the article of life and property. If its propriety in that case can be generally admitted, I suppose little distinction can be drawn between defence of person and goods, and protection of reputation. . . . I shall leave the question with the casuists, however; only observing, that what I have written will not avail either the professed duelist, or him who is the aggressor in a dispute of honour. I only presume to exculpate him who is dragged into the field by such an offence, as, submitted to in patience, would forfeit for ever his rank and estimation in society. [Ch. 16]

Even without the disclaimer of aggression, the letter insists on the defensive role of honor by pressing the analogy to property. In these terms Arthur Mervyn attempts to justify the duel between Mannering and "Brown" in India, before the action of the romance. Significantly, the text of *Guy Mannering* is vague as to who challenged whom on this historic occasion. At one point (Ch. 21) it seems that the Colonel must have been the "aggressor"; but he himself refers to the event impersonally—a trifle "which occasioned high words and a challenge" (Ch. 12). The fact that *both* Mannering and the hero are gentlemen is responsible for the vagueness: either is justified in defending his honor, but neither in forcing someone else to defend his. A duel between characters of such equal merit poses an awkward problem for Scott. He relegates it, of course, to past times and foreign lands. When Guy Mannering again confronts his future son-in-law in Scotland, he is happy to find him still alive, and Scott records his "joy at finding himself relieved from the guilt of having shed life in a private quarrel" (Ch. 50). Gentlemen in the Waverley Novels are frequently compelled to defend their honor, but as for the spirit of honor that goes beyond defense, Scott concurs with the Bailie in *Rob Roy*—"Honour is a homicide" (Ch. 26).

The long soliloquy in *The Fortunes of Nigel* (Ch. 22) clearly expresses the hero's wish to be independent, to act for himself, to exercise "his own free agency." But immediately after expressing these thoughts Nigel resolves to surrender himself, a course of action that he somehow *deduces* from his decision to be free. This sequence of resolutions is something more than a symptom of psychological ambivalence: it reflects on an individual scale the political theory that freedom is based on the restraint of law. Nigel responds to this theory instinctively when he converts his longing for freedom into the impulse to surrender. The passive hero believes in "free agency," but his rigid posture in the romance is hardly that of a free agent. He is irrevocably committed to the laws and morality of society as he finds them; he instinctively moves to conform with authority. He represents, in Coleridge's terms, "the mighty instincts of *progression* and *free agency*."[16] The hero stands for civilization—the civilization that has brought material progress and political liberty. But this progress and liberty are conceived as contractual benefits. Individuals voluntarily surrender their prerogatives to complex social restraints and to the rule of law, in order to gain certain advantages and in order to escape from the unruly past, when the sway of passion and force prohibited social gains.

At the same time this political framework does have its psychological impact. It requires the individual to submit not only to an authority outside of himself but also to an authority within. In the estimation of Burke, "Men are qualified for civil liberty in exact proportion to their disposition to put moral chains on their own appetites."[17] The Waverley Novels project an ideal, but not an ideal life for the hero. He is bound and tied by his own determination to merge his interests with those of society. His only diversions are to watch the activities of others, to protest his innocence, and to nurse his anxiety. The dark heroes and heroines of the romance are much more free; and they are much more alive, though the plot frustrates their projects. The passive hero and his blonde heroine look forward to a relaxation of "circumstances" that will permit them to marry; but they are too

[16] *Coleridge's Miscellaneous Criticism*, ed. Thomas Middleton Raysor (London, 1936), pp. 341–42.

[17] Quoted by Cobban, *Edmund Burke and the Revolt against the Eighteenth Century*, p. 56.

prudent to be passionately in love. The absence of passion is balanced by the depth of commitment: either party is willing to sacrifice himself for the other. But if life is the career of the passions, or of independent action, the passive hero is far from eager to live.

The hero not only seems to shun life in this sense: he frequently tempts death. The Waverley Novels frame countless perils of life and death, and the hero, as a matter of course, has to be rescued time and again. Yet he sometimes deliberately provokes these situations of life and death. By turning again and again to authority he seems sometimes to ask for punishment. When Nigel Olifaunt surrenders himself, after vowing to "live or die, sink or swim," he is much more likely to suffer harm than good at the hands of the authorities. The hero's anxieties have suggested that he cannot totally identify himself with law and order—that he cannot identify himself as closely as he would like to. As if he had a grudge on this score, he sometimes responds by stretching to the breaking point his relation to the abstract structure of his own society. When Francis Osbaldistone hears that he is under suspicion for highway robbery, he does not for an instant entertain Diana Vernon's idea of running for the border, but instead heads directly for the justice of the peace. Diana exhorts him to "make the best of your way before they can serve the warrant"; and Frank replies, "That I shall certainly do; but it shall be to the house of this Squire Inglewood—Which way does it lie?" (Ch. 7). In the sequel a word from the heroine to Squire Inglewood is sufficient to clear Frank of all suspicion. Instead of shaking hands and departing, however, the hero testily insists on his due: "Pardon me, sir . . . but I have not heard the nature of the accusation yet" (Ch. 8). Thus the hero incites the authorities to combat at the same time that he submits.

The hero's tendency to provoke trouble for himself is intensified by his pride. The hero of Scott has a haughty streak in him; his sense of honor is often characterized by pique and resentment. Edgar Ravenswood is the extreme example: he seems unable to avoid offending his benefactor the Marquis of A———, and even Lucy, to say nothing of his enemies. Ravenswood behaves in this way because his fortunes have fallen to such a low ebb. Because honor and property are parallel concepts, the sense of honor may compensate for the loss of property. Poor gentlemen are traditionally more sensitive to honor than rich gentlemen. The haughtiness of heroes varies inversely with their fortunes. There is something of Edgar Ravenswood in all of Scott's heroes, but especially those who are in financial straits. The denouement of *The Bride of Lammermoor* fairly predicts that the ultimate destination of this piqued sense of honor is death.

The most impoverished hero in the Waverley Novels is undoubtedly Sir Kenneth in *The Talisman,* since his fortunes are at such extreme odds with his actual rank as Royal Prince of Scotland. Sir Kenneth dishonors himself by failing to guard the standard of King Richard. As a result of this disgrace, not only is Richard prepared to execute the hero, but the hero is prepared to die. "I have deserted my charge—the banner intrusted to me is lost—when the headsman and block are prepared, the head and trunk are ready to part company" (Ch. 15). Saladin intervenes and saves the hero from death by persuading the king to give him Sir Kenneth as a slave. But this lease on life merely deepens the hero's despair into a mood that is frankly suicidal. Scott records the "disgust which [Sir Kenneth] felt against swallowing any nourishment" and the wish that his horse would "stumble so effectually as at once to break my neck and her own" (Ch. 22). In a short time Saladin and the hero encounter in the desert a force of Templars. It is also suicidal for Kenneth to meet the Templars, but he angrily protests Saladin's intention to retreat.

> "Yonder," he said, "are my companions in arms—the men in whose society I have vowed to fight or fall—on their banner gleams the sign of our most blessed redemption—I cannot fly from the Cross in company with the Crescent."
>
> "Fool!" said the Hakim [Saladin]; "their first action would be to do thee to death, were it only to conceal their breach of the truce."
>
> "Of that I must take my chance," replied Sir Kenneth; "but I wear not the bonds of infidels an instant longer than I can cast them from me."
>
> "Then will I compel thee to follow me," said El Hakim.
>
> "Compel!" answered Sir Kenneth, angrily. "Wert thou not my benefactor, or one who has showed will to be such, and were it not that it is to thy confidence I owe the freedom of these hands, which thou mightest have loaded with fetters, I would show thee that, unarmed as I am, compulsion would be no easy task.". . .
>
> Sir Kenneth had no time to note what ensued; for, at the same instant, the Hakim seized the rein of his steed, and putting his own to its mettle, both sprang forward at once with the suddenness of light, and at a pitch of velocity which almost deprived the Scottish knight of the power of respiration, and left him absolutely incapable, *had he been desirous,* to have checked the career of his guide. [Ch. 22]

The conditional mood of the protest, and especially the words that I have italicized, prove that the hero's protest is merely habitual and formal. It seems that in this case he has two interests, one ideal and the other practical. Before being forcibly dragged away, he must protest his readiness to die—in this case to die at the hands of the Christians, under "the sign of our blessed redemption." If it were not for

Saladin, Sir Kenneth would indeed die. The dark hero compels him, in effect, to live.

The likely consequence of placing oneself at the mercy of one's own society, in such cases, is ominous. Nigel is asking to have his hand cut off, Frank to be hanged for robbery, and Sir Kenneth to be slaughtered on the spot. Each effort of the hero to hang himself, so to speak, enlists the hostile aspect of his society—the same aspect that his anxiety has discovered to us. He keeps offering himself up to the very forces that presumably support his existence. And each of these instances involves the hero's honor. Nigel wishes to follow the "manliest and most proper course"; Frank is concerned for his reputation; and Sir Kenneth, we may interpolate, is not only bent on suicide but reluctant to retreat under any circumstances.

Honor that scorns ambition and admits only a defensive concern for reputation seems to have become merely another word for virtue; and virtue, at the time of the Waverley Novels, means self-restraint. But honor retains a specific meaning that goes beyond either virtue or reputation in themselves. Honor, whether ancient or modern, is also a pledge. It is a pledge of a particular kind, distinguished by the particular security it offers. The security is life itself. The restraint of the passive hero is self-imposed but also self-guaranteed. The hero stakes his life as security for his commitment to society. Though he will never force a duel on someone else, he is prepared, as in old times, to defend his reputation with his life. Honor is always equivalent, in some sense, to sacrifice. Honor means the readiness to accept death rather than break a promise, a moral code, the law, or any of the abstract relations of society to which the hero is committed. Even where death is not literally in question, honor implies some partial disadvantage to the hero. He is confronted with the paradox that any acts that redound to his material advantage are suspect. His acts must redound only to the credit of his virtue, his ability to restrain himself; his acts must visibly triumph over some other kind of self-interest—an interest in love or in property. A hero must continually give himself up.

Pacifying the sense of honor, therefore, does not make it any less compelling. To the original burden of self-sacrifice, implicit in every definition of honor, is added the modern burden of self-restraint. The interdict on violence obliges the hero to observe more and more strictly the rules of truth-saying and promise-keeping with which civilization has replaced violence. Implicit in any breach of faith is the return of violence or the overthrow of civilization. In the scene in *Kenilworth* (Ch. 31) in which Tressilian incurs the suspicion of madness, he in effect punishes himself every time he ventures to speak.

As the logical climax of his effort to convince the Queen of his rationality and the truth of what he says, Tressilian offers his life: "I will lay down my head on the block." In the previous chapter the hero's anxiety about his dress, we recall, has been compared with that of "the doomed criminal who goes to certain execution." The Waverley Novels, like the contemporary arguments against dueling, insist that honor must no longer lead to homicide; but the possibility of suicide remains. Without that possibility the concept of honor would merge with the larger concept of self-restraint; honor pledges an individual life on behalf of an abstract ideal, and always prefers death to dishonor.

24. Immortality

The wise Saladin, philosopher and physician of *The Talisman* as well as warrior, well understands the threat of death inherent in Sir Kenneth's dishonor. He offers his protection and at the same time cautions against suicide:

> "Thou art, then wilfully determined not to fly to the Saracen host?" said the physician—"Yet, remember, thou stayest to certain destruction; and the writings of thy law, as well as ours, prohibit man from breaking into the tabernacle of his own life."
>
> "God forbid!" replied the Scot, crossing himself; "but we are also forbidden to avoid the punishment which our crimes have deserved."
> [Ch. 14]

The hero's religious protestation against suicide is thus balanced by the dictate of honor: he is "forbidden to avoid the punishment." He refuses to draw the connection between this sentiment and suicide: Saladin, however, makes the connection explicit; and the emotions of the hero, following this scene (Chs. 15 and 22), also make the connection. The hero's sense of honor constantly reminds him that he deserves punishment if he has offended society or failed in his promises. In *Guy Mannering*, when Sir Robert Hazelwood refuses to believe that "Brown" is "Captain in his Majesty's ———— regiment of horse," the hero replies, "I shall willingly submit to any punishment which such an imposture shall be thought to deserve" (Ch. 43). The hero of *Rob Roy*, as we have seen, finds it "the most provoking thing on earth, that every person will take it for granted that I am accessory to a crime which I despise and detest, and which would, moreover, deservedly forfeit my life to the laws of my country" (Ch. 11). The passive hero acknowledges on principle that the state, not the individual, has authority over life and death. His sense of honor acts as the representative of the state within him.

The heroes of Scott also accept the possibility of death indirectly by their preference for the military profession. Heroes do not regularly earn a living, but when pressed by circumstances they favor, at least in theory, military employment. Harry Bertram is not the only one "whose genius [has] a strong military tendency." Even Francis Osbaldistone "would choose the army . . . in preference to any other active line of life" (Ch. 2). The tendency is strongest with two unhappy heroes, Henry Morton and Edgar Ravenswood, who both resolve to become soldiers of fortune on the Continent in order to relieve their distress at home. This preference receives an interesting corroboration in *The Broad Stone of Honour*, where Kenelm Digby offers only four professions to gentlemen without means and then virtually retracts all choices but one: the solemn ministry of the church is hardly to be undertaken with a view to its "emoluments and comfort"; a career in Parliament brings very doubtful associations, and it is hard to imagine what motives "would lead any gentleman of elevated sentiments to *solicit* an appointment in public life"; the law is probably not even "consistent" with the order of gentlemen, since a lawyer must be able to argue both sides of the same question; but as for the army, "you will be sensible that this must be a profession highly honourable, and worthy of your rank." Digby embellishes this choice with his usual instances, including that of John of Bohemia, whom age and blindness could not deter from battle: "Placing him in the midst of them, and interlacing their bridles, they spurred forward their horses, and were almost immediately slain."[18]

None of the heroes of Scott is as blind as the King of Bohemia, and when they thrust themselves forward, they are not immediately slain. That is precisely the point, and a central fact of the Waverley Novels—a fact so obvious that its significance escapes our notice. The hero never does die. No matter how many times he may offer himself up, romance solemnly refuses to let him die. The passive hero of romance is immortal. He survives all threats of death, whether engendered by his enemies or provoked by his own testy sense of honor, and lives happily ever after. This infinite future life is his highest reward and is intimately associated with property, the title to which also lives indefinitely into the future. For even if one imagines—contrary to the suggestion of the romance—that the physical death of the hero does occur at some future time, his property will still survive. The hero earns this reward, not by work or by action of any kind, but

---

[18] *The Broad Stone of Honour*, pp. 454–90.

by reiterating his readiness to die at any moment. He turns instinctively to face death in this life in the hope that he will live forever. In order to save himself from violence, including the violence of death, he sacrifices his individual claims to society. In the same hope of immortality he shuns killing others. In fiction, at least, he is rewarded. The hero never dies because he never kills.

There is ample evidence to support this rule. In the Waverley Novels a hero never kills anyone. The clear exceptions, so far as I can see, are only three. Henry Wynd, who slaughters five Highlanders in *The Fair Maid of Perth* (Ch. 34), does not have the rank of a gentleman. In *The Fortunes of Nigel* the hero shoots an anonymous assistant villain who is trying to stab Martha Trapbois (Ch. 24). In *Anne of Geierstein* the hero slays Rudolph Donnerhugel, his hapless rival, in combat (Ch. 35). The last case, then, is the only instance in the Waverley Novels in which a proper hero kills another principal, villain, or rival. There seem to be no extenuating circumstances or explanation of this one instance—but it is, of course, the opposite case that cries out for explanation. Why should a hero *not* kill his rival, met fairly in battle in the year 1474? Even the soldier heroes, however, are exempt from the necessity of killing. The gentlemen heroes often bear arms through part or all of the story, but also without harming anyone. Some heroes have undoubtedly killed people on appropriate military occasions in past times; a few are supposed to have impressive military records. But the reader never sees them in action. Their current military deeds Scott either restricts or suppresses altogether. The result is very curious. In *Old Mortality* Henry Morton fights valiantly at Bothwell Brig. In defense of the bridge, one assumes, the hero must kill a good number of the enemy. The text, however, yields only this: "Morton and Burley fought in the very front of their followers" (Ch. 32). The hero's activity impends upon this single verb: "Morton *fought*." Also to the surprise of the reader who returns to *Old Mortality*, the action at the bridge occupies only two or three pages. To the attack on Glasgow, where Morton is in full command, Scott devotes exactly two paragraphs (Ch. 26). The generality of "Morton and Burley fought" may be contrasted with the display of Burley's solo triumph at Drumclog: "with a laugh of savage joy, [Burley] flourished his sword aloft, and then passed it through his adversary's body" (Ch. 16).

Here the resources of tentative fiction come to Scott's aid. With the exceptions noted, it is impossible to demonstrate from the text of the Waverley Novels that any hero kills anyone in the course of the action. In *The Betrothed* the Constable de Lacy slays Gwenwyn, the Welsh chieftain, in battle. The fair Eveline has vowed to wed her deliverer;

but Scott's heroines are not won by violence, even honest violence. The Constable has proved himself too active as well as too old for a proper hero, and he gives over his rights to his nephew Damian. Of Damian de Lacy's unsuccessful encounter with some later assailants of Eveline, the reader hears, *after* the event, that "two or three" had been "cut down by Damian in his furious onset" (Ch. 25). "Cut down" in such a context puts the fate of the banditti well out of doubt without insisting that the hero's blows were fatal. The tentative language surrounding such rare moments in the Waverley Novels consistently guards the hero from the implication of killing. Wherever possible Scott avoids the situation altogether—unconsciously, perhaps, but nonetheless effectively. Here is Roland Graeme's contribution to the battle of Langside in *The Abbot*: "Roland paused not a moment, but pushing his steed down the bank, leaped him amongst the hostile party, dealt three or four blows amongst them, which struck down two, and made the rest stand aloof" (Ch. 37). The impression given is that of startling or frightening the enemy away. The account of "three or four blows" shares the indefiniteness of the "two or three" victims of Damian. Roland pushes and leaps his steed, and deals out blows, but does nothing to the enemy very directly. Instead the effective action is thrust on the subordinate verbs, and the isolated "blows" do the deed, if deed is done.

This eccentricity of heroes in the heat of battle reminds us of Quentin Durward's failure to slay the Boar of the Ardennes, and the awkward substitution of Balafré at the last minute. Why does the hero himself not slay this monstrous villain? He is militarily entitled to do so; he has a chivalric motive; he serves to gain the hand of the Countess; he has virtually killed his man already; and Scott's interruption of the act is nothing if not gratuitous. In *The Talisman* Sir Kenneth has two excellent opportunities to do away with treacherous enemies. He stops a desperate would-be assassin of Richard by seizing the wretch's arm: when King Richard himself is apprised of the situation, *he* has no hesitation in turning about and smashing the villain's brains out with a stool (Ch. 21). Kenneth wounds the guilty Conrade in the lists; but it is medically ascertained by Saladin that Conrade was not *mortally* wounded, and he perishes instead by the hand of the Templar (Ch. 28). The most famous of such contrivances occurs in the denouement of *Ivanhoe* (Ch. 43). Rebecca will burn at the stake unless a champion appears to prove her innocence against the formidable Bois-Guilbert. At length the wounded Ivanhoe arrives in the lists. Every motive urges a personal triumph over the Templar: justice, valor, Ivanhoe's personal concern for Rebecca, and the very historical institution that Scott intends to portray. No possible discredit could attach to a victory of the wounded knight over the wicked Templar in the fierce disinterestedness of a trial by combat. Yet at the pitch of battle, "unscathed" by Ivanhoe, Bois-Guilbert dies "a victim to the violence of his own contending passions."

Confronted by such phenomena as these, one feels the presence of some profound law of the Waverley Novels. Such instances do not leave one content with the proposition that Scott's heroes are committed to nonviolence. They are instances of nonviolence so arbitrary as to demand a motive deeper than that of the preservation of society. They are, in truth, the outward expression of a bargain with fate. They reveal a mythic confidence that those who have sacrificed themselves to society have gained rather than lost by the sacrifice. On behalf of the individual who has sacrificed so much for the preservation of society this romance challenges the potency of death. The hero is threatened, but never dies; and by refusing to kill, he hopes never to experience death. If Quentin Durward were to slay the Boar of the Ardennes, or if Ivanhoe were to slay Bois-Guilbert, their own immortal life would be cast in doubt, since those who inflict death must admit its potency.

The villains and dark heroes who do inflict death in the Waverley Novels, also suffer death. The passive hero takes the opposite course. He refrains from killing and proclaims instead his own readiness to die. When Francis Osbaldistone avows that he would "deservedly forfeit his life" if he were guilty, he is proclaiming his innocence in the most emphatic way he knows. He does not actually expect to die. He is saying that he is the one person who ought *not* to die. As a selfish individual, he insists, he is already dead. The immortality that a hero so achieves is obviously not the same as the eternal life promised by Christianity—though the degree of deliberate confusion between the two would be hard to measure. This is the immortality of rank and of property. Like Burke in his *Thoughts and Details on Scarcity* and Paley in the *Reasons for Contentment,* Scott recommends the Christian promise of immortality chiefly to the lower ranks.

The contrast of the dark hero is again instructive. The dark hero perishes at the end of the romance. His career is active, passionate, and independent; he is much more alive than the passive hero, but he *uses up* life, and dies. The passive hero expends neither his own life nor that of others; but, in the course of the story, the dark hero kills his enemies. For him death is murder, the destruction of life. He practices it on others because in due time it will be practiced upon himself. Saladin, in *The Talisman,* has perhaps the most symbolic stature of all such heroes. Saladin possesses the life-giving talisman; he heals the sick and wounded, man and beast; his admiration for women is frankly sexual; he places a high value on his own skin and would rather retreat than lose his life unnecessarily. He also respects the life of others. He saves Sir Kenneth from execution when Sir Kenneth would rather die; and from murder against his will. But Saladin also kills. Nothing can be more striking than the contrast between Sir Kenneth, who vows that his own "head and trunk are ready to part company" (Ch. 15), and Saladin, who removes "the head" from "the trunk" of the Templar at a single blow (Ch. 28). The passive hero surrenders the power of life and death to a political authority, and thereafter no longer believes in death. Saladin retains his power over life and death by remembering that he is mortal. Among the luxuries and trophies in his tent is a banner with the inscription, "SALADIN, KING OF KINGS—SALADIN, VICTOR OF VICTORS—SALADIN MUST DIE" (Ch. 28).

There is one area in which a passive hero may display a certain initiative—in the cause of peace. In *Old Mortality*, for example, Henry Morton is himself largely responsible for the attempt to negotiate with the Duke of Monmouth (Ch. 30). The hero is obviously much more at home as a peacemaker than as a warrior, and it is amusing to watch Waverley racing ahead over the battlefield in order to rescue Hanoverian officers, and then being commended for his distinguished service by the Chevalier (Chs. 48, 50). The hero's longing for peace, however, has an emotional as well as a moral cast. Harry Bertram voices this emotion near the end of *Guy Mannering*. He is imprisoned for the night (under a warrant drawn up by the villain) in the House of Correction:

> "When will this uncertainty cease, and how soon shall I be permitted to look out for a tranquil home, where I may cultivate in quiet, and without dread or perplexity, those arts of peace from which my cares have been hitherto so forcibly diverted? . . . Happy friend!" he said, looking at the bed where Dinmont had deposited his bulky person, "thy cares are confined to the narrow round of a healthy and thriving occupation!—thou canst lay them aside at pleasure, and enjoy the deep repose of body and mind which wholesome labour has prepared for thee!"
> [Ch. 48]

Bertram here anticipates the peace and contentment promised in the denouement of each of the Waverley Novels—the benefits assured to him by civilization. In the final pages the reader does not hear of the hero's death, and hears only the promise of his marriage. His "dread and perplexity," however, give way to tranquillity and certainty—the certainty that he will live forever without pain. After this, nothing else happens. This is the immortality promised to the passive hero.

A distinction can be drawn between tranquillity and happiness. A despairing moment in *Old Mortality* (Ch. 39) teaches that "virtuous resolution and manly disinterestedness seldom fail to restore tranquillity even where they cannot create happiness." Perhaps virtuous resolution and manly disinterestedness do *not* produce happiness, even at the end of the story. The immortality granted the hero has a rather negative atmosphere. One receives the impression not of the hero longing to live beyond the pages of the romance but of longing to be released from life, to be free from turmoil and anxiety. He has demonstrated his utter loyalty to society, and now he would enjoy its blessings. But it is hard to see why this pleasure should suddenly become a positive thing, when the hero has hitherto pleaded merely his willingness to suffer and to sacrifice himself. He will never, after all, enjoy the "healthy and thriving occupation" of Dandie Dinmont. The future life of the passive hero is something weary and doubtful to contemplate; and again one is compelled to wonder if Thackeray, in *Rebecca and Rowena*, did not very seriously contest the happiness of the happy ending of *Ivanhoe*, when he set the hero in search of Rebecca again.

IX

OLD MORTALITY

"But whither," said Morton, in the bitterness of his heart, "am I now to direct my course? or rather, what does it signify to which point of the compass a wretch so forlorn betakes himself? I would to God, could the wish be without sin, that these dark waters had flowed over me . . . !

—*Old Mortality*

What an overwhelming obstacle to civilization aggression must be if the defence against it can cause as much misery as aggression itself!

—Freud, *Civilization and Its Discontents*, trans. Joan Rivière

25. Henry Morton

*O*LD *MORTALITY* is Scott's highest achievement in historical and political fiction. As a work of art coming to grips with moral conflict, it rivals *The Heart of Mid-Lothian* in complexity; as an act of courage in exploring the validity of an armed revolution against the state, it strains the already taut thematic lines of the Waverley Novels. In the ranting of Mause Headrigg and the Cameronian preachers Scott demonstrated his ear for fantastic but significant rhetoric; in the skirmish at Drumclog he achieved a rendering of military action worthy of Tolstoy.[1] More importantly, he attempted in every chapter of *Old Mortality* to make the private and public pieces of his fable cohere. The involvement of Waverley in the Stuart rebellion of 1745 is accidental and melodramatic in contrast with the involvement of Henry Morton with those who, in 1679, "without leaders, without money, without magazines, without any fixed plan of action, and almost without arms, borne out only by their innate zeal, and a detestation of the oppression of their rulers, ventured to declare open war against an established Government" (Ch. 18). In *Old Mortality* Scott carefully motivates his hero: Henry Morton is vindicated by a theory of political right and by history, as well as by honor and his affection for Edith Bellenden.

[1] The similarity to Tolstoy is also remarked by V. S. Pritchett, *The Living Novel* (New York, 1947), p. 69.

Old Mortality confronts the reader with the anomaly of a proper hero in the improper act of leading an assault on the government. For Morton is unquestionably a proper hero: this is not the case of Henry Wynd of Perth, who is an artisan, but of Henry Morton of Milnwood, a gentleman, the son of Silas Morton, who fought for Cromwell but also for the restoration of Charles II. As a consequence, the hero finds himself in a much more tortuous predicament than anyone in *The Fair Maid of Perth*, and the tension of *Old Mortality* divides the allegiance of the hero as well as the nation. The fact that Morton is active, and yet so typically inactive also, provided Adolphus with a final test, in his description of the heroes of Scott:

> In all the works of the novelist, there is no character of the same class more vigorously drawn, or more variously illustrated than that of Henry Morton: his qualities are such as at once compel our sympathy and command our respect, and many principal events of the story receive their whole impulse and direction from his will. But, during those scenes with the insurgents at Drumclog, those scenes so animated and intensely agitating . . . Henry Morton is quietly seated on a hill, awaiting the event, and only contrives at the close of the engagement to incur some danger by interposing on behalf of Lord Evandale. When the resolution is taken to defend the castle of Tillietudlem . . . Henry Morton is hearing sermons at the fanatical camp. When his fellow rebels appear before the council, and the enthusiast Macbriar is enduring torture with a martyr's constancy, Henry Morton is standing aloof with his pardon in his hand, though not an unconcerned, yet a passive spectator. When the gallant Evandale falls a victim to his own high spirit, and the baseness of his enemies, Henry Morton, though hastening to his rescue, comes too late to succour or to assist personally in avenging him.[2]

Adolphus graciously passes over some of the hero's more extraordinary shifts of direction—such as when Morton, an officer of the insurgents, leads the besieged royalists to safety (Ch. 28). At the other extreme, Morton distinguishes himself at Bothwell Brig as the one proper hero in Scott who actually inspires and leads into battle a dark hero, John Balfour of Burley.

Scott enlists for this hero a justly famous retainer or "trusty squire" (Ch. 32), whose adventures closely parallel Morton's. Cuddie Headrigg's marksmanship at the "wappenschaw" is second only to that of the hero and Lord Evandale; he contemplates military service as an alternative to domestic success; and even reflects the hero's indiffer-

---

[2] [Adolphus], *Letters to Richard Heber*, p. 140.

ence to the intramural debates of the Presbyterians: "I sae nae sae muckle difference atween the twa ways o't as a' the folk pretend" (Ch. 7). Cuddie's love relations also correspond to those of the hero: Jenny Dennison is the counterpart of Edith Bellenden, and Tam Halliday is the noncommissioned counterpart of the rival, Lord Evandale. This subplot is extremely useful to the author. The usual facility and "address" of the lower ranks in the Waverley Novels allow Cuddie and Jenny Dennison to slip between enemy lines—and to trespass the moral lines of Scott's romance—with much greater agility than the hero and heroine dare to display. Between them they lift much of the burden of heroism from Henry Morton—by urging him to retreat in good time, by employing the practical advantages of attachments in the enemy camp, by being less scrupulous of honor and more direct in self-interest, and finally, when that act becomes timely, by shooting the villain dead.

But not all of Cuddie Headrigg's actions are as definite as the destruction of Basil Olifant at the end of the book. Viewed in another way, his parallel actions subvert the precarious ambivalence of the hero by caricaturing it. At the siege of Tillietudlem (Ch. 25), for example, it falls within Cuddie's power to take the castle by means of a familiar pantry window. With friends on both sides of the wall, Cuddie approaches this weak spot in the royalist defenses "not very willingly," and is repulsed by a pot of scalding "kail-brose." At the same ineffectual siege Morton, similarly unwilling, commands his marksmen to fire only upon the red-coats and "to save the others engaged in the defence of the Castle; and, above all, to spare the life of the old Major." When Cuddie is brought before the Scottish Privy Council for his action against the crown at Bothwell Brig, he is granted a free pardon (Ch. 36). The comic evasiveness of the Scottish peasant, however, comes perilously close to mocking the manner in which the Council, and the author, are willing to slur over Henry Morton's complicity in the same event. Was Cuddie even present at the battle of Bothwell Brig? "I'll no say but it may be possible that I might hae been there. . . . It's no for me to contradict your Lordship's Grace's honour. . . . How can ane mind precisely where they hae been a' the days o' their life?" The Council can hardly afford to address the same question to the hero himself—and in fact they do not cross-examine him. A bond for his release has been prepared in advance. This is the scene to which Adolphus objects because of its damaging contrast of the hero with Ephraim Macbriar. "'Were you at the battle of Bothwell Bridge?' was, in like manner, demanded of [Macbriar]. 'I was,' answered the prisoner, in a bold and resolute tone."

As Jenny Dennison remarks, "Forby that, it's maybe as weel to hae a friend on baith sides" (Ch. 24). Cuddie and Morton are, precisely, on both sides. But if that is the case, from what we know of the Waverley Novels how is it possible for Henry Morton to escape the consequences, to return from exile, to marry Edith Bellenden, to inherit property, and to live forever after? The answer is that only history can save him. When Morton returns from exile in 1689, history has vindicated his position. Scott can accept the compromise of past history—above all, the great compromise of 1688. The ending of *Old Mortality* is full of absurdities, but without pausing ten years for the historical Revolution to complete itself, the individual "revolution" of Henry Morton would violate the canon of the Waverley Novels. In those last awkward chapters *Old Mortality* straddles the great representative event of civil society. For Burke the Glorious Revolution was the act of "necessity," and when Morton returns to Scotland, he may be thought to confront a new reality altogether. Burley and Claverhouse, the fierce opponents of the earlier action, are now conspiring together against the political settlement. The joining of two such implacable enemies is meant to underline the stature of Henry Morton, who now comes into his own as the passive and loyal hero of the new era. When Lord Evandale, also, rejects the Revolution, Scott can easily dispose of Morton's rival in love.

Morton's infraction of the rules is also mitigated throughout the earlier portion of the romance by his ambiguous military policy, his respect for private property, his gallantry toward Evandale, and his efforts to make peace. In one bitter moment he speaks, in clearly unheroic language, of "vengeance" for his wrongs (Ch. 14); but in general he believes his decision to join an armed uprising to be based solely on principle. As the proponent of "reason and mildness," in a letter to Major Bellenden, Morton has not consciously acted from passion: "I do not share the angry or violent passions of the oppressed and harassed sufferers with whom I am now acting." His statement allows the Major to observe angrily that Morton is "without even the pretext of enthusiasm" (Ch. 25). The hero's emotional responses to his fellow insurgents are in fact the very opposite of enthusiastic. In the Presbyterian camp, where his protests against extremism far outweigh his cooperation in the revolutionary council, Morton is continually at odds with the other leaders and their partisan followers. He is personally uncomfortable in their midst; his feelings range from distaste to disgust. The people he admires are the Bellendens and Evandale: Morton "felt fully the embarrassment of his situation, yet consoled himself with the reflection, that his newly-acquired power in the insurgent army would give him, at all events, the means of extending

to the inmates of Tillietudlem a protection which no other circumstances could have afforded them" (Ch. 23).

Much of the hero's discomfort can be traced to his rank. Though
poor and dressing "with great simplicity," he possesses "a superior
rank to the vulgar" (Ch. 3). In the course of the rebellion he associates himself, as the heroine sharply reminds him, with "brutal clowns"
(Ch. 29). At the same time, his rank as a gentleman has great usefulness. It is hard to find any other grounds for his rescue by Claverhouse after the battle of Bothwell Brig. Claverhouse, apparently the
hero's most formidable enemy, now makes himself responsible for
Morton's return to society, stands security for him, sees to his personal needs, and treats him "rather as a friend and companion than
as a prisoner." He deprives Morton of his firearms but not of his
sword—"in those days, the distinguishing mark of a gentleman" (Ch.
35). Even before the battle Claverhouse announces his intention to
befriend the hero. His interest has two sources: Morton's own generosity to Evandale, and his rank as a gentleman. "I trust I shall always
make some difference between a high-minded gentleman, who,
though misguided, acts upon generous principles, and the crazy fanatical clowns yonder, with the bloodthirsty assassins who lead them"
(Ch. 30).

When Scott has Edith Bellenden and Colonel Claverhouse refer to
the insurgents as "clowns," he calls attention to their class prejudice.
A true gentleman never mocks the lower ranks in either word or
thought. As they ride to Edinburgh Morton openly disputes the un-
democratic views of Claverhouse, who is himself too bloodthirsty.
Scott carefully rejects *both* "the fanaticism of honour and that of dark
and sullen superstition" (Ch. 35). This ride, nevertheless, is a critical
moment in *Old Mortality*. The rebellion, put down by force, is at an
end. The hero is a prisoner of Claverhouse and the government
again, just as he was at Drumclog, where the rebellion began. And
Claverhouse, whatever his prejudices, is a member of Morton's own
class. Morton's fate is undecided, but he has escaped "the cares of his
doubtful and dangerous station among the insurgents." Scott states
the hero's emotional relief in unmistakable terms: "his hours flowed
on less anxiously than at any time since his having commenced actor
in public life." In other words, if I may oversimplify this paradox, as a
prisoner of his own society, Morton is free again. He is also "free"
from freedom itself: "He was now, with respect to his fortune, like a
rider who has flung his reins on the horse's neck, and, while he aban-
doned himself to circumstances, was at least relieved from the task of
attempting to direct them." Morton's anxiety during the course of
the rebellion and his relief at his recapture by Claverhouse suggest

that, in emotional terms at least, the action of *Old Mortality* consists of an excursion, not an actual revolution. The revolution—the Glorious Revolution of 1688—takes place while Morton is in exile.

The off-stage revolution explains Morton's return and his claim to futurity but does not so easily explain how such a hero could become involved in an insurrection in the first place—*before* 1688. Granted that his experience is characteristically temporary, Morton, unlike the heroes who abandon themselves to circumstance throughout the romance, actively participates in a forbidden action. The process of his involvement is as diffuse as one might expect. It begins when Morton gives a night's shelter to Burley, who once saved the life of Morton's father. He is not aware of the nature of Burley's villainy, but fully conscious that it must be against the law to shelter him: "the punishment of the law shall fall upon myself, as in justice it should, not upon my uncle" (Ch. 5). His initial attitude toward the state is therefore typical of the passive hero—namely, that he deserves punishment if he has offended the law. This helps to explain Morton's captious and self-defeating behavior when Sergeant Bothwell arrives to arrest him. Bothwell charges, "You broke the law," and Henry has no answer. "Henry was silent" (Ch. 8).

By honoring his father's debt, and in ignorance of Burley's activities, Morton does break the law. His first instinct is to accept the consequences. But once apprised of the extreme penalty, and having seen the administrators of the law act with arbitrary violence and scorn for procedure, he gradually comes to feel that he has been wronged. In his despair he states to Edith that he might have given "temporary refuge" to Burley even if he had known the extent of his crimes (Ch. 10). He openly challenges the military administration of the law. By the time he has been sentenced to death and reprieved (Ch. 13), he is convinced that he has been wronged. He no longer imagines that he has broken any law. But he does not therefore set himself up as a judge of right and wrong: he appeals to a doctrine of rights and due procedure, to a concept of law of higher authority than the arbitrary rulings of military commanders and an oppressive government. Morton might very well appeal to Blackstone, who describes one of the auxiliary rights of Englishmen as "that of having arms for their defence, suitable to their condition and degree, and such as are allowed by law." Blackstone hardly conceives of organized revolution, but such arms may be used for "resistance and self-preservation," at least, "when the sanctions of society and laws are found insufficient to restrain the violence of oppression."[3]

---

[3] *Commentaries,* 1: 143–44.

When Edith Bellenden first hears of Morton's arrest (Ch. 10), she exclaims, "he must be totally innocent, unless he has been standing up for some invaded right." Few heroines in the Waverley Novels are so politically astute as to admit some other motive than innocence. But political rights are as central to *Old Mortality* as moral scruples are in *The Heart of Mid-Lothian*. Heroes are accustomed to depend upon the civil authorities, but Henry Morton must "resist any authority on earth . . . that invades tyrannically my chartered rights as a freeman" (Ch. 14). Scott does not define the nature of these rights very precisely. They are the same rights of Englishmen that Blackstone recommends as "highly necessary to be perfectly known and considered by every man of rank and property."[4] The rights that Morton defends seem anterior to some kinds of law, since it is the business of the government—"that used to be more tenacious of our liberties" (Ch. 10)—to ensure them. Yet they are not "natural" but "chartered" rights. Blackstone seems to have the same difficulty.[5] The chapter on "Absolute Rights" in the *Commentaries* manages to qualify even the absolute: thus the absolute right of "personal liberty consists in the power of locomotion . . . without imprisonment or restraint, *unless by due course of law*" (my italics).[6] Similarly, Morton writes to Major Bellenden that he shall "no longer submit to have my own rights and those of my fellow-subjects trampled upon, our freedom violated, our persons insulted, and our blood spilt, *without just cause or legal trial*" (Ch. 25; my italics). In this letter Morton appeals to due process of law; he wishes to "substitute the authority of equal laws to that of military violence." His argument comes down to the familiar choice between force and law. As a hero of the Waverley Novels Morton continues to conceive of his liberty as subordinate to law, and merely demands that the government also subordinate itself to law. His position contrasts with that of Claverhouse, who boasts of taking "vengeance" under law (Ch. 10) and of his willingness to "find" a law to suit his purposes (Ch. 12). The additional liberty propounded in *Old Mortality* is that "permitting all men to worship God according to their own consciences" (Ch. 25)—a right that Morton defends with dignity against the intolerance of both sides. But religious liberty, too, is not an absolute value; it serves the broader interests of society. Scott's summary of the intentions of William III after 1688 reflects the hero's intention: that is, "to tolerate all forms of religion *which were consistent*

---

[4] Ibid., p. 144.

[5] Cf. Daniel J. Boorstin, *The Mysterious Science of the Law* (Cambridge, Mass., 1941), pp. 161–66.

[6] *Commentaries*, 1: 124.

with the safety of the state" (Ch. 37; my italics). As in the *Commentaries* of Blackstone,[7] the one right that approaches an absolute in *Old Mortality* is the right of property. Henry Morton is neither leveler nor libertine, but a sore-beset defender of the British Constitution. By a slight anachronism, the constitution he defends is that of 1688, but even in 1679 (Chs. 2–36) he consistently refers to himself and his followers as "subjects" of the king.

In his rationalization of the laws of England, Blackstone hits upon more than one true end of civil society. The rights of Englishmen, including the right of property, are one such end, and "the principal view of human law is, or ought always to be, to explain, protect, and enforce such rights."[8] Elsewhere he suggests that peace is the ultimate end of society: "for peace is the very end and foundation of civil society."[9] Peace is also the aim of the hero of the Waverley Novels. The reader never does perceive Morton's actual decision to join the insurrection. The narrative leaves him on the hilltop at Drumclog (Ch. 17) and discovers him next in the rebel camp (Ch. 21). Even then Scott refrains from "detailing at length the arguments by which [Burley] urged Morton to join the insurgents." Once hostilities have commenced, however, the passive hero can pursue an active end: to civilize the conflict, reduce bloodshed, and bring about an armistice. Morton cannot very well start a civil war: he simply joins, in his words, "a cause supported by men engaged in open war, which it is proposed to carry on according to the rules of civilised nations, without in any respect approving of the act of violence which gave immediate rise to it" (Ch. 21). It will give him pleasure "to be the means of softening the horrors of civil war" (Ch. 22). In battle he demonstrates "as much skill in protecting his own followers as spirit in annoying the enemy" (Ch. 25). And his most logical and confident function is that of truce envoy to the Duke of Monmouth: "Our avowed object is the re-establishment of peace on fair and honourable terms of security to our religion and our liberty. We disclaim any desire to tyrannise over those of others" (Ch. 30).

The values of liberty and peace, however, would be better studied in Blackstone or Burke, if the only significance of *Old Mortality* were historical and political. We are obliged to take seriously the issues of romance. The politics of this romance are those of the Whig Revolution of 1688 and the Tory Reaction of Scott's lifetime; but the hero of the romance is a near cousin of Edgar Ravenswood, who, in his de-

[7] Cf. Boorstin, pp. 166, 186.
[8] *Commentaries*, 1: 124.
[9] Ibid., p. 349.

spair, would leave Scotland altogether. In *Old Mortality* Scott even argues a connection between love and politics. Interpretations that would reduce the Waverley Novels to historical dialectics or the hero to a "symbolic observer" must balk at soliloquies like the following:

> "Farewell, stern enthusiast!" said Morton, looking after [Burley]. "In some moods of my mind, how dangerous would be the society of such a companion! If I am unmoved by his zeal for abstract doctrines of faith, or rather by a peculiar mode of worship . . . can I be a man, and a Scotchman, and look with indifference on that persecution which has made wise men mad? Was not the cause of freedom, civil and religious, that for which my father fought? and shall I do well to remain inactive, or to take the part of an oppressive government, if there should appear any rational prospect of redressing the insufferable wrongs to which my miserable countrymen are subjected? —And yet, who shall warrant me that these people, rendered wild by persecution, would not, in the hour of victory, be as cruel and as intolerant as those by whom they are now hunted down? What degree of moderation, or of mercy, can be expected from this Burley . . .? I am weary of seeing nothing but violence and fury around me—now assuming the mask of lawful authority, now taking that of religious zeal. I am sick of my country—of myself—of my dependent situation—of my repressed feelings—of these woods, of that river—of that house—of all but—Edith, and she can never be mine! . . . Her grandmother's pride—the opposite principles of our families—my wretched state of dependence—a poor miserable slave, for I have not even the wages of a servant,—all circumstances give the lie to the vain hope that we can ever be united. Why then protract a delusion so painful?
>
> "But I am no slave," he said aloud, and drawing himself up to his full stature—"no slave, in one respect surely. I can change my abode—my father's sword is mine, and Europe lies open before me, as before him and hundreds besides of my countrymen, who have filled it with the fame of their exploits." [Ch. 6]

It can be argued that this is bathos, that this is not Scott at his best. For the moment we are concerned not with the quality but with the swiftness of the transition in midspeech—the transition from "my country" to "myself," from politics to love. The transition takes place in a mood of despair from which the hero finally recovers by resolving to leave the country and become a professional warrior. "Perhaps," he concludes, "some lucky chance may raise me to a rank with our Ruthvens, our Lesleys, our Munroes, the chosen leaders of the famous Protestant champion, Gustavus Adolphus—or if not, a soldier's life or a soldier's grave."

26. Life and Death

The relation of love and politics raised in the soliloquy in Chapter 6 of *Old Mortality* is explored in Chapter 13, where Morton is tried for his life by Colonel Claverhouse. The violence threatened to the hero in this scene is tentative: that is, he is condemned to be shot, but he is also reprieved. The prose of the chapter is also tentative: though approaching a crisis in the action, Scott devotes more space to discursive speculation on the hero's predicament than to simple narration of the event. He studies the formation of the event—or near event—in abstract terms, discovering the connection between the hero's private fortunes in love and the public "circumstances of the times"—the juncture of passion and history that is presumably at the heart of historical romance. At the point where politics and love converge, Scott postulates nothing less than a "revolution" of the hero's character. This wealth of material gives us an opportunity to examine the substance of romance in sequence, to test our understanding of the Waverley Novels not by selected detail but by interpreting each detail as it presents itself.

As he is marched in for trial at the end of Chapter 12, Morton overhears and misconstrues Edith Bellenden's delicate effort to persuade Lord Evandale to plead for the hero's life. He is struck with the false impression that Edith asks the favor of intercession by right of an attachment to Evandale. Chapter 13 begins with the following short paragraph, which announces that the next few pages will be concerned with abstract relations and states of mind:

> To explain the deep effect which the few broken passages of the conversation we have detailed made upon the unfortunate prisoner by whom they were overheard, it is necessary to say something of his previous state of mind, and of the origin of his acquaintance with Edith.

The fact of Morton's emotion, obliquely asserted in this sentence, has not yet been established by the narrative. The conversation referred to has been treated solely with respect to the position of Edith and Lord Evandale. Up to this point, and in the pages that follow, Scott avoids the statement of fact that Morton *was* deeply affected. The fact must be inferred from the slight concrete evidence of a sigh supported by a series of general causes, supplied by the author, that make a deep effect probable. This etiological bias takes command in the first sentence. The language—the relative clauses, the reference to origins or conditioning of the effect, and the call for an orderly exposition—already conforms to a scientific method.

The explanation of the deep effect consists first in a summary of Morton's character. He possesses talent, courage, and enthusiasm; his own intelligence and his frequent visits to Major Bellenden's home have freed him from the "fanatic zeal" and "puritanical spirit" that presumably animated his father.

> Still, however, the current of his soul was frozen by a sense of depen-
> dence—of poverty—above all, of an imperfect and limited education.
> These feelings impressed him with a diffidence and reserve, which effec-
> tually concealed from all but very intimate friends, the extent of talent
> and the firmness of character which we have stated him to be possessed
> of. The circumstances of the times had added to this reserve an air of in-
> decision and of indifference; for, being attached to neither of the fac-
> tions which divided the kingdom, he passed for dull, insensible, and un-
> influenced by the feelings of religion or of patriotism. No conclusion,
> however, could be more unjust; and the reasons of the neutrality which
> he had hitherto professed had root in very different and most praise-
> worthy motives. He had formed few congenial ties with those who were
> the objects of persecution, and was disgusted alike by their narrow-
> minded and selfish party-spirit, their gloomy fanaticism, their abhorrent
> condemnation of all elegant studies or innocent exercises, and the en-
> venomed rancour of their political hatred. But his mind was still more
> revolted by the tyrannical and oppressive conduct of the Government—
> the misrule, license, and brutality of the soldiery—the executions on the
> scaffold, the slaughters in the open field, the free quarters and exac-
> tions imposed by military law, which placed the lives and fortunes of a
> free people on a level with Asiatic slaves. Condemning, therefore, each
> party as its excesses fell under his eyes, disgusted with the sight of evils
> which he had no means of alleviating, and hearing alternate complaints
> and exultations with which he could not sympathise, he would long ere
> this have left Scotland, had it not been for his attachment to Edith
> Bellenden.

The transition from self-doubts to political principle is again swift and interesting. We gather that Morton feels his isolation deeply, that he would enjoy the company and sports of the ruling class, but upholds the political rights of the Covenanters. The passage clearly supports David Daiches' contention that Henry Morton is an "intelligent lib-eral in a world of extremists."[10] But Scott does not introduce this sub-ject in order to assert the dignity of the intelligent liberal: the gist of the argument is defensive. The hero seems "dull, insensible, and unin-fluenced by the feeling of religion or of patriotism"—charges from

[10] *Literary Essays* (Edinburgh and London, 1956), p. 110.

which he must be vindicated. Though Scott asserts that the "indeci-sion" and "indifference" of Morton are superficial, he also suggests, by means of a metaphor, that Morton is thwarted by something within himself: "the current of his soul was frozen" by his various feel-ings of inadequacy.

The last sentence in the paragraph signals a transition from politics to love again. The discussion of Morton's political dilemma has been introduced, oddly enough, "to explain the deep effect" of overhear-ing Edith pleading to his rival for assistance. The statement that Mor-ton would "have left Scotland, had it not been for his attachment to Edith Bellenden" goes back to the long soliloquy in Chapter 6. Here Scott similarly links the political stance of his hero to the love affair by posing Morton's longing to leave Scotland (because of his disgust with the times) against his longing for Edith. From a following para-graph of stock phrases and gentle irony we learn that Edith and Mor-ton have, in the name of "friendship," exchanged letters and enjoyed numerous meetings in the open air. Still another paragraph reintro-duces the theme of Morton's self-doubt. The lovers seem altogether submerged in the discussion of cause and effect:

> It followed, as a consequence of this state of things, as well as of the diffi-dence of Morton's disposition at this period, that his confidence in Edith's return of his affection had its occasional cold fits. Her situation was in every respect so superior to his own, her worth so eminent, her ac-complishments so many, her face so beautiful, and her manners so be-witching, that he could not but entertain fears that some suitor more fa-voured than himself by fortune, and more acceptable to Edith's family than he durst hope to be, might step in between him and the object of his affections. Common rumour had raised up such a rival in Lord Evan-dale, whom birth, fortune, connections, and political principles, as well as his frequent visits at Tillietudlem, and his attendance upon Lady Bellenden and her niece at all public places, naturally pointed out as a candidate for her favour. It frequently and inevitably happened, that engagements to which Lord Evandale was a party interfered with the meeting of the lovers, and Henry could not but mark that Edith either studiously avoided speaking of the young nobleman, or did so with obvi-ous reserve and hesitation.

Like the first sentence of the chapter, the first sentence of this para-graph announces an attempt to deduce the facts from a number of rather vague generalizations. Instead of being presented with the stated history of the case, the reader is instructed in what must have "inevitably happened." The general sense of the passage is made intel-ligible only by numerous phrases. Eliminating the eight prepositional phrases from the first sentence, for example, we have simply, "It followed that his confidence had its cold fits." In threading his way through these qualifying phrases Scott seems instinctively to avoid making the lovers either subject or object of his sentences. Instead he employs an impersonal construction, or invokes "her situation" and "common rumour," or denies a contrary possibility. In each of these respects the denotation of actual objects is diminished, and the reader is presented with a network of relations between rather dimly conceived elements—what "followed, as a consequence of this state of things, as well as of the diffidence of Morton's disposition at this time."

The following two pages concern the rival, Lord Evandale. But Evandale's very existence can be deduced (Morton fears "some suitor more favoured than himself") from the hero's state of mind and circumstances. The fact that Edith has visited Morton in his cell the night before, with obvious risk to her own reputation, cannot assuage the jealous anxiety of a hero "ingenious in tormenting himself":

> The visit which he received from Edith during his confinement, the deep and devoted interest which she had expressed in his fate, ought of themselves to have dispelled his suspicions; yet, ingenious in tormenting himself, even this he thought might be imputed to anxious friendship, or, at most, to a temporary partiality, which would probably soon give way to circumstances, the entreaties of her friends, the authority of Lady Margaret, and the assiduities of Lord Evandale.

Scott's summary of the hero's "previous state of mind" and his "acquaintance with Edith" has, of course, interrupted the linear action of *Old Mortality*. At this point in the chapter Scott introduces a soliloquy for the hero that is appropriate to the subject at hand. Just as casually, the paragraph following the soliloquy places it in time and returns the narrative to a point just *before* the conclusion to the previous chapter:

> "And to what do I owe it," he said, "that I cannot stand up like a man, and plead my interest in her ere I am thus cheated out of it?—to what, but to the all-pervading and accursed tyranny, which afflicts at once our bodies, souls, estates, and affections? And is it to one of the pensioned cut-throats of this oppressive Government that I must yield my pretensions to Edith Bellenden?—I will not, by Heaven!—It is a just punishment on me for being dead to public wrongs, that they have visited me with their injuries in a point where they can be least brooked or borne."
>
> As these stormy resolutions boiled in his bosom, and while he ran over the various kinds of insult and injury which he had sustained in his

own cause and in that of his country, Bothwell entered the tower, followed by two dragoons, one of whom carried handcuffs.

Politics and love are fused, at least, in the heat of Morton's imagination: he somehow owes his failure in love, and therefore all his feelings of inadequacy and frustration, to the government. In the accomplished person of Lord Evandale the object of Morton's anxiety and self-doubt merges with a symbol of the reigning classes. Though unqualified metaphor is almost nonexistent in this chapter, we have twice been notified of the chill in Morton's soul. Here, as is sometimes the case with other heroes of Scott, he becomes hot ("resolutions boiled") only in the act of verbalizing his indignation. When Scott frankly endorses Morton's charge of "insult and injury," the line between the author's judgment and the hero's heat becomes a very fine one: the strident voice is amplified by the romance, in the sense of daydream, that the hero is enacting. The hero who is continually acted upon here exhibits a certain justifiable paranoia.

The stridency of the complaint obscures its logic. We know from the thematic structure of two separate worlds in the Waverley Novels that the raging of love against the government makes a certain amount of sense. Morton is confronted by "circumstances," the word which, especially in this chapter, represents the reality posed by the accepted morality and powers that be. He has already meditated upon the realities of his situation in respect to property, education, and family—abstract relations that obtain for Evandale but not at present for Morton. He now confronts a tyrannical government. Morton's love longings are characterized by a rather petulant anxiety; his attitude toward public affairs, by disgust. In neither area has he been in a position to act. Now, Scott will argue, despair of love will prompt him to political action. Morton will act out his private antagonisms and disappointment against the political sector of the "reality" that confronts him.

When Bothwell approaches to put on the irons, Morton threatens to brain him with an oaken seat. Bothwell scoffs at this "youngster"— an emphasis that Claverhouse also brings to bear in this chapter— and advises him to be "prudent," because he has just heard Miss Bellenden ask Evandale to intercede. This information—not merely, as we have supposed, the fragments of conversation that Morton himself overhears a moment later—completely disarms the hero. "Morton, thunderstruck by this intelligence, no longer offered the least resistance." This flashback, and the long account of Morton's state of mind and circumstances, have finally prepared the reader for the "deep effect" promised in the first sentence of the chapter:

And as [Bothwell] spoke, he and his party led their prisoner towards the hall. In passing behind the seat of Edith, the unfortunate prisoner heard enough, as he conceived, of the broken expressions which passed between Edith and Lord Evandale, to confirm all that the soldier had told him. That moment made a singular and instantaneous revolution in his character. The depth of despair to which his love and fortunes were reduced—the peril in which his life *appeared* to stand—the transference of Edith's affections, her intercession in his favour, which rendered her fickleness yet more galling,—*seemed* to destroy every feeling for which he had hitherto lived, but at the same time awakened those which had hitherto been smothered by passions more gentle though more selfish. Desperate himself, he determined to support the rights of his country, insulted in his person. His character was *for the moment* as effectually changed as *the appearance* of a villa, which, from being the abode of domestic quiet and happiness, is, by the sudden intrusion of an armed force, converted into a formidable post of defence.

Scott no sooner presents this "revolution"—a revolution in character presented as *logically* implied by all that has gone before—than he partly withholds his conviction in it. I have italicized the words that convey this qualification. In the next few pages, Morton is reprieved from death: but even in advance of the reprieve, the language of tentative fiction betrays that the peril is only apparent. Adolphus observed that Scott, in both prose and verse, prefers simile to metaphor.[11] Here, where Scott employs a simile, he compares Morton merely to "the appearance" of a villa, despite the fact that his subject is a deep change of character.

Nearly half of Chapter 13 has been concerned, in abstract terms, with Morton's state of mind and circumstances; now the main action of the chapter proves to be based on a rational error. Morton's despair, and hence his revolution of character and sudden nationalism, are based on a mistake: he has falsely concluded that Edith does not love him. The error is that of a person "ingenious in tormenting himself."

Granted that the peril, and the revolution, are tentative or imaginary, the argument displays a certain logic. Deprived of love, Morton resolves to "support the rights of his country." His previously announced alternative to love, first sounded in Chapter 6 and reiterated in the present chapter, was to leave his country altogether. Are these two resolutions, both vociferated in despair and both aborted by the plot, actually very different? Both resolutions, if carried out, would re-

[11] [Adolphus], *Letters to Richard Heber*, p. 52.

move the hero from the action of the romance. Supporting the rights of his country under the present circumstances is suicidal. Morton's despair, and so forth, "seemed to destroy every feeling for which he had hitherto lived." The same despair produces defiance of a government that does not respect his rights. But Morton is chained fast by Claverhouse—who speaks "coolly," "calmly," and is "totally unmoved," and who forthwith orders Bothwell to draw up a firing squad. The hero's new stand implies martyrdom at best. In the remaining pages of the chapter Morton defies Claverhouse to take his life: but that is precisely what Claverhouse wishes and intends to do.

Lady Margaret and Major Bellenden plead for the hero without success. At the intercession of Evandale, however, Claverhouse agrees to suspend the sentence of death.

> [Claverhouse] then stepped forward to the table, and bent his eyes keenly on Morton, as if to observe what effect the pause of awful suspense between death and life, which seemed to freeze the bystanders with horror, would produce upon the prisoner himself. Morton maintained a degree of firmness, which nothing but a mind that had nothing left upon earth to love or to hope, could have supported at such a crisis.

But heroes are even more unpredictable than tyrants on some issues. Sometimes they seem to prefer death to life. When the "awful suspense between death and life" has been resolved in favor of life, Henry Morton continues to protest: "'If my life,' said Morton, stung with the idea that he owed his respite to the intercession of a favoured rival, 'if my life be granted at Lord Evandale's request'—." Claverhouse orders him away before he can finish; and Bothwell declares, as he forces Morton off, "Have you three lives in your pocket, besides the one in your body, my lad, that you can afford to let your tongue run away with them at this rate?"

The verse tag for this chapter is taken from *Othello*: "O, my Lord, beware of jealousy!" Morton experiences nothing of Othello's impulse to murder the woman in the case: he shares some of the impulse to destroy himself. In his gruff way Bothwell comments significantly on the passive hero who would stubbornly provoke his own death. A few hours later at Drumclog, Burley slays Bothwell (Ch. 16). Bothwell himself is clearly not afraid to die; but his courage in the face of death differs from Morton's "firmness" in the present chapter. Would he contest a last minute reprieve on so nice a point of honor? When Bothwell dies, he dies by the violent hand of the enemy; the death that Morton almost dies is a death exacted by his own world. The tentative aspect of Morton's encounter with death also constitutes a difference. Bothwell is transfixed three times by a sword; for the hero, however, death can have only the mental substance of a fear or a wish.

The threat of execution in Chapter 13 is the first turning point in *Old Mortality*: it makes the hero's rebellion an act of self-defense, as it were. The scene has an exact counterpart at the end of Morton's adventures among the insurgents. Scott seldom designed his fictions so symmetrically. In Chapter 33 the hero's life is again threatened by his own side—this time by the Covenanters. After the defeat at Bothwell Brig Morton stumbles into a nest of fanatical Cameronians. "He hath burst in like a thief through the window," exclaims Habakkuk Mucklewrath; "he is a ram caught in the thicket, whose blood shall be a drink offering" (Ch. 33). This time Scott strains for an out-and-out nightmare effect; but, as in the former chapter, the responses of the sacrificial ram tend to provoke rather than assuage the intentions of his persecutors. This time it is Claverhouse who comes to the rescue at the last minute. Chapter 33 thus forms the second turning point in the plot, the end of the hero's sojourn with revolution. After such thanks for his services, Morton clearly has no further obligations to the insurgents. The fact that Ephraim Macbriar is present at this scene and consents to the intended slaughter probably accounts for his subsequent torture by the Privy Council.

27. The Denouement

The last eight chapters, in which "Captain" Morton returns as "Major General Melville," have frequently embarrassed even stalwart admirers of *Old Mortality*. The conclusion of *The Heart of Mid-Lothian* rambles on with little reward for the reader; the conclusion to *Old Mortality* rewards the reader too profusely. It consists of a succession of extravagant scenes and stock situations that destroy the narrative illusion. The gratuitous promotion of the hero, his return as a wandering stranger, the unbelievable "ghost" scene, the unspoken parallels to Odysseus[12] but also to Hamlet, the sudden introduction of a new villain, the patience of Evandale, the fidelity of Edith, and the obliteration of Burley in a mist of Satanism and sublime nature are further weakened, if that is possible, by the lapse of ten years, which divide this rush of events from the main and superior part of the action. *Old Mortality*, in short, succumbs to the stock material of fairy tales—but with the important result that the denouement overflows with the-

---

[12] Cf. Christabel F. Fiske, *Epic Suggestion in the Imagery of the Waverley Novels* (New Haven and London, 1940), pp. 2–3.

matic significance. If one can suspend impatience and regret for the failure in quality, the last chapters even supply a certain degree of psychological insight into the hero.

A common villain hardly seems necessary in a romance possessed of such extreme representatives of violence as Burley and Claverhouse. And in fact, Basil Olifant, the villain, never does appear in person except to be shot in the last pages. He is not a mere afterthought, however, but the craven enemy of property who prefers to operate in the shadows. The threat to property gradually supplants the political issues and the resulting melodrama seems to cheapen the achievement of *Old Mortality*. The threat is important, nevertheless, in this particular romance. Henry Morton has taken political risks, but his respect and defense of private property place him above and beyond the insurrection in general. Though the rebellion of 1679 is primarily religious and political, one consequence is that seven of Lady Margaret's tenants have refused to pay their rent (Ch. 12). Morton promises to respect the Bellendens' property (Ch. 25). And Edith Bellenden states that her "private family" is "only in arms for the defence of the established government, and of our own property" (Ch. 29). Property becomes a standard that flies above the temporary conflict—a standard by which both sides can win. It becomes the basis of the historical settlement of 1688. Lord Evandale has already pointed out that even "those in the upper ranks" have become discontented with the present government (Ch. 25). Burley, on the other hand, "treated with contempt the remonstrances of those who reminded him, that the terms granted to the garrison [by Morton] had guaranteed respect for private property" (Ch. 30). He seizes a deed that enables Basil Olifant to possess the estate of Tillietudlem.

Basil Olifant is chiefly characterized as a turncoat. We hear that he changes his political and religious allegiance with every change of the wind: his being consists solely of the greed for property. He thus serves as a foil for the hero, whose concern for property is characteristically unselfish. In fact, the unselfishness of the hero in *Old Mortality* is so pronounced as to approach self-defeat. If one puts aside the doctrine of rights and the process of Morton's involvement in history, the plot of *Old Mortality* can be viewed as a contest in unselfishness between Morton and Lord Evandale—Scott calls it a "race of generosity" (Ch. 24). The entire action consists of a series of payments on debts of honor: Morton shields Burley because Burley has served his father; Evandale intercedes for Morton to oblige Edith; Claverhouse listens because he is indebted to Evandale for some service at the

Privy Council; Morton responds by rescuing Evandale at Drumclog; Burley cannot prevent him because he is obliged to Morton for shelter. Morton then runs significantly ahead in the "race of generosity" by again saving Evandale from certain death (Ch. 28): from this moment Evandale becomes Morton's leading advocate among the various civil authorities and is instrumental in freeing him from complicity in the rebellion. This exchange between the rivals in love continues after the intervention of 1688 and Morton's return from exile. At the cottage of Fairy Knowe, in the most elaborate scene of the denouement, the "dead" hero overhears evidence from her own lips that Edith still loves him, but generously resolves to depart because she is now engaged to Evandale (Chs. 38 and 39).

The latter incident defies every probability of real life, but no scene in the Waverley Novels more nicely defines the meaning of honor. Morton is now "conscious that he was still beloved by Edith, yet compelled, by faith and honour, to relinquish her for ever" (Ch. 39). In other words, honor compels him to maintain the general belief that he is dead. Shortly afterward he consciously longs for death. The sense of honor inexorably opposes the will to live:

> An hundred times he was tempted to burst upon their interview, or to exclaim aloud, "Edith, I yet live!"—and as often the recollection of her plighted troth, and of the debt of gratitude which he owed Lord Evandale (to whose influence with Claverhouse he justly ascribed his escape from torture and from death), withheld him from a rashness which might indeed have involved all in further distress, but gave little prospect of forwarding his own happiness. He repressed forcibly these selfish emotions, though with an agony which thrilled his every nerve.

With his talk of "rashness" and "selfish emotions" Scott is surely editorializing. His argument is hardly objective. He has distorted Morton's "prospect for . . . happiness." If the hero would only exclaim aloud, "Edith, I yet live," he would be more likely to *gain* "his own happiness"—and probably that of the others as well. The scene makes sense only as a triumph of honor, or selflessness, over life itself.

A short soliloquy that follows this extraordinary argument helps to clarify the conflict involved. For one thing, the soliloquy stresses the absolute power of the "plighted troth" even when opposed to human happiness. Scott, of course, is not the only novelist to exaggerate the binding force of such an engagement—the plot of *Sense and Sensibility*, for example, turns on an issue equally nice. Edith's "resolution" to marry Evandale, however reluctant, is a contract—one inseparable promise in the network of relations celebrated by the Waverley Novels. Morton would therefore be wrong to disturb even the factual assumptions on which her resolution is based.

> "No, Edith!" was his internal oath, "never will I add a thorn to thy pillow—That which Heaven has ordained, let it be; and let me not add, by my selfish sorrows, one atom's weight to the burden thou hast to bear. I was dead to thee when thy resolution was adopted; and never—never shalt thou know that Henry Morton still lives!"

Another aspect of the soliloquy is puzzling. What precisely does Morton mean by a thorn in Edith's pillow or the burden she must bear? By such proverbial metaphors he must refer to Edith's particular unhappiness in marrying one she does not love. He would not increase this unhappiness by informing her that she might have married the one she does love. The language may also hint that the sexual aspect of marriage is a disagreeable burden for a woman in any case. Morton, unwilling to add a thorn and a burden, keeps repudiating his "selfish" interest, and we are reminded that honor not only resists life in general but love in particular. The conflict of love and honor is, of course, traditional in romance.

In both of the above passages the expressions "selfish emotions" and "selfish sorrows" can be fairly translated as "sexual interests." One does not expect Scott to use very explicit language in this area; nor is there any reason to insist that he was consciously thinking in sexual terms. The same use of "selfish" can be demonstrated from other contexts in the same chapters. When Evandale proposes that Edith fulfill her engagement immediately, because he is departing on a dangerous adventure, she accuses him of "indelicate importunity. There is more selfishness than generosity, my lord, in such eager and urgent solicitation." When he hastens to point out that his only purpose in marriage is to assure her of his property, in case of his death, Edith sees that "Lord Evandale's suit was urged with delicacy" after all (Ch. 38). Again, in the extravagant final interview of Morton and Burley, "in a situation that appeared equally romantic and precarious," the word "selfish" is used with the same reference. The interview contains an oddly appropriate twist: Burley offers to throw over his alliance with Basil Olifant and surrender the deed of Tillietudlem, if only Morton would seek Edith Bellenden for himself instead of giving her up to Evandale. He thus gives Morton the opportunity to reply, "I came in hopes to persuade you to do a deed of justice to others, not to gain any selfish end of my own" (Ch. 43). This penultimate chapter of *Old Mortality* is itself a concoction of romantic excesses: "the dark mountain-stream made a decided and rapid shoot over the precipice, and was swallowed up by a deep, black, yawning gulf," and the figure of Burley "seemed that of a fiend in the lurid atmosphere of Pandemonium." But down with the torrent pours a surfeit of thematic associations: "selfishness" associated with nature, but also with violence and the devil; the respect for property joined to the belief that "there are some who are willing to sacrifice their happiness to that of others."

Because the hero in the Waverley Novels seeks only to sacrifice himself, some chance event or friendly agent must finally frustrate his intention and operate to his material interest. In *Old Mortality* the villain shoots Lord Evandale, Cuddie Headrigg shoots the villain, and the hero comes to life again (Ch. 44). But *Old Mortality* is a very distinctive romance. Henry Morton becomes more involved in forbidden activities than any other hero; he is also more ambivalent. In the last eight chapters Scott manages to contrive some tension between the rumor that Morton is dead and the palpable fact that he is alive. The hero himself consciously subscribes to the rumor; but unconsciously and in spite of himself, as it were, he desires to live. And in the latter desire he is to some extent successful. This ambivalence explains the ghost scene (Chs. 38 and 39). As Morton secretly departs, resolving "to relinquish her for ever," he attempts "to steal one last glimpse" of Edith through the window of the cottage. But what he actually wishes is not to see Edith but *to be seen*—to signal to her that he is alive. His unconscious wish, if that is what it is, bears fruit: Edith sees him—or his "ghost"—clearly enough to render her unable to marry Evandale. The ghost is doubly interesting because Scott cites in a note a source for the episode in Defoe's *History and Reality of Apparitions*, in which the "ghost" is a male heir about to be deprived of his rightful property.

The explanation that Morton unconsciously hopes to be discovered is an interpolation on my part and not given directly in the text. But the romance abounds in evidence of similar ambivalence on the part of the hero. He is at least partly conscious of it himself. When Morton originally resolves to leave Scotland, he carefully plans to take some "irrevocable step" in that direction *before* saying farewell: "another walk by Edith's side, and my resolution would melt away." And when his resolution is blocked by his uncle, he is "not altogether displeased" (Ch. 6). At the end of the story, wavering between life and death, the hero's secret desire to be recognized—and thus to live—betrays him at every turn. "'Old Alison,' he thought, 'will not know me'"; but when he visits her on that supposition, she of course recognizes him (Ch. 39). He dresses himself in his former clothes—though "it had occurred to him more than once . . . that his resumption of the dress which he had worn while a youth . . . might render it more difficult for him to remain *incognito*" (Ch. 41). In fact, Scott makes use of another ambivalent act to explain Morton's failure to communicate with Scotland during his years of exile:

> During his residence abroad he had once written to Edith. It was to bid her farewell for ever, and to conjure her to forget him. *He had requested her not to answer his letter, yet half hoped, for many a day, that she might transgress his injunction.* The letter never reached her to whom it was addressed, and Morton, ignorant of its miscarriage, could only conclude himself laid aside and forgotten, *according to his own self-denying request.* [Ch. 39; my italics]

Was ever such a hero wooed and wed? Scott invokes in *Old Mortality* not chance alone but chance in conjunction with the dire vagary of the hero. Why, then, did Morton return at all? Why any of this tortured pretense that he is dead? Morton yielded, answers Scott, "to the impulse of an inconsistent wish" (Ch. 39). The same inconsistent wish is at work in the ghost scene. The disconcerting thing about the end of *Old Mortality* is that the hero comes close to a decisive action without knowing it and that Scott comes close to producing a tragedy without knowing it. For the inconsistent wish may operate even when Morton overhears the plot against Evandale's life. What should he do? "To Fairy Knowe? —no; alone I could not protect them. —I must instantly to Glasgow. Wittenbold, the commandant there, will readily give me the support of a troop, and procure me the countenance of the civil power" (Ch. 43). The decision to defer to higher authority is exemplary in the hero of civil society, but fatal to his rival. Wittenbold and the dragoons, "accompanied by Morton and the civil magistrate," arrive too late (Ch. 44). Yet the odds, when Evandale confronts the villains himself, are exactly four against four: the addition of Morton alone would clearly have defeated the murderers without recourse to the authorities. The hero's misjudgment is thoroughly motivated, however, if one takes into account his inconsistent wish.

The final chapters of *Old Mortality* leave the reader in a rather cheerless and helpless state of mind. The very loneliness of the hero is affecting. It overwhelms even the bad taste of the romantic trappings and the excessive improbability of this part of the book. For Morton is engaged in a hopeless circus of fictional contrivances—the high wire of selfless property, the race of generosity, and the contest of life and death. The ideal of civil society endues this dream—or nightmare—with endless thematic significance. But the significance itself seems barren so far as the individual is concerned.

The Waverley Novels would be a curious set of documents if Scott allowed his heroes to complete their several gestures toward death.

Even as the romances stand, the euphoria promised in the final pages is somewhat deathlike. The Waverley Novels are romance, however—the kind of fiction that projects a moral and dreamlike arrangement of things; they are "to the grown man what play is to the child."[13] As in the play of children, even disagreeable emotions are allayed by projecting them into fiction. The only way to cure the heroes' anxieties altogether would be to attack their origins in real life, and that would imply an attack not only on anxiety but on the very premise of the romance, the achieved stability of civilization in property and law—an adjustment tantamount to holding the French Revolution in England. Desires and fears and ideals are also a part of history, and the Waverley Novels originate in a particular age and nation. But they are not narrowly a product of their time either. Edmund Burke was convinced that "it is not a question between France and England; it is a question between property and force."[14] In fiction Scott never directly treats the French or any other revolution of the "horrid servile description," yet the Waverley Novels tell an extraordinary tale of property and force.

[13] Robert Louis Stevenson, "A Gossip on Romance," *Longman's Magazine* 1 (1882): 77.

[14] *Letters on a Regicide Peace*, in *Works*, 5: 325.

CONTRAST OF STYLES IN

THE WAVERLEY NOVELS

S IR WALTER SCOTT'S first novel was begun and then put aside, and a number of beginnings and statements of intent are still discernible in its pages.[1] Intermingled with the hero's nearly involuntary journey toward the highlands, these statements of the literary adventure are one of the attractive things about *Waverley*. The anti-novelistic deliberations of chapter 1, the qualified comparison with Cervantes in chapter 5, the measuring of narrative pace against the claims of historiography in the same chapter, assume for us an importance that Scott could not appreciate in 1814, before the Waverley Novels became a major event in European literature.

One such statement, the opening paragraph of chapter 19, bears on the subject of this essay. It serves as a transition from Waverley's encounter with the cateran, Donald Bean Lean, to the description of the highland chief (and Stuart courtier) Fergus Mac-Ivor. Because the emphasis is now upon the characters the hero meets rather than his own frame of mind, the allusion to Spanish literature is this time to the picaresque rather than the quixotic:

> The ingenious licentiate, Francisco de Úbeda, when he commenced his history of La Picara Justina Diez,—which, by the way, is one of the most rare books of Spanish literature,—complained of his pen having caught up a hair, and forthwith begins, with more eloquence than common sense, an affectionate expostulation with that useful implement, upbraiding it with being the quill of a goose,—a bird inconstant by nature, as frequenting the three elements of water, earth, and air, indifferently, and being, of course, "to one thing constant never." Now I protest to thee, gentle reader, that I entirely dissent from Francisco de Úbeda in this matter, and hold it the most useful quality of my pen, that it can speedily change from grave to gay, and from description and dialogue to narrative and character. So that, if my quill display no other properties of its mother-goose than her mutability, truly I shall be well pleased; and I conceive that you, my worthy friend, will have no occasion for discontent. From the jargon, therefore, of the Highland gillies, I pass to the character of their Chief.

[1] From *NOVEL: A Forum on Fiction* 6 (1973). Copyright © 1973 NOVEL Corp. Reprinted with permission.

The important message here is not the amusing reduction of Scott's narrative inspiration to a mere pen, or, under the same figure, the metempsychosis of his muse as Mother Goose, but the cheerful acknowledgment of the mutability of styles. Though *La pícara Justina* (1605) exploited to some extent the contrast of a low style with the style of its writer and readers, Úbeda viewed his fouled pen and his goose (a duck in the original) as appropriate to the moral inconstancy of the world, not the inconstancy of style. Scott faithfully reproduces the irony of Úbeda—his is only a mock disagreement with a mock expostulation—but he brings the irony to bear on certain technical questions. He refers to the transition "from description and dialogue to narrative and character" and, more importantly, to the determination of style by genre and by social class, according to whether the subject is grave or gay, and having to do with gillies or chiefs. The little moral irony with which Úbeda exposes the real world is as nothing compared with this last problem, which bears directly on the perplexing question of Scott's realism.[2]

Of the alternative methods of representing reality that Erich Auerbach traced in Western literature, the separation and the mixture of styles, Scott instinctively and consciously chose the latter. He regularly assigned a high style to his protagonists and historical personages, and a low style (usually dialect) to the lower ranks of society and the comic characters (who are usually one and the same). The two styles in uncomplicated form—in direct discourse, that is—may be represented by two scenes from *Waverley* that are virtually emblems of the hero's adventures. In that novel one cannot aspire higher in society than the company of Prince Charles: he may be said to provide the climax of the action when he sweeps aside Fergus Mac-Ivor and introduces himself to the hero, with the words, "I beg your pardon for interrupting you, my dear Mac-Ivor; but no master of ceremonies is necessary to present a Waverley to a Stuart" (Ch. 40). That is the high style. There is a still higher style in the Waverley Novels—notably in some of the soliloquies of the gentlemen heroes. Northrop Frye would probably call the Prince's words, and the ordinary address of the heroes, a middle style.[3] But I do not wish to try to untangle middle styles here, since higher and lower are sufficient to establish the contrast in styles that is the important phenomenon.

The low style may be illustrated by a second emblematic scene of the same hero's progress, when Waverley dons his tartans and fighting gear prior to the battle of Preston and turns to ask Callum Beg,

[2] I am grateful to Angel Gonzáles Araúzo for helping to interpret Úbeda's introduction.

[3] *The Well-Tempered Critic* (Bloomington: Indiana University Press, 1963), pp. 93–108.

in straightforward English, "How does it look?" The lowly Callum replies, in dialect, that it looks like the highlander painted on the signboard of a certain inn: "Like the bra' Highlander tat's painted on the board afore the mickle change-house they ca' Luckie Middlemass's" (Ch. 44). Scott explains that Callum intends the comparison as a compliment. But we hear it unmistakably deflate the hero; and in truth it subverts the entire aspect of dressing-up that seems to characterize Waverley's adventure. The dialect and (in this case) unconscious impertinence compensate just as effectively for Callum's inferior social standing as the bullet that he will send after the hero during the march to England. "Waverley," writes Scott, "asked him no farther questions."

Scott's method is never methodical. The assignment of low style to low characters and high style to their superiors in the Waverley Novels is not uniformly consistent. Gentlemen who are treated comically frequently speak a dialect, and gillies may suddenly lapse into precise English. On the journey into the highlands Evan Dhu explains, in dialect, the relation of Donald Bean Lean to his chief—that is, Mac-Ivor—until Waverley makes the mistake of referring to Mac-Ivor as Evan's "master" (Ch. 18). " 'My master?—*My* master is in heaven,' answered Evan haughtily; and then immediately assuming his usual civility of manner—'But you mean my Chief;—no, he does not shelter Donald Bean Lean, nor any that are like him; he only allows him (with a smile) wood and water.' " As soon as the flash of indignation is well passed, however, Evan resumes the dialect: "Ah! but ye dinna see through it. When I say wood and water, I mean the loch and the land," etc. He even retraces his words and translates back into dialect. Quite evidently Scott did not introduce dialect into *Waverley* in order to produce, as if for sociological purposes, a phonetic account of the way such persons spoke. Evan's momentary inconsistency of speech answers a literary purpose—the expression of pride and independence by means of an elevation of style.

But there is a more obvious reason for suspecting that Scott's mixed styles do not derive simply from a principle of verisimilitude, and that reason is Shakespeare. There are perhaps two thousand specific allusions to Shakespeare in the Waverley Novels, but all such allusions together do not add up to a relation between the two writers as important as this mixture of styles. For the novel, between gentlemen and the lower ranks of society, Scott reintroduced what William Empson called the "tragic king—comic people" convention of the dramatist.[4] Roughly the same compromise between classical decorum and medieval realism is reached by Scott as by Shakespeare. High and

---

[4] *Some Versions of Pastoral* (Norfolk, Conn.: New Directions, 1960), p. 41.

low styles are mixed within a single work, but distributed according to the old criteria of genre and of social class.

In his chapter on Shakespeare, Auerbach concedes that the "conception of the sublime and tragic is altogether aristocratic," but calls attention mainly to the very pronounced mixing of styles in the plays, in three important respects: scenes of tragic or public action may alternate with comic scenes; within serious scenes fools and other comic characters "accompany, interrupt, and . . . comment upon what the heroes do, suffer, and say"; and some tragic characters (he is thinking especially of Hamlet and Lear) "have their own innate tendency to break the stylistic tenor in a humorous, realistic, or bitterly grotesque fashion."[5] The interweaving of tragic and comic scenes Scott carries out even in a determinedly tragic story like *The Bride of Lammermoor*, in which the low antics of Caleb Balderston generate an underplot so contrasting in style to the main action that some distinguished readers have been unable to hear its brilliant commentary on the theme of fallen fortunes and lost honor. And this tendency is present, borrowed primarily from Shakespeare's history plays, in Scott's first novel. The chapter that relates the death of Colonel Gardiner, for example, a real historical person whose bravery Scott documents with a note and fixes with a look of reproach at the hero, concludes with the comic catastrophe of the Laird of Balmawhapple. The irreverent account by Lieutenant Jinker, in dialect, is ironically elevated in turn (actually contrasted with the death of Gardiner) by the summary, in the high style, "Such was the elegy of the Laird of Balmawhapple" (Ch. 47). As for Auerbach's second point, the Waverley Novels also contain an extraordinary collection of fools and comic characters who encounter or follow the high characters and comment on the action. The sexton in *The Bride of Lammermoor*, who officiates at weddings with his fiddle and at funerals with his spade, is copied from Shakespeare (the chapter tag is from the grave diggers' scene in *Hamlet*). But again, such characters were boldly forecast in *Waverley* when Scott described Davie Gellatley as "not much unlike one of Shakespeare's roynish clowns" (Ch. 9). Only the last tendency mentioned by Auerbach—the incongruous plunge of a high character into a low style—is not represented in the Waverley Novels: perhaps because Scott, in a relatively more democratic age, was yet more aristocratic and classical in outlook than Shakespeare; or perhaps because, after the French revolution, the gentlemen of England were too apprehensive of the future to tolerate, in fiction, a breach of decorum.

[5] *Mimesis*, trans. Willard R. Trask (Princeton: Princeton University Press, 1953), p. 315.

Such a substantial source as Shakespeare confirms the literary, as opposed to the descriptive or sociological, thrust of Scott's effort, but does not really explain what mixed styles achieve. As in the case of Shakespeare, it is much easier to experience the achievement than to explain it. An explanation is likely to seek some extraliterary dimension of the problem: some inherent condition of society, or possibly, as Auerbach seems to argue, an historical event as compelling as the passion of Christ, in which high and low affairs mingled with centuries-long effect.[6] Georg Lukács argued that, as a great popular writer, "Scott aims at portraying the totality of national life in its complex interaction between 'above' and 'below' "; and that " 'below' is seen as the material basis and artistic explanation for what happens 'above.' " It will be agreed that some such interaction exists in most societies, and Lukács would be the last to argue that its literary portrayal could be narrowly representational or descriptive in a sociological sense. He even has the temerity to use *Ivanhoe* to illustrate his point, and cites the hero and King Richard as belonging "above," and Wamba and Gurth and especially "the leader of the armed resistance," who is Robin Hood, among those "below." And he seems to relay this message, at least momentarily, in terms of the problem of style: "While on the whole the historical tendencies 'above' receive a more distant and generalized expression, we find the true heroism with which the historical antagonisms are fought out, with few exceptions, 'below.' "[7]

It is a little unclear whether Lukács is writing of society or of literary artifice, but I believe he means the latter in relation to the former. He would deny that the totality of society can be described, and would agree that contrast of styles is one way to construct an impression of totality. He discovers the "generalized expression" of that which is "above" in the Waverley Novels, and the materiality of that which is "below." But beyond that, I hesitate to follow him. He may be hinting that the proletariat is always the "material basis" of society, whereas, to the extent that Scott believes that the real force behind events comes from below, he is more likely to be thinking of the fist of Dandie Dinmont that in *Guy Mannering* can deliver a blow "which an ox could hardly have received without the same humiliation" as the smuggler who is attempting to prevent the hero's escape (Ch. 48). Moreover, the "generalized expression" of force exerted by the

---

[6] *Mimesis*, pp. 40–49; and *Dante: Poet of the Secular World*, trans. Ralph Manheim (Chicago: University of Chicago Press, 1961), pp. 11–20.

[7] *The Historical Novel*, trans. Hannah and Stanley Mitchell (London: Merlin Press, 1962), p. 49.

nobility is illogically contrasted by Lukács with the guts of the lower ranks, not their style. He too willingly confuses verisimilitude and certain moral values that he shares with Scott, as when he writes on the following page of *The Historical Novel* that "Historical authenticity means for [Scott] the quality of the inner life, the morality, heroism, capacity for sacrifice, steadfastness, etc. peculiar to a given age."

What actually results from the contrast of styles in the Waverley Novels is much more problematic than even Lukács suggests, and it has to be studied first in the technical achievement rather than in a vision of society. Scott believed as firmly in the difference of social ranks as any Marxist can with good countenance believe, but his stylistic account of this difference is nearly always ironic. The low style in the novels invests the serious action with vitality, but not typically by the kind of direct contribution made by Dandie Dinmont's fist. More often the low style assures the vitality of the whole by making the serious action struggle to be heard. The low style competes with the high, and in memorable scenes nearly overwhelms its seriousness.

The Heart of Mid-Lothian well repays study in this respect. The seriousness here comes not from "above" but from the deliberate descent to humble life that characterizes this novel. The crisis of extramarital love and pregnancy that forms the subject of one of the early chapters is something that Scott would not think of introducing among his other heroes and heroines, and he uses the lowliness of the protagonists to heighten the dignity of his subject. " 'To be come of honest folk' . . . is an advantage as highly prized among the lower Scotch, as the emphatic counterpart, 'to be of a good family,' is valued among their gentry. The worth and respectability of one member of a peasant's family is always accounted by themselves and others, not only a matter of honest pride, but a guarantee for the good conduct of the whole" (Ch. 12). But once he has established the high seriousness of the lower Scotch and has introduced Reuben Butler to the cottage with his melodramatic message for Jeanie from George "Robertson," Scott virtually surrenders his chapter to the comic encounter of Bartoline Saddletree and David Deans. A great dialectic in dialect takes place between the amateur enthusiasts of religion and of law. To read the chapter carefully is an hilarious experience. Yet Scott dares use it to forward his serious action; he creates within it sufficient suspense with which to conclude the first volume of the 1818 edition; and he puts over the serious content in competition with two of the most compulsive dialecticians in the Waverley Novels. Somehow the distress and predicament of David Deans emerge clearly because they are so nearly buried in endless discourse. Seriousness becomes real through the struggle to be heard, as dullness and sorrow drag at the sheer verbal energy of the encounter and produce sudden silences.

The low style is characterized by the obtrusiveness of things, and by the freedom to descend to details. This is why the catalogue is a prominent device in the dialect passages. What is your General Assembly, demands David Deans, "but a waefu' bunch o' cauldrife professors and ministers, that sate bien and warm when the persecuted remnant were warstling wi' hunger, and cauld, and fear of death, and danger of fire and sword, upon wet brae-sides, peat-haggs, and flow-mosses, and that now creep out of their holes, like bluebottle flees in a blink of sunshine, to take the pu'pits and places of better folk—of them that witnessed, and testified, and fought, and endured pit, prison-house, and transportation beyond seas?" The more unnecessary the piled-up detail, the more it obtrudes itself in the name of reality. Saddletree gropes in his pocket for the indictment against Effie Deans and comes up with the wrong document: "This is no it—this is the information of Mungo Marsport, of that ilk, against Captain Lackland, for coming on his lands of Marsport with hawks, hounds, lying-dogs, nets, guns, cross-bows, hagbuts of found, or other engines more or less for destruction of game, sic as red-deer, fallow-deer, cappercailzies, grey-fowl, moor-fowl, paitricks, herons, and sic like . . ." (Ch. 12). Such catalogues of irrelevant detail always verge on the unpredictable, since it is never certain what they will include or where they are tending. They halt when the speaker runs out of breath.

Mischance, the unpredictable aspect of things, is closely associated with the low style. When Waverley departs from his own society and from the company of those who speak in his own style, he stumbles into a world of accident as well as romance. When Guy Mannering loses his way at the beginning of Scott's second novel, the advice given him by a cottager makes the way seem more precarious than do the dark and the sound of the sea. "Ow, man! ye should hae hadden *eassel* to Kippletringan—ye maun gae back as far as the Whaap, and haud the Whaap till ye come to Ballenloan, and then————" (Ch. 1). Unintelligible local directions, in dialect, become the standard joke that Scott refines in *Old Mortality* in the person of Goose Gibbie, whose misdirections affect the action so decisively that he begins to represent the accidental in human history. "Upon this ludicrous incident," wrote Scott in his own review of "Tales of My Landlord"—referring merely to the first of Gibbie's mishaps—"turns the fate . . . of the principal personages of the drama."[8]

Scott represents ongoing life in its stubborn obtrusiveness and mis-

---

[8] *Quarterly Review* 16 (1817): 448.

chance by means of his low style, but if this vitality is the "material basis" for the main action, it is so obliquely and indirectly. The low style is a foil for the high. Since it is unfamiliar to the hero, it may even sound to his stiff upper ear the note of danger, as when Waverley hears the foreign chatter of the highlanders around him at Preston and is frightened by the forces on his own side. He is equally intimidated by the unfamiliar Biblical style of Gifted Gilfillan, the first of Scott's Covenanters. "I wish the young gentleman may be safe with him," the kindly Mr. Morton exclaims to the magistrate who commits the hero to Gilfillan's charge (Ch. 32). Similarly, the scene of Henry Morton's arrest in *Old Mortality* is one of Scott's astonishing amalgams of low with high styles, comedy with political principle, local accident with complication of the public and private action. And no one would deny that Mause Headrigg's irrepressible voice, a composite of Scottish dialect and Covenanting jargon borrowed from the Bible, constitutes at first a potential and then an actual threat to the hero. Due to his heritage, his principles and feelings, the position of Henry Morton is already ambivalent; the intrusion of the low style at this critical juncture circumscribes this ambivalence with materiality and makes it suddenly consequential. Scott repeatedly shows that his heroes are victims of circumstances, but to dramatize circumstances most effectively he employs direct discourse in the low style. The outbursts of Mause Headrigg are endangering because they provoke the government as well as amuse the reader, and because they correspond in some way to the hero's private resentment of his situation. The story of Cuddie Headrigg and Jenny Dennison in *Old Mortality*, the most carefully developed underplot in the Waverley Novels, operates by contrasting style and parallel action to explain and make real the history of Morton and Edith Bellenden. It is just as inadequate to say of Scott as of Shakespeare, that scenes of comedy in the low style are brought in to supply "comic relief" from the serious action. Comic relief relieves to the extent that it criticizes or drives home the superior action.

Almost all Scott's low characters are impertinent. What they speak in dialect draws itself up against the high style and the assurance of life that the high style connotes. There is nothing intrinsically funny about dialect, and yet almost every line in dialect in the Waverley Novels is pointed and entertaining, because it punctures the high style and the reader's accustomed level of hearing. Scott usually guarantees this effect by making sure that what the low character says is pointed, critical, and even affronting—apart from the way he says it. Mause Headrigg and Caleb Balderston, or Andrew Fairservice in *Rob Roy*, are much more typical Scott creations than Wamba and Gurth, and even the latter have a certain impertinence. And impertinence is a relation, not a quality of mind; it does not exist in itself, but as it violates social propriety or accepted thought. Its equivalent in the theory of style is the breach of decorum or uniformity, and it is therefore the characterological equivalent of the contrast of styles.

The best way to understand the relation of impertinence in the Waverley Novels is to think about dialect jokes. Dialect jokes clearly reflect the classical criteria, of genre and social class, for the differentiation of styles. They may be told for or against an inferior or minority class. The scurrilous dialect joke exalts the joker by excluding and deprecating the inferior class: even Scott and Shakespeare are guilty of this kind of joke, when they create for a gull or scoundrel some mock French, or German, or Dutch accent. The better kind of dialect joke deprecates the majority or more powerful class by excluding *them* from the minority. The joker may come from either class. Even when a dialect joke is told by a minority, for or against itself, the principle of exclusion still operates: the joke may express pride of nationality or contempt of self, but always the difference of social groups. Hence there is an appropriate mixture of styles. The joke may be related entirely in dialect, but by a speaker and for an audience who ordinarily employ some ostensibly higher style. To assure a contrast of style, however, the typical dialect joke does not need to make itself heard against the normal speech of the audience. The necessary two styles are built into the narrative of the joke, and the speaker modulates from one to the other. For dramatic purposes the thickest dialect is crowded into the end of the joke, along with the impertinence. Here is where the licentiousness occurs, and sometimes only here, if the joke has a single impact. As the decorous becomes indecorous, the low style comes into play. So much is this the case that frequently, in a gathering of a clan dedicated to the retailing of such jokes, an outsider can understand all but the last line, which may pass the region of dialect straight into a foreign language.

One can perceive just this kind of joke in a well-known passage from *The Heart of Mid-Lothian*:

> "The case of Effie (or Euphemia) Deans," resumed Saddletree, "is one of those cases of murder presumptive, that is, a murder of the law's inferring or construction, being derived from certain *indicia* or grounds of suspicion."
>
> "So that," said the good woman, "unless poor Effie has communicated her situation, she'll be hanged by the neck, if the bairn was still-born, or if it be alive at this moment?"
>
> "Assuredly," said Saddletree, "it being a statute made by our Sovereign Lord and Lady, to prevent the horrid delict of bringing forth children

in secret—The crime is rather a favourite of the law, this species of mur-
ther being one of its ain creation."

"Then, if the law makes murders," said Mrs. Saddletree, "the law
should be hanged for them; or if they wad hang a lawyer instead, the
country wad find nae faut." (Ch. 5)

The collision of Mrs. Saddletree's remark about lawyers with the
pseudolegal style of her husband need not be stressed; but the contrast of that last remark, in dialect, with her own language leading up
to it, is a trick that is almost concealed from us. Mrs. Saddletree ordinarily speaks in dialect, but here her normal speech is suppressed so
that it can break out afresh in the punch line. Until that line, only
the word "bairn" and possibly "if it be alive" signal her dialect; and
one clause, "unless poor Effie has communicated her situation," is so
patently in the high style that it easily balances these two signs of the
low. The last speech, moreover, is neatly divided between an independent clause in the high style that states the justice of her position and
another in the low style that makes it concrete (a lawyer instead of
the law) and gives it a personal and national animosity. I do not believe Scott had to try very hard to write in this way, and yet the effect
is brilliant. The impertinence not only goes straight to the main issue
of this novel, the law presumptive that in effect legislates the existence of a crime, but also hits at the particular use of hanging por-
trayed in *The Heart of Mid-Lothian.* Just as Porteous is hanged for all tyrants, and Effie to be hanged for all unwed mothers without children,
one lawyer would satisfy Mrs. Saddletree for all law—and possibly all
husbands.

There is one famous speech in *The Heart of Mid-Lothian* that would
seem to be very far from being a joke: Jeanie Deans's plea to Queen
Caroline to remit the death penalty against Effie, which concluded
the third volume in the 1818 edition. The awesome difference in
rank between Jeanie and the Queen calls for a very dignified use of
the low style: in order to lay bare the high style in which the speech is
actually constructed and to show where the overlay of dialect has
been concentrated, I shall transcribe the spellings that indicate a dialect pronunciation into cognate English forms, in brackets.

"If it like you, madam," said Jeanie, "I would [have gone] to the end of
the earth to save the life of John Porteous, or any other unhappy man in
his condition; but I might lawfully doubt how far I am called upon to be
the avenger of his blood, though it may become the civil magistrate to
do so. He is dead and [gone] to his place, and they that have slain him
must answer for their [own] act. But my sister, my [poor] sister, Effie,
still lives, though her days and hours are numbered! She still lives, and a

word of the King's mouth might restore her to a broken-hearted [old] man, that never, in his daily and nightly exercise, forgot to pray that his Majesty might be blessed with a long and a prosperous reign, and that his throne, and the throne of his posterity, might be established in righteousness. O madam, if ever [you knew] what it was to sorrow for and with a sinning and a suffering creature, whose mind is [so] tossed that she can be neither [called] fit to live or die, have some compassion on our misery!—Save an honest house from dishonour, and an unhappy girl, not eighteen years of age, from an early and dreadful death! Alas! it is not when we sleep soft and wake merrily ourselves, that we think on other people's sufferings. Our hearts are waxed light within us then, and we are for righting our [own wrongs] and fighting our [own] battles. But when the hour of trouble comes to the mind or to the body—and seldom may it visit your [Ladyship]—and when the hour of death comes, that comes to high and low—[long] and late may it be yours!— Oh, my [Lady], then it [isn't] what we [have done] for [ourselves], but what we [have done] for others, that we think on [most] pleasantly. And the thoughts that [you have] intervened to spare the [poor] thing's life will be sweeter in that hour, come when it may, than if a word of your mouth could hang the [whole] Porteous mob at the [end of one rope]." (Ch. 37)

The dialect spellings that I have replaced are, in order: *hae gaen, gane, ain, puir, auld, ye kend, sae, ca'd, ain wrangs, ain, Leddyship, lang, Leddy, isna, hae dune, oursells, hae dune, maist, ye hae, puir, haill, tail of ae tow.* A glance at the speech will show that fully half of these indications are concentrated in the last two sentences, or one fourth of the entire speech. A number of words (*so, called, ourselves, long*) occur twice in the speech, first in English and then in dialect. By this simple index the famous plea of Jeanie Deans before the Queen has the common pattern of a dialect joke. I do not mean to overlook some other slight indications of dialect in the grammar or the three or four suggestions of the Bible—"avenger of his blood," "days and hours are numbered," "established in righteousness," "waxed light within us"—with which Scott characterizes his heroine. But the increasing weight of dialect is clear, especially in the peroration. Not once, in transcribing the dialect spellings into accepted English, have I needed to use anything but a cognate form—until the last phrase, "the tail of ae tow," which is figurative, concrete, and a thoroughly local expression.

Moreover, the last clause of the speech is impertinent. Hanging the murderers of Porteous is just what the Queen would like to do, and the phrase in dialect belittles that ambition. The Queen's wishes are both exaggerated (to "hang the haill Porteous mob") and made small ("at the taill of ae tow"). Jeanie knows the identity and whereabouts of the principal murderer; and the Queen has uncannily hinted that Jeanie knows. Recourse to a joke permits the low character to duck the issue and stand up to the high. Jeanie's rational argument for closing the social distance between herself and the Queen is sententious and is spoken in what Frye calls the "high demotic" style: the argument, namely, that death comes "to high and low" alike. That argument, too, contains a threat, but not a threat pointed by Jeanie herself. Jeanie's last clause, on the other hand, returns more aggressively to the subject of hanging, with something of the feeling expressed in Mrs. Saddletree's joke. The recourse to dialect signals the difference in social class, and the humor bridges this difference.

Scott does not make Jeanie deliver this speech in as disembodied a way as I have given it here. He mentions her tears and "her features glowing and quivering with emotion"; and there is also the appeal of her cleanly dress, which is remarked frequently in the novel and might be said to be in the "low hieratic" style. Nevertheless, Jeanie manages to please and persuade the Queen by means of something like a dialect joke, and there is also impertinence here. The entire interview begins with an unconscious hit at the Queen ("there are mony places besides Scotland where mothers are unkind to their ain flesh and blood") and another at Lady Suffolk, who is also present ("for light life and conversation, and for breaking the seventh command"). Such impertinence can only add to the unconscious irony of the Queen's final rejoinder to Jeanie's speech, in the high style: " 'This is eloquence,' said her Majesty to the Duke of Argyle."

The daring of Scott, in this matter of the contrast of styles, should not be underestimated. Another exceptional heroine, Lucy Ashton, speaks in the high style throughout *The Bride of Lammermoor*. Then the shrill and piercing cry is heard on her wedding night, the family rush into the bridal chamber, discover the husband, wounded, lying athwart the door, and Lucy insane and dabbled with blood in the corner of the chimney. Bucklaw is carried off and then Lucy—"not without the use of some force." As they carry her over the threshold, she looks down and exclaims: "So, you have ta'en up your bonny bridegroom?" (Ch. 34). The contrast of this style with everything she has said before is complete. She has never before exhibited the least tendency to speak in dialect, nor has she ever uttered the least irony or resentment. Scott adapted the line from his source, which he gives in the 1830 introduction to the novel as, "Tak up your bonny bridegroom." Like the teller of a dialect joke (a rather grim one this time) he keeps the dialect out of hearing until the last dramatic moment. All of the impertinence that poor Lucy Ashton can muster has to be compressed in a single line. The descent in style signifies her madness, but her madness cannot conceal—indeed, it reveals—her protest. Dialect now excludes from her company forever each principal character of her story, not excepting the Master of Ravenswood. In terms of the ancestral and historical themes of this novel, dialect seems to link the heroine with the uncultured past. The Master perishes and she becomes, as the title suggests, the bride of the place. Her one line in dialect recalls similar lines in the border ballads, which often stab from below in the same way.

Much of what I am saying is not new. Any literary history informs us that Scott was a close student of the English drama and that he caused dialogue and dialect to become staples of novel-writing. What students of the novel continue to ignore, even after the advances of the last ten years, is that there is a Scott problem. We know that the Waverley Novels are, with Shakespeare's plays, one of the two largest exports of English literature; that they contributed in some immeasurable way to nineteenth-century realism as well as historical romance. But we understand very little of what the Waverley Novels are like or how they exerted this influence. We do not understand, even after Edgar Johnson's comprehensive biography,[9] why Scott's personal interest in drama, in romance, in balladry, in anecdote, and in jokes was compatible with his interest in history and in politics, or how his literary ambition squared with his ironic self-deprecation. To put it bluntly, we understand not the origin, the nature, or the result of Scott's realism. Students of the novel should therefore try to put together what we have learned about Scott's themes and their historical context with a study of his narrative methods. Scott himself was a deeply experienced student of literature and not the least of our critics of the novel. His transformation of Úbeda's expostulation to his pen into an apology for the mixture of styles shows him aware, from the writing of *Waverley*, of the literary contrivance in his representation of reality. The inclusive picture of society in the Waverley Novels does not result from a collection of data from all walks of life, but from the contrast of styles. To what extent is this true also of nineteenth-century realism, at least until the Armageddon of style in Joyce's *Ulysses*? If there is some truth in what Empson said of English drama—that it may not have outlived the double plot—it may be no less true to say that the English novel has not outlived the contrast of styles.

[9] *Sir Walter Scott: The Great Unknown*, 2 vols. (New York: Macmillan, 1970). My review can be found in *Studies in Scottish Literature* 9 (1971): 59–66.

HISTORY AND REVOLUTION IN

OLD MORTALITY

S COTT HELPED to create a history or myth for his own time, but he was also a serious historian of past times and particular places. As Fredric Jameson has observed, historical novels have built into them a formula for realism, since the fictional part always invites comparison with a reputed external reality: "The very structure of our reading of the historical novel involves comparison, involves a kind of judgment of being."[1] In order to study Scott's achievement as an historical novelist and his contribution to realism, clearly one should not try to generalize about his entire output, because generalization quickly blurs this sort of comparison and judgment. The following essay therefore returns to a single text, *Old Mortality*—a great novel in its own right and, as it happens, the text that Georg Lukács seems to have had most in mind when he wrote on Scott in *The Historical Novel*.[2]

By birth and temperament Lukács was much closer to a nineteenth-century critical perspective than appears from his current readership. His books were simply not available in English until well after World War II. *The Historical Novel* was first published in a Russian translation in 1937 and only twenty-five years later in English. In some ways the outlook of the book seems older still. Lukács's theory of the novel as a genre was Hegelian; he saw the Waverley Novels through the eyes of Balzac and appreciated their contribution to history much as Augustin Thierry did. Some of his views were adopted from the lesser-known Otto Ludwig, whose novel studies were chiefly directed at the English practice of Scott, Dickens, and George Eliot.[3] Without doubt, *The Historical Novel* is solidly based in bourgeois as well as Marxist opinion, and this eclecticism can only be helpful in approaching the novelist whom it champions.

Lukács recognizes that Scott's idea of history cannot be met with in some explicit theory but only in his practice. He argues that this idea rises above any personal prejudice (the politics of the novelist and

---

[1] Fredric Jameson, *Marxism and Form: Twentieth-Century Dialectical Theories of Literature* (Princeton: Princeton University Press, 1971), p. 196.

[2] Georg Lukács, *The Historical Novel*, trans. Hannah and Stanley Mitchell (London: Merlin, 1962).

[3] Otto Ludwig, *Romane und Romanstudien*, ed. William J. Lillyman (Munich: Hanser, 1977), pp. 533–672.

the critic are hardly in sympathy) as well as any tendencies toward romanticism, in which he sees the decline of the historical novel after Scott. He is quick to point out that Scott does not write directly of the present or "raise the social questions of contemporary England in his novels."[4] These are important concessions, since for Lukács as for many moderns the test of historicism is conceiving of the present as occurring in historical time.[5] He firmly believes that historicism is endemic in literary realism itself. "Thus with Balzac the historical novel which in Scott grew out of the English social novel, returns to the presentation of contemporary society"; and precisely because realism has been the end of novel-writing all along, "the age of the classical historical novel is therewith closed." For Lukács—and this may be his most important lesson for the study of literature in English—the historical novel is not a genre apart but a phase of realism.

> Its classical form arises out of the great social novel and then, enriched by a conscious historical attitude, flows back into the latter. On the one hand, the development of the social novel first makes possible the historical novel; on the other, the historical novel transforms the social novel into a genuine history of the present, an authentic history of manners, something which the novel of the eighteenth century was already striving for in the works of its most eminent representatives.[6]

"Genuine" and "authentic," I take it, because there is no other mode but the historical for comprehending social existence. Though the teleology of Lukács's thought may be apparent—realism is the end of the novel—such passages provide a sharp corrective to the careless way of thinking that isolates Scott's achievement from the history of the novel. In the nineteenth century, one did not have to be a Marxist to appreciate these continuities.[7]

Lukács scorns the old-fashioned search for sources and games of precedence. The modern consciousness of history arose in many minds of different nations at roughly the same time. "It is certain that Scott had no knowledge of Hegel's philosophy," he writes, "and had he come across it would probably not have understood a word. The new historical conception of the great historians of the Restoration actually makes its appearance later than the works of Scott and some of its problems are influenced by them." He is aware of the stirrings

---

[4] Lukács, *The Historical Novel*, p. 33.

[5] Cf. Jameson, *Marxism and Form*, pp. 320–22.

[6] Lukács, *The Historical Novel*, pp. 85, 169.

[7] For Lukács, however, "realism is not one style among others, it is the basis of literature." See *The Meaning of Contemporary Realism*, trans. John and Necke Mander (London: Merlin, 1962), p. 48.

of the Scottish enlightenment—if only because, as a Marxist, he is bound to know of Adam Smith. But these stirrings were "a product of realistic instinct and did not amount to a clear understanding of history as a process, of history as the concrete precondition of the present."[8] That this last remark is too offhand has been made clear by at least two recent critics who argue that the teaching of Scottish philosophers *about* history made a direct impression on the Waverley Novels.[9] But not surprisingly Lukács several times stresses Goethe's relation to Scott, whose first publication was a somewhat rocky translation of *Götz von Berlichingen*.[10] He is also thoroughly cognizant of the military and political conditions that enforced a new interest in history, though here his emphasis is mainly French. Enlightenment histories of the classical world helped clear an intellectual path for the French Revolution, which then gave a tremendous and varied impetus to history writing in the following century. The reasons for that outpouring of history have been summarized by Lionel Gossman as follows:

> The role of history in the political programs of the first half of the nineteenth century was crucial. By discovering the hidden anonymous history of the nation beneath the outmoded histories of its rulers and its narrow ruling class, historians were expected to provide the legitimation of a new political order, a new state, and at the same time to impose the idea of this state on the consciousness of its citizens. Since history's objective was at once revolutionary (to furnish a basis for a new political order) and conservative (to found and authorize that order by revealing it to be the culmination of a continuous historical development, albeit a long-concealed, underground one), part of its aim was to achieve in itself a reconciliation of the investigative and disruptive practice of historical scholarship with the narrative art that establishes connections and asserts continuities.[11]

Upon this well-prepared ground fell the Waverley Novels, with their own husks and kernels of history, though whether the novels flour-

---

[8] Lukács, *The Historical Novel*, pp. 30, 21.

[9] Avrom Fleishman, *The English Historical Novel: Walter Scott to Virginia Woolf* (Baltimore: Johns Hopkins University Press, 1971), pp. 37–54; and John MacQueen, *The Enlightenment and Scottish Literature*, vol. II: *The Rise of the Historical Novel* (Edinburgh: Scottish Academic Press, 1989), pp. 8–13, 30–37.

[10] See G. H. Needler, *Goethe and Scott* (Toronto: Oxford University Press, 1950), for a more specific though rambling account of the relationship.

[11] Lionel Gossman, "Jules Michelet and Romantic Historiography," in *Between History and Literature* (Cambridge, Mass.: Harvard University Press, 1990), p. 153. Gossman notes that he read Lukács's *Der Historische Roman* as a student in Glasgow in 1947 (p. 2).

ished more because of their specific historical actions or because of the promise of stability they conveyed is another matter.

Against Lukács, I believe that the fable of the Waverley Novels was a double one: action and change occur only in past times, whereas the relation of things as they stand, enhanced by the prescriptive right to property, is conceived as more or less unchanging.[12] Lukács recognizes the double fable of history in the nineteenth century, but following Marx he attributes it to bourgeois humanism. "The important bourgeois humanists of this period find themselves in a paradoxical situation: while they comprehend the necessity of revolutions in the past and see in them the foundation for all that is reasonable and worthy of affirmation in the present, nevertheless they interpret future development in terms of a henceforth peaceful evolution on the basis of these achievements."[13] Lukács admires the Waverley Novels too much, however, to pin this label on their author. Thus he may argue that progress for Scott is "always a process full of contradictions, the driving force and material basis of which is the living contradiction between conflicting historical forces, the antagonisms of classes and nations." A "living" contradiction suggests, without quite pointing to any grounds for the idea in the novels, that change will continue into the future, obedient to dialectical materialism. Later, in contrasting the novelist with Balzac, he tempers this judgment considerably by noting that "Scott himself lived in a period of English history in which the progressive development of bourgeois society seemed assured, and thus he could look back upon the crises and struggles of the prehistory with epic calm."[14] Lukács is right about the epic calm and perfectly just in finding such a double outlook on history paradoxical. The irony is that nineteenth-century doctrines of history, including the Marxist, all share in this paradoxical thinking insofar as they posit both progress and an end to progress.[15]

It is principally dialectical thinking that allows Lukács to assimilate such conservative writers as Scott and Balzac to his version of history in the first place. Even so, he obviously values the specific interpreta-

---

[12] Cf. Alexander Welsh, *Reflections on the Hero as Quixote* (Princeton: Princeton University Press, 1981), pp. 130–48.

[13] Lukács, *The Historical Novel*, p. 29. In his essay "Class Consciousness," Lukács quotes Marx's caricature of the bourgeois idea: "Thus there has been history, but there no longer is any." See *History and Class Consciousness: Studies in Marxist Dialectics*, trans. Rodney Livingstone (Cambridge, Mass.: MIT Press, 1971), p. 48.

[14] Lukács, *The Historical Novel*, pp. 53, 84.

[15] Cf. Mircea Eliade, *The Myth of the Eternal Return*, trans. Willard R. Trask (New York: Pantheon, 1954), p. 149; and my "Opening and Closing *Les Misérables*," *Nineteenth-Century Fiction* 33 (1978): 8–23.

tions of the past that he finds in the Waverley Novels. These he treats, from their pastness, as so many demonstrations of necessity, with tragic implications for individuals:

> Scott then becomes a great poet of history because he has a deeper, more genuine and differentiated sense of historical necessity than any writer before him. Historical necessity in his novels is of the most severe, implacable kind. Yet this necessity is no otherworldly fate divorced from men; it is the complex interaction of concrete historical circumstances in their process of transformation, in their interaction with the concrete human beings, who have grown up in these circumstances, have been variously influenced by them, and who act in an individual way according to their personal passions. Thus, in Scott's portrayal, historical necessity is always a resultant, never a presupposition; it is the tragic atmosphere of a period and not the object of the writer's reflections.[16]

One quality of the novels registered here is their secularism. Scott was so respectful of established Christianity, so tolerant of dissenters (despite his humor at their expense), so sympathetic with Catholicism or Jewishness in females, that we may no longer appreciate the degree to which the Author of Waverley ought to come across as a voice of the Enlightenment. Thus, for example, his novels affected "the first unsettlement" of Mary Ann Evans's faith.[17] Lukács is also picking up the freedom from prejudice that Scott at his best conveys. The novels account for many circumstances, many individual courses, without the imposition of "the writer's reflections." In the very repetition of "necessity," however, can be heard the critic's own doctrine of history, a teleology of things to come. Scott's teleology approaches safely to the present, with a sense of necessity more akin to the bourgeois humanist distinction between past and future. With few exceptions the principal action in each novel is comic rather than tragic. Necessity is a premise frequently called upon, but always as a constraining leash upon events rather than a force, "resultant" or otherwise. In the same vein Edmund Burke allowed that necessity might bring about a revolution, but instanced the Revolution of 1688. "*Necessity*, in the strictest moral sense in which necessity can be taken," Burke admitted as a justification of the British revolution, peaceable and a safe number of generations in the past.[18] "Necessity" was a word to conjure

---

[16] Lukács, *The Historical Novel*, p. 58.

[17] J. W. Cross, *George Eliot's Life as Related in Her Letters and Journals*, 3 vols. (New York: Merrill and Baker, n.d.), 1: 369.

[18] *Reflections on the Revolution in France*, in *The Works of Edmund Burke*, 12 vols. (Boston: Little, Brown, 1865–1871), 3: 254.

with well before dialectical materialism, but it was then conjured with rather differently. Radical and conservative assumptions of inevitability stop history at widely different stations, future and past.[19]

When Lukács writes of Scott's heroes, he concedes that "petty aristocratic-conservative prejudices" may have played a part in their composition. But this he admits only in passing, since he believes that the choice of such unheroic heroes "is the clearest proof of Scott's exceptional and revolutionary epic gifts." He immediately observes that the hero's passivity signifies "a renunciation of Romanticism, a conquest of Romanticism." His approach to the hero, derived from Hegel and from Otto Ludwig, is generic rather than historical—that is, it is historical only in the broad sense that the modern novel has supplanted the ancient epic. The hero's role is dictated by the kind of fiction he serves, and in novels he stands for the ongoing life shared by others. In historical drama one finds high moments of history and world-historical characters; in novels, the portrait of an age, "held together at the centre by the historical novel's 'middle-of-the-road hero.' " As Lukács explains, "those very social and human characteristics which banish such figures from drama or permit them only a subordinate, episodic role, qualify them for their central position in the historical novel."[20] He spells out this thesis with considerable subtlety and touches only lightly the argument, ventured by Scott himself, that this hero is a mere convenience to authors and their readers. Lukács's generic view of the matter is certainly more persuasive than any thesis that attempts to explain away the hero. But he gains very little by ignoring the hero's politics, which are in no way inconsistent with his generic role, or for that matter, with some future peasant or proletarian revolution. Lukács seems only wistful or sentimental in his apology for conservative prejudices in the Author of Waverley, since these prejudices (Scott would think of them as principles) constitute the theme of the novels and hold them together "at the centre." Lukács's determination to overlook the politics, one might say, results in neglect of the plot.

Many of Lukács's insights are confirmed and others qualified by *Old Mortality*, a novel about revolution. Specifically, *Old Mortality* describes events in the west of Scotland in the month of June 1679. More broadly, it concerns the Revolution of 1688. Near the end a

---

[19] Cf. Fredric Jameson, *The Political Unconscious: Narrative as a Socially Symbolic Act* (Ithaca: Cornell University Press, 1981), pp. 19–20, 101–2.

[20] Lukács, *The Historical Novel*, pp. 33, 128.

span of ten years is omitted from the narrative, which starts over again "in a new era, being the year immediately subsequent to the British Revolution" (Ch. 37). Thus the time scheme quite blatantly responds to one of the distinctions Lukács draws between drama and novel: whereas drama treats the crises of history, "the novel portrays more what happens before and after these crises, showing the broad interaction between popular basis and visible peak."[21] Scott did not confine himself to facts, as facts are generally understood, but by focusing especially on some lesser-known events prior to 1688 he was able to construct a model of revolution. Though the model is concrete and specific to Scotland, it raises important questions right and left.[22] Can political authority be supplanted by a force that has no preexistent authority of its own? Is revolution a decision on the part of certain leaders or an event beyond their control? Is political murder, committed for or against the state, a justifiable recourse? To employ force against a government or against a people is to kill in order to attain one's ends, but the nice question of whether the end justifies the means becomes, in the moment of revolution, a series of worrisome decisions about details.

The wider events adumbrated in *Old Mortality* can be summarized as follows. The Restoration of Charles II in 1660 signaled the return in Scotland of the earlier Stuart policy of direct interference with church polity and ritual. In the years that followed, the country was ruled through the Scottish Privy Council, which chiefly occupied itself with the punishment of religious recusants. By 1666, the year of the Pentland Rising, the practice of holding conventicles, or field meetings, had been forced on the Presbyterians. The Duke of Lauderdale, now the most powerful agent of the king in Scotland, briefly adopted a more conciliatory stance and issued letters of "indulgence," which permitted ministers to return to their churches if they acknowledged the episcopacy and the supremacy of the crown. Few ministers responded, however, and the repressive measures of the government increased.[23] Landowners and masters were held responsible for the conformity of their tenants and servants; certain offenders were intercommuned, and then it became an offense to associate with them. The more extreme Presbyterians—or Covenanters, as they

---

[21] Ibid., p. 150.

[22] On such make-believe history, or what I refer to as modeling, see David Brown, *Walter Scott and the Historical Imagination* (London: Routledge, 1979), pp. 173–83. Brown also carefully positions himself with respect to Lukács (pp. 195–209).

[23] See Richard L. Greaves, *Enemies under his Feet: Radicals and Nonconformists in Britain, 1664–1677* (Stanford: Stanford University Press, 1990), pp. 49–103, 235–41.

were called, from their hope to restore the solemn League and Covenant of 1643—began to carry arms to their conventicles in self-defense. On 3 May 1679, James Sharp, the Archbishop of St. Andrews, was murdered in Fife. On 29 May, at Rutherglen near Glasgow, about eighty persons publicly burned the most hated acts of the Council. This group formed the nucleus of the insurgents at Drumclog, where on 1 June they repulsed an attack by John Grahame of Claverhouse, more or less as described in the novel. The victory over government troops drew more Presbyterians to arms, and for a brief while they were able to occupy Glasgow. But on 22 June they were decisively defeated at Bothwell Bridge on the Clyde. In 1681 James, Duke of York, succeeded Lauderdale as Royal Commissioner for Scotland, and the government continued to busy itself with the remaining hard-core Covenanters. After the succession of James to the throne in 1685, the issue of Catholicism brought opposition to the monarchy to a head both in England and in Scotland; by the end of 1688, London and Edinburgh were filled with supporters of William of Orange.[24]

The Revolution of 1688 was only superficially a dynastic revolution. It was the culmination of changes in the class structure of the nation, of violent political and religious contention, of an evolving political ideal that would come to be called the British Constitution, and of much weariness. It may even be called the end of the Reformation in England and Scotland. By studying a popular rising of 1679, Scott came closer to the heart of all this change than he would have if he had chosen to describe the flight of James II from England. Lukács, drawing on Balzac, makes the general point as if he had *Old Mortality* in mind:

> What matters is that we should experience the social and human motives which led men to think, feel and act just as they did in historical reality. And it is a law of literary portrayal which first appears paradoxical, but then quite obvious, that in order to bring out these social and human motives of behaviour, the outwardly insignificant events, the smaller (from without) relationships are better suited than the great monumental dramas of world history.[25]

The rising in Scotland was a direct action by the lower classes, supported by a few middle-class leaders. Instead of anticipating Lukács's

---

[24] For the general history I have drawn mainly on George Clark, *The Later Stuarts, 1660–1714*, 2d ed. (Oxford: Clarendon, 1955), pp. 263–93.

[25] Lukács, *The Historical Novel*, p. 42. In "Balzac and Stendhal," Lukács quotes at length from Balzac's review of Eugéne Sue to make the same point: see *Studies in European Realism*, no trans. (New York: Grosset and Dunlap, 1964), p. 70.

script for "the poetic awakening of the people," however, Scott's model of revolution descends to the most practical matters. To be effective militarily, the insurgents must outnumber the trained soldiers who can be brought against them, yet their numbers pose an even more serious problem of organization. They have neither an army nor political experience, and when they fall into groups of manageable size, these groups do not subordinate themselves one to another but quite the opposite. Throughout the central chapters of *Old Mortality*, which describe the actions of the Presbyterians from the unexpected victory at Drumclog to their overwhelming defeat at Bothwell Bridge, Scott seldom removes his eye or ear from the chaotic and fractious state of the insurgent forces.

The Covenanters in the novel elect leaders from a carefully chosen slate of officers, the composition of which has been worked out with those concerned by one man, John Burley. This is the revolutionary council: three extremists and three moderates. The strictly balanced council forms the "front"—to use a curiously ambiguous term of modern revolution—behind which two rival individuals, Burley and Henry Morton, struggle for influence. Again it must be stressed that Scott has constructed a model of revolution and not written a history as usually conceived. Neither of Scott's leaders bears any resemblance to Robert Hamilton, the leader of the historical rising. Though Burley was among the actual murderers of Archbishop Sharp, he did not play the further role ascribed to him in the novel. Morton, the hero of the novel, has only fictional being. As Lukács remarks, "historically unknown, semi-historical or entirely non-historical persons play this leading role," and he includes Burley in the handful of examples he names. "The popular character of Scott's historical art manifests itself in the fact that these leader figures, who are directly interwoven with the life of the people, in general are more historically imposing than the well-known central figures of history."[26]

The imaginary Burley is one of Scott's most brilliant historical conceptions. While the narrator presents Burley as motivated by a personal drive for power, demonstrates his deceitfulness, and hints that his destructive passions are only kept in check by a ruthless will, he also grants the man less dubious advantages as a leader: fearlessness, rhetorical power, and a rapid insight into the motives of other people. All these qualities, good and bad, make Burley the successful—or nearly successful—leader of revolution. When the political ends of the Covenanters are hopelessly confused, Burley is sustained by his

---

[26] Lukács, *The Historical Novel*, p. 38. On social class in *Old Mortality*, see also Brown, *Walter Scott and the Historical Imagination*, pp. 68–91.

strong personal motive; when his fellow insurgents tend to take opposite courses, Burley pulls them together, if necessary by telling a different lie to each one. The contrast with Ephraim Macbriar, who possesses as much courage and fanaticism as his fellow revolutionary, but is too sincere in his religion to resort to deceit or bribery, or even to accept the assistance of the moderate Presbyterians, merely proves that without men such as Burley there can be no effective fighting force and no revolution. The conclusion clearly emerges that the drive for individual power and the willingness to use underhanded means are perquisites of direct action.

This conclusion would be less surprising if Scott went on to argue that revolution is therefore an unacceptable recourse. But in fact Scott believes in the historical necessity of this particular revolution; when his hero accedes to one phase of it, he does so with sufficient awareness of Burley's vices. Morton senses that this man is not to be trusted but does so anyway because he has grasped the importance of Burley's role. The motives that cause Morton to join in armed rebellion seem to arise purely from the situation. Though he too may have certain personal motives, these are never consciously selfish, and at every step Morton attempts to justify himself intellectually. He assures Major Bellenden, for example, in a letter advising the surrender of the Tower of Tillietudlem, that he does not share any of "the angry or violent passions" of the other insurgents (Ch. 25). Though Scott takes some pains to impress us with Morton's intrepidity, what finally impresses us is this hero's intelligence.[27] He soon realizes that the military objectives of the revolution must be pursued with an enthusiasm far out of proportion to his own commitment and confidence in their success—if not, the military consequences will be disastrous. He knows that order and discipline are necessary to victory, but learns that these are not wholly compatible with enthusiasm. In the upshot he elects to fight for a negotiated compromise, only to learn that compromise is the gift of time and that negotiation is an impractical military objective. Because of his original diffidence, his loyalty to a class that is opposed to revolution, and his intelligence, Morton becomes the technical adviser in someone else's civil war—a role still widely available to his descendants, apparently, in today's postcolonial conflicts.

Of the various factions of insurgents after the victory at Drumclog,

---

[27] Cf. Francis R. Hart, *Scott's Novels: The Plotting of Historic Survival* (Charlottesville: University Press of Virginia, 1966), pp. 70–86. Hart treats Scott as a champion of "natural humanity and personal fidelity" whose studies of "the politics of survival" speak to the present time (p. 338).

"it seemed likely that those of the most violent opinions were, as is usual in such cases, to possess and exert the greater degree of energy" (Ch. 23). Scott shares with Burke the notion that revolution means the release of a terrible "energy" that in a viable society is held under restraint of law, property, rank, and the collective prudence of its leaders. Yet he makes Burley argue that "it is not men of sober and self-seeking minds, who arise in these days of wrath to execute judgment and to accomplish deliverance" (Ch. 22). When Henry Morton joins the rebellion, Scott acknowledges in effect the justice of Burley's observation: revolutions do not originate from totally civilized imaginations. Morton does not wish to be on the side of Burley and Macbriar, but the revolution is already under way. Scott would hardly allow his hero to associate with such radicals in 1816, when he wrote this novel, but the Revolution of 1688 holds a special place in his thinking. Both Scott and Burke endorse the victory of the propertied classes symbolized by that date in history, and Scott more nearly faces up to the kinetic energies that gave it being than does Burke, who in his anxiety to establish the permanence of 1688 treats it as an exception of almost supernatural necessity. The novelist's advantage here stems from his need to imagine the event concretely.

The release of energy implicit in revolution, for this way of thinking, is analogous to the release of a person from the restraint of reason. The presence, and even popular effectiveness, of the mad preacher Habakkuk Mucklewrath among Scott's insurgents underlines the analogy. But if revolution is an irrational act, how can a theory of revolution be propounded? Or how can a rational decision be formed to join it? Since the hero of Scott is distinctly rational, this dilemma is a factor in the almost tortuous process by which Morton is drawn into open rebellion. He can appeal, it is true, to a sanction for the use of force in English common law. He argues that due process has been abridged by the government in its effort to subdue the Covenanters by military means, and common law allows that subjects have a right to bear arms in self-defense—the very principle written into the Constitution of the United States in 1791. But that hardly decides the momentous questions of how far the principle can be applied or when one is justified in firing the first shot. Judith Wilt has summarized the hero's role this way:

> Morton's fundamental cast of mind is defensive, a cast adapted to preserving and opening at least two, preferably three, sides to every issue. Syntactically . . . this means keeping the frame of the sentence open for the qualification, the condition, the provision; tactically it means defending, preserving, defiles, causeways, passages, and, above all, bridges. Now

that the word is the sword, and the private speakers of reason are detached from home and committed to enactment, the novel moves to the battlefield and to the bridges on these battlefields which separate, that is, join, the antagonists.[28]

Instead of law and rationality, revolution borrows or invents an ideology, which justifies change and gives coherence to the purposes of those bent upon supplanting political authority. The role of ideology is represented in *Old Mortality* by the language and religious zeal of the Covenanters, who exploit every justification of righteous violence to be found in the Bible. (Their Biblical phraseology is supported by specific allusions, paraphrases, and recitations from both the Old and New Testaments that add an important dimension to this novel. When Burley uses language that Morton characterizes as dangerous, for example, he is actually paraphrasing John the Baptist foretelling the coming of Christ.) But ideology is seldom an unmixed blessing, even for revolutionaries, and Scott displays some of its divisive effects and the way it can distort both practical and humanitarian issues. The Covenant itself had become an impractical creed by 1679. The exclusive establishment of Presbyterianism in England and Scotland had been the least realistic provision of the Solemn League and Covenant in the first place. Still, the struggle had an important bearing on the way relations of church and state would be conducted in the future. The extreme Presbyterians of the novel presciently call Morton an Erastian: the settlement of 1688 was, indeed, an Erastian settlement. Never again would religion be so consequential in the affairs of state as it had been in the seventeenth century. The Revolution brought an end to a certain ideological conflict.

Ideology does not play a strictly parallel role for the powers that be. The appeal of the government in Scott's novel is to personal loyalty and to order and possession, and despite our modern view that ideology is inescapable, such sentiments need not be formulated as distinctly as a program for change. Scott shows rulers face just as dire problems in the use of force as revolutionists do. For both, every recourse to extreme measures will narrow the alternatives. The choice of clemency, on the other hand, though attractive to outside observers, will seem dangerous to the government and very likely be unwelcome to revolutionists. Can a government negotiate with armed rebellion without in some sense conceding the justice of its cause? Can it entertain a political compromise without vitiating its military posi-

---

[28] Judith Wilt, *Secret Leaves: The Novels of Walter Scott* (Chicago: University of Chicago Press, 1985), p. 98. For Morton's interaction with Burley, see pp. 98–103.

tion? These are questions, still common today, that are clearly set forth in *Old Mortality*. The individual stances of such persons as Claverhouse, General Dalzell, and the Duke of Monmouth further suggest how government policy is modified by character. Better still, the character and behavior of Sergeant Bothwell show an aspect of repressive government not always delineated in political and historical treatises. Scott mingles respect for Bothwell's usefulness as a military tool with just exposure of his repellent qualities as a political agent. The man's self-importance, his catering to rank, his crude mimicry and jocularity, and his brutality bring home the peculiar irritations and eventual disaster of a military police.

Revolution means a time of assassinations on one side and summary executions on the other. The several deliberate killings in *Old Mortality* might seem to provide the thrills of historical romance: this is so because Scott writes of torture and murder as things of the past, marking them off from the achieved civilization of the present. But in the Second Treatise on government in 1690, Locke virtually defined political power as the power to exact the penalty of death.[29] Revolution claims this power for itself, a power that goes to the very heart of the nature of the state, though in normal times it may be expressed in more disguised forms. To have a theoretical justification for taking life is to be either a soldier, an executioner, or a revolutionist. Scott condemns execution without trial but does not argue that the state has no right to put persons to death by due course of law, or to sacrifice lives in warfare, and he gives full play to Claverhouse's opinion of the justice of executing Henry Morton on the spot. He does not countenance Burley's argument that the assassination of Archbishop Sharp was divinely appointed, but he allows Burley to speak certain cogent ironies:

> You are of the opinion that the justice of an execution consists, not in the extent of the sufferer's crime, or in his having merited punishment, or in the wholesome and salutary effect which that example is likely to produce upon other evil-doers, but hold that it rests solely in the robe of the judge, the height of the bench, and the voice of the doomster! Is not just punishment justly inflicted, whether on the scaffold or the moor? (Ch. 21)

---

[29] "Political power, then, I take to be a right of making laws, with penalties of death, and consequently all less penalties for the regulating and preserving of property, and of employing the force of the community in the execution of such laws . . . and all this only for the public good." John Locke, *Two Treatises of Government*, ed. W. S. Carpenter (London: Everyman's, 1988), Bk. II, Ch. 1, p. 118.

Scott knows that history absorbs assassinations and summary executions with very little discomfort. His hero is repelled by the thought that Burley is a murderer, yet he states that he will not judge the murder Burley has already committed and cites as precedent for it a murder committed by Robert the Bruce.

The conflict of Covenanters and royalists in the novel provides a good many lessons in the inertia and momentum of events—or the difficulties of keeping up with history while attempting to direct it. The leaders on both sides have done their best to time their military efforts wisely but have not always succeeded. Claverhouse's decision to advance from an unfavorable position at Drumclog is based on his estimate of the consequences of not advancing at that particular moment—if his scouts had given him sufficient intelligence of the enemy, he explains, he could have retreated without loss of face. His defeat, however, brings all the consequences he dreads and more. Every commitment to military force is an amplification, whether the participants will it or not, of political purpose; and a defeat redoubles the political consequences of every commitment. Among the insurgents, Scott writes, were some who "felt themselves rashly embarked in a cause which they had neither courage nor conduct to bring to a good issue, yet knew not how to abandon for very shame" (Ch. 22). The downward course of conflict is as difficult to control as the upward, and most wars, once begun, elude the capacity of human courage or conduct to bring them to a good issue. At Bothwell Bridge, Morton reminds his followers that if they are defeated the rebellion, "far from being useful to the country, would be rendered the apology for oppressing it more severely" (Ch. 29). But once again the hero's intellectual grasp exceeds his ability to act. He sees that in order to stay abreast of events the insurgents must either advance to the attack, retreat in good order, or actively sue for peace, but he presents these alternatives as choices to a mob incapable of choice and too late turns to the bridge with the remnant who will follow him. The ambiguities of power affect the insurrection at every level: "The wiser, or more timid part of the assembly, were already withdrawing from the field" (Ch. 31). Even the decisive event of the battle cannot finally clarify whether those who withdraw are more properly called wise or timid. In the long run a compromise is reached but not by the combatants themselves. In the view of history perhaps every revolution fails, but so does every counterrevolution. By the same token, both succeed, for every determined use of force takes its effect one way or the other on the mass that is history. One of our legacies from Scott and his contemporaries is this historical perception. Once we perceive that revolution cannot achieve its full ends, and that counterrevolution is likely to be similarly wasteful, we cannot eagerly wage one or the other. We are then in the position of Henry Morton in his most modern aspect—heroes in exile, waiting for history to take its course.

Those who move more comfortably with history in *Old Mortality* come from what Scott called the lower ranks of society. It was too early in the nineteenth century for him to think of such people as the working classes, and insofar as he conceives of their economic role, this is well concealed within a Shakespearean literary convention of high and low characters in the same action. Thus Scott endows his low characters with wit and address that manners and morals prohibit to his heroic company. A few, like Neil Blane and Jenny Dennison, are neutral in the conflict that divides the nation, yet they are active in a persistent economic fashion. Just as Burley is able to serve a revolution by obeying his personal drive for power, the innkeeper and the waiting-lady can keep their heads above the fray by looking first to their material interests. Scott treats these characters humorously but also endows them with great confidence in history. He does not patronize them and is critical of those who hold themselves aloof from the lower ranks. Note how Morton regards his inferiors with scrupulous respect. The hero is never tempted, with Claverhouse, to make invidious comparisons to his own bloodline or to speak of them, as even Edith Bellenden does at one point, as "clowns" (Ch. 29). In *Old Mortality*, at least, Scott extends to a handful of sharply individualized low persons the function of living *in* history, of surviving from day to day in a material mode opposite to the hero and heroine's far more abstract commitment to property. But though Scott does not patronize, he does not exalt "the people"—as Lukács is wont to say, a little anachronistically, while writing perceptively of these relations.

"The interaction between 'above' and 'below,' the sum of which constitutes the totality of popular life, is thus manifested in the fact that, while on the whole the historical tendencies 'above' receive a more distinct and generalized expression, we find the true heroism with which the historical antagonisms are fought out, with few exceptions, 'below.' "[30] If one takes into account the whole tendency of the historical novel to deal with the concrete and particular experience, which Lukács also celebrates, then there is some validity to privileging the popular experience of revolution. Even so, in a given instance, Scott is likely to treat heroism as a virtue paralleled on different social levels. For example, though the hero once cites St. Paul as his authority, hardly anyone in *Old Mortality*, despite its many preach-

[30] Lukács, *The Historical Novel*, p. 49.

ers, figures as a practicing Christian except one Bessie Maclure, a woman who has lost two sons to the brutality of the reigning government yet shelters Lord Evandale when he is wounded. She, too, is waiting patiently for history to pass, and it may be significant that the final Revolution gives her essentially what she wants: freedom of religious conscience. Bessie Maclure, however, is a peasant counterpart of Lord Evandale himself: both exhibit generosity and fairness that transcend the political conflict. With her, of course, these virtues are Christian principles, whereas in Evandale they are what Burley calls "heathen virtues," or the code of honor.

What Lukács's somewhat formulaic attention to the people of Scott's novels ignores is the traditional function of Scott's humor. To be sure, the words and actions of the lower ranks tend to subvert the language and formal political stance of the protagonists. In the pattern derived from Shakespeare—especially his English history plays and above all *Henry IV*—the antics of the low characters dramatically challenge the propriety, and hence the destiny, of those above them. Moreover, as is the case with many other novels in English, the humor of Cervantes supports that of Shakespeare. Cuddie Headrigg, the plowman turned servant, is the Sancho Panza of *Old Mortality*. Scott deliberately points Headrigg's career in revolution—and his ultimate escape from the consequences—in the same direction as Morton's, but with a different style, comprising both dialect and serio-comic actions. The parallel even makes for narrative convenience at times, since Cuddie can accomplish certain things, such as escaping sudden death and running for help, that are beneath the dignity of heroes. More important, without compromising principles entirely, Cuddie gives expression to that hope for material survival that we must assume is hidden somewhere in the hero's mind or body. He has the same impatience with doctrinal differences among the Presbyterians, the same awe of Burley, the same timidity of violence, the same longing for a just peace and a woman's love as the hero, but expresses these motives and feelings outright. Without doubt his materiality, like that of Sancho Panza, calls the idealism of his master into question. It may be noticed, for example, that Cuddie has a reputation for enjoying food, whereas Morton's appetite is never mentioned, except in two instances when he feels particularly unable to eat. It is hard to calculate, obviously, the effect of such humorous interplay of styles, but the novel is neither a celebration of the role of the people in history nor an uncritical, incautious, or humorless celebration of propriety.

Dialect gives the low characters an independent voice. That they use a good many Scottish words makes them more pointedly local than the high characters, but Scott was not finally attempting a phonetic transcription of the way people spoke in a certain district. Their language is closely related to that of dialect jokes, and frequently in the Waverley Novels a joke that begins in standard English unobtrusively slips into dialect for the punch line. Nevertheless, dialect contributes to the Shakespearean and Cervantine realism of the novel, since it is used to puncture the refined language and idealistic thought of the principal characters. Writing in dialect also seems to have released Scott's store of wit and his power of metaphor. It is not that the characters speak in broad Scots that is important, but what they actually say; and what they say is usually something brightly impertinent. "I am sure they belie baith Cuddie and me sair, if they said he wadna fight ower the boots in blude for your leddyship and Miss Edith, and the auld Tower—ay suld he, and I would rather see him buried beneath it, than he suld gie way; but thir ridings and wappenshawings, my leddy, I hae ne broo o' them ava—I can find nae warrant for them whatsoever" (Ch. 7). The reader may conceive the general resemblance between Mause Headrigg's position here and that of Ailie Wilson, who in dialect advises her master to get his throat paved with stone if he insists on drinking his soup before it cools. Such speeches are antiauthoritarian, but Scott no more suggests the speakers or their heirs will subsequently come into power than Shakespeare holds out hope for Falstaff and his cronies.

The speeches of Mause and Gabriel Kettledrummle are charged with sudden quotations and daring analogies from the Bible, and like dialect in the last line of a joke, a ready allusion often works best in the peroration of a speech. Again, it is not that they use Biblical language that is crucial but the sly appositeness of what they say. When Kettledrummle is in immediate need of some doctrinal justification for his noncombatant role at Drumclog, for example, he boldly compares himself to Moses directing the battle against Amalek, and generously confers the ancillary roles of Aaron and Hur upon Morton and Cuddie. This was the occasion on which Moses had the power of turning the battle in Israel's favor merely by raising his hands. "But," as related in Exodus, "Moses' hands were heavy; and they took a stone, and put it under him, and he sat thereon; and Aaron and Hur stayed up his hands, the one on one side, and the other on the other side; and his hands were steady until the going down of the sun."[31] As is often the case in the Covenanters' appeals to Scripture, Kettledrummle seizes one of those texts that are precisely most difficult for the modern imagination to accept. The character's impertinence and

---

[31] Exodus 17:20.

Scott's subversive humor are directly at odds with the seriousness of the revolutionary crisis, yet the effect is not to cast doubt on the representation but to surround it with vitality.

The lowest of the low characters in *Old Mortality*, named Goose Gibbie from his humble duties on the farm, may be thought of as a personification of the accidental in history. He is treated with the broadest possible humor—so broad that only a child could heartily laugh at him. Yet this figure of low comedy intervenes in the story three times, each time in critical fashion. Scott was certainly aware of this, since he wrote of Gibbie's equestrian catastrophe at the wappenschaw, in his own review of the novel, "Upon this ludicrous incident turns the fate . . . of the principal personages of the drama."[32] A moment's reflection shows that this is quite true: Goose Gibbie's performance leads to the discharge of Cuddie Headrigg from Lady Margaret's service, which brings Mause Headrigg to old Morton's home at the wrong moment, which contributes to Henry Morton's arrest, and so on. Then at the end of the novel another failure on the part of Gibbie contributes to the death of Lord Evandale and the eventual marriage of the hero. By means of Gibbie, Scott evidently shows the power of accident in human affairs. It is true that his third performance in *Old Mortality*—carrying Edith Bellenden's letter to Major Bellenden—is successfully completed. But here Gibbie's close association with the accidental is spoken unmistakably by Jenny Dennison, who cautions, "He'll maybe no ken the way, though it's no sae difficult to hit, if he keep the horse-road, and mind the turn at the Cappercleugh, and dinna drown himsell in the Whomlekirn-pule, or fa' ower the scaur at the Deil's Loaning, or miss ony o' the kittle steps at the Pass o' Walkwary, or be carried to the hills by the whigs, or be taen to the tolbooth by the red-coats" (Ch. 10). This may be a fresh rendering of a fairly standard joke, but it will be noticed that assigning proper names to such local hazards makes them unique, proof against theory and generalization, and as stubborn in their existence as the low characters.

The hero and heroine of *Old Mortality* have not this degree of individual presence. They speak well but rather stiffly in English, and their love story may at first seem to have little to recommend it for its own sake. A few of the chapter epigraphs in the novel may help to modify this criticism—the epigraphs in the Waverley Novels are often more suggestive with respect to the story as a whole than to the particular

---

[32] *Quarterly Review* 16 (1817), rpt. in Walter Scott, *On Novelists and Fiction*, ed. Ioan Williams (London: Routledge, 1968), p. 246.

chapters they introduce. Just as several quotations from *Henry IV* remind one that the contrasting styles of Scott's realism derive in part from Shakespeare, some lines from Dryden's "Palamon and Arcite" and from *Two Nobel Kinsmen* (identified simply as "Fletcher") point up the highly literary cast of the rivalry of Morton and Evandale for Edith Bellenden. The motifs of imprisonment in a tower, of exile that would be welcome for political reasons but not for love, of the maiden reluctant to commit herself, and even soliloquy—which Scott regularly adopts for his heroes—lead the reader back to Chaucer's *Knight's Tale* and Boccaccio's *Teseide*.[33] The chief resemblance to the story of Palamon and Arcite is developed at the end of the novel: in a sudden reversal Evandale dies so that the hero can live after all and possess the heroine. For the tournament in the older story Scott has substituted a revolution, but history in a true historical novel is still literary. The modernization, or pacification, of the code of honor evident in the Waverley Novels prevents rivals from fighting it out like Palamon and Arcite but not from vying with one another in selflessness, or from preferring their own deaths to life without love. The question remains whether this conventional relation of death to love is as profound, or as demonstrable in real life, as that between death and politics, and whether both relations belong in the same novel. No one ever really dies for love, Rosalind claimed in *As You Like It* (a play that Scott calls upon for another epigraph), whereas it is all too obvious that men and women die for national or political causes. When, early in the novel, the hero despairs of the heroine's love, he feels that he will die, much as he feels ten years later when, thought to be dead, he is seen by Edith at the window. Persuaded that she is indifferent, however, he first turns upon the government, defying Claverhouse and his redcoats. In broad thematic terms the conventions with which Scott worked have a certain logic. Dying for love is allowable if the reader can be persuaded that there is only one love object for each hero or heroine. The power of the state over lives of individuals traditionally conflicts with love. A speech of Dryden's Arcite, for example, suggests that Claverhouse might better worry about Morton's love than his political interest:

> Law is to Things which to free Choice relate;
> Love is not in our Choice, but in our Fate:
> Laws are but positive: Love's Pow'r we see
> Is Natures Sanction, and her first Decree.

---

[33] See Jerome Mitchell, *Scott, Chaucer, and Medieval Romance: A Study in Sir Walter Scott's Indebtedness to the Literature of the Middle Ages* (Lexington: University Press of Kentucky, 1987), pp. 102-5. Mitchell finds this story recurrent in the Waverley Novels.

Each Day we break the Bond of Humane Laws
For Love, and vindicate the Common Cause.
Laws for the Defence of Civil Rights are plac'd,
Love throws the Fences down, and makes a general
    Waste.[34]

The first and last couplets are Dryden's embellishments on Chaucer's poem, but in any event this Arcite speaks in something like the language of early modern political theory. The form of necessity he invokes—Eros—might be thought of as medieval or as still more modern than the rest. It is very difficult to imagine why Scott needs to engage with this earlier literature at all, in his realist mode, if it does not pose some rules to be followed. As Robert C. Gordon has recently been arguing, precisely when Scott's contribution to history is the issue, the conventions of love and honor need to be taken into account.[35] One of the many hats worn by the Author of Waverley was that of editor of Dryden: his knowledge of the theater did not stop with Shakespeare or with Beaumont and Fletcher—whom he also edited—but was extensive and international. If not love itself, then literary convention may be a form of historical necessity.

Georg Lukács, in his warm testimonial to Scott, did not forget to indicate Goethe's influence, but at the same time he probably failed to do justice to the wider influence of earlier literature on the novels. In his treatment of the common people, especially, he neglected the conventions of English drama exemplified by Shakespeare's history plays, though he obviously knew the plays and used them to make generic distinctions in *The Historical Novel.* He may have been tempted to adopt an anachronistic view of "the people" because of the belief, expressed elsewhere, that class consciousness could not affect the course of history before the capitalist era. Since "bourgeoisie and proletariat are the only pure classes in bourgeois society," and the state itself was not fully identified with economic interests before then, possibly Lukács was not very curious about the specific fate of "other classes (petty bourgeois or peasants)" in seventeenth-century Scotland.[36] But such omissions or different emphases do not diminish the value of his account of the Waverley Novels as much as his refusal to

---

[34] "Palamon and Arcite," Bk. I, ll. 327–34, from *Fables Ancient and Modern* (1700): in *The Poems of John Dryden*, ed. James Kinsley, 4 vols. (Oxford: Clarendon, 1958), 4: 1476.

[35] Robert C. Gordon, "Scott, Racine, and the Future of Honor," in *Scott and His Influence*, ed. J. H. Alexander and David Hewitt (Aberdeen: Association for Scottish Literary Studies, 1983), pp. 255–65; and "The Marksman of Ravenswood: Power and Legitimacy in *The Bride of Lammermoor*," *Nineteenth-Century Literature* 41 (1986): 49–71.

[36] Lukács, "Class Consciousness," pp. 55–59.

examine the fate of the higher ranks in society, including the destiny of the middle-of-the-road hero. Determined not to taint Scott with the charge of bourgeois humanism, Lukács virtually ignores the plot of the novels, which not only rewards the strictest respect for property but reflects a political theory of the permanence of the British Constitution, a kind of end of history. The plot of the Waverley Novels is unfortunately every bit as metahistorical as Lukács's own beliefs, but metahistorical in an opposed direction.

Lukács is hardly alone in neglecting novel plots, the study of which demands sorting out protagonists from other characters, a sense of where the reader's attention has been rhetorically directed, and above all consideration of the outcome of an action. Thus historians often admire some parliamentary maneuver in a Trollope novel—or feminists, the behavior of a special heroine—without concerning themselves with the resonant affirmation of a society of landed gentlemen with which the Trollope novel typically concludes. Still, Lukács labors under a particular difficulty in this regard, because he insists so upon endings—upon closure—within his definition of nineteenth-century realism. That insistence can be found almost anywhere in his writings, from his fixed admiration of Scott to what I take to be his misreading of Joyce's realism. Some praise accorded Tolstoy, for example, he summarizes this way: "The profound realism of Tolstoy's world thus rests on his ability to present an intricate and differentiated world and yet to make it quite clear, by poetical means, that underlying all this diversity of manifestations there is a coherent, unified foundation to all human destinies."[37] That "yet" is Lukács's slight acknowledgment that realism's detailed representations do not of themselves confer any outcome upon events; the outcome must be imposed "by poetical means." The association of strong closure with realism is all the more evident when Lukács dismisses myriad forms of modernism, most of which he dislikes:

> Whereas in life 'whither?' is a consequence of 'whence?', in literature 'whither?' determines the content, selection, and proportion of the various elements. The finished work may resemble life in observing a casual sequence; but it would be no more than an arbitrary chronicle if there were not this reversal of direction. It is the perspective, the *terminus ad quem*, that determines the significance of each element in a work of art.[38]

[37] Lukács, *Studies in European Realism*, p. 177.
[38] Lukács, *Contemporary Realism*, p. 55. For his belief that Joyce's realism goes nowhere, see pp. 17–19.

Thus for this critic to neglect the regular denouement of virtually all Scott's novels runs counter to his inmost beliefs about literature, about realism. But in English literature the property plot, a reaffirmation of bourgeois humanism, supplied conventional endings for novels throughout the nineteenth century, or until the advent of modernism. It is as if, for Lukács, the shape of bourgeois fiction were always pleasing regardless of its politics.

Twenty years ago, Fredric Jameson chided us for viewing "our culture, indeed, as a vast imaginary museum in which all forms and all intellectual positions are equally welcome side by side, providing they are accessible to contemplation alone." Thus, among other things Marxian, we failed to understand Lukács's lifework, committed as it was to a particular and continuous vision of society.[39] Because of my own reading of the Waverley Novels, however, and this perceived contradiction in Lukács's thinking about them, I felt immediately that I would have to pick and choose among the positions taken in *The Historical Novel.* Lukács assuredly resides in my imaginary museum, a formidable display alongside other authorities on Scott and the historical novel, but museums for the contemplation of theories are useful, even necessary institutions.

[39] Jameson, *Marxism and Form,* pp. 160–63.

PATRIARCHY, CONTRACT, AND REPRESSION

IN SCOTT'S NOVELS

THOUGH SCOTT'S contribution to historical consciousness and to historiography undeniably rests upon specific achievements such as *Old Mortality*, his success as a creative mythographer of the nineteenth century followed from the continuities, the similarities of action, in the twenty-seven novels he composed from 1814 until his death in 1832. Mainly, I have argued, Scott promulgated during the long century of his fame a double fable of past actions and present stability in the social scheme of things. But this double fable and the confidence underlying it were not untroubled. Dramatically, the promised outcome of the plot is challenged beforehand, by intrusions of the low style and even heroic misgivings—Shakespearean techniques that Scott uses to dramatize modern forms of uncertainty. Judith Wilt, exaggerating a little, locates in *Old Mortality* "the single most poignant and typical gesture of all the protagonists in all the Waverley Novels." The instance she singles out is when "Morton comes home from his truant activism, his captaincy, at the revels, to knock on the door of home with 'a sort of hesitating tap, which carried an acknowledgment of transgression in its very sound, and seemed rather to solicit, than command attention.'"[1] The narrator's "acknowledgment of transgression" seems to say it all. A certain authorial irony plays about the expression even before the critic lays hold of it, but that degree of perspective is still consistent with Scott's helping to define modern behavior.

Implicit in civilization itself, in the pacification of behavior and commitment to property celebrated in the Waverley Novels, is a persistent drama involving not only past historical actions but the immediate reactions of the protagonists. Both aspects of this drama make their contribution to civilization: the dynamic of the myth is the same as that of each novel, a bearing of actions upon outcome. The protagonists' actions—most likely their inactions or restraint—certify their worthiness to benefit from society. The inward drama often discovers heroes voluntarily submitting themselves to civil, or even military, authorities in order to affirm their commitment to society. Typically—and here I differ slightly from Wilt—they do not seek to identify with a father, or male head of the family, but with an authority to whom

[1] Judith Wilt, *Secret Leaves: The Novels of Walter Scott* (Chicago: University of Chicago Press, 1985), p. 86.

they have contractually agreed to give way. Their "acknowledgment of transgression" thus corresponds to a newer idea of authority in which they actually participate. On behalf of civilization, an inward affirmation of loyalty is enacted repeatedly in the Waverley Novels. Scott dramatizes, in order to resolve, the very antagonisms that Nietzsche and Freud will decree are unresolvable. Just so, without Scott and other novelists there would be less understanding of the burdens of a social contract for Nietzsche and Freud to work on.

Scott's first move as a novelist in 1814 was to pluck Edward Waverley from the library at Waverley-Honour and cause him to take up a commission with a regiment stationed in Scotland, in the year 1745 (he was supposedly writing *Waverley* "sixty years since," as the subtitle has it). Being unused to discipline and curious about his relations in Perthshire, the young hero directly requests a leave of absence and rides off to visit the Baron Bradwardine at Tully-Veolan. Thence he gets a chance to trek to the highlands in pursuit of the Baron's rustled cows, while he remains largely oblivious to the political rising on behalf of the most romantic of lost causes, the return of the Stuarts to the throne of England and Scotland. Sometime after he has become the guest of the chieftain and Stuart conspirator Fergus Mac-Ivor, he is apprised by a letter from Rose Bradwardine that sojourning in the highlands has brought him under suspicion.

> How *he* himself should have been involved in such suspicions, conscious that until yesterday he had been free from harbouring a thought against the prosperity of the reigning family, seemed inexplicable. . . . Still he was aware that unless he meant at once to embrace the proposal of Fergus Mac-Ivor, it would deeply concern him to leave this suspicious neighbourhood without delay, and repair where his conduct might undergo a satisfactory examination. (Ch. 28)

In this typical turn of the Scott hero's adventures, note two things: the threatened danger comes from the more civilized Hanoverian settlement to which the hero already subscribes; and his immediate response is voluntarily to resubmit himself to that establishment for "examination." What this voluntary examination would consist of is a little unclear, for when the hero turns southward for the purpose— after an interlude with a blacksmith that enacts the politics of the day in the low style—he is promptly arrested for high treason and undergoes a formal examination preliminary to a criminal trial. It is Waverley's revulsion from this treatment that throws him temporarily into the Stuart rebellion after all.

The reader may not exactly be surprised by Waverley's arrest, since it was precisely such danger that Rose Bradwardine warned of, and quite a few times heroes in novels by Fielding or Smollett had been arrested before this. Waverley himself is surprised, indignant, exasperated, and ashamed, though only a few days before he decided "to repair where his conduct might undergo a satisfactory examination." Thus in his first novel Scott invented an action in which the hero ambiguously invites and resists his own arrest—a posture so modern that it more nearly resembles a novel by Kafka than any by Scott's predecessors. Waverley demands of the local magistrate, a retired major, to hear the charges against him. Besides the military crimes of desertion and inciting mutiny, he finds himself accused of high treason, or "the highest delinquency of which a subject can be guilty."

> "And by what authority am I detained to reply to such heinous calumnies?"
> "By one which you must not dispute, nor I disobey."
> He handed to Waverley a warrant from the Supreme Criminal Court of Scotland, in full form, for apprehending and securing the person of Edward Waverley, Esq. suspected of treasonable practices and other high crimes and misdemeanours.

Because Waverley and other of Scott's heroes are so consciously committed to authority and to correct legal procedure, the voices of incrimination in such a scene are partly internal. In the present instance, the narrator explains the internal case this way: "Although Edward's mind acquitted him of the crimes with which he was charged, yet a hasty review of his own conduct convinced him that he might have great difficulty in establishing his innocence to the satisfaction of others." In the course of his formal "Examination" (the chapter title), the hero inwardly conducts his own review of the case, and now the question inevitably arises, of the "satisfactory examination" he has promised himself earlier: Satisfactory to whom? There follows an elaborate Kafkaesque sequence over the personal papers he has about him, one of which he tries to conceal because he treasures it as a love-gift from Flora Mac-Ivor but which Major Melville, the magistrate, sees in a political light; the paper consists of a poem, no less, not addressed to Waverley at all but to the memory of one Captain Wogan who deserted the Puritan for the Royalist side in 1648, and who bore the same forename as our hero.[2] After these embarrassments, the prisoner—"for such our hero must now be called"—recovers his presence of mind and defends himself as best he can against

---

[2] The story of Edward Wogan was given by Clarendon: see *The History of the Rebellion and Civil Wars in England*, ed. W. Dunn MacRay, 6 vols. (Oxford: Clarendon, 1888), 5: 313–15.

the circumstantial evidence, but there comes a point when Melville speaks of an incident at Tully-Veolan (the Baron defended the hero's honor while he slept) that "cannot be charged against you in a court of justice" but ought nevertheless to be answered. It is as if all the hero's shortcomings, even incidents of which he was not conscious, are matters for examination.

> This was too much. Beset and pressed on every hand by accusations, in which gross falsehoods were blended with such circumstances of truth as could not fail to procure them credit—alone, unfriended, and in a strange land, Waverley almost gave up his life and honour for lost, and leaning his head upon his hand, resolutely refused to answer any further questions, since the fair and candid statement he had already made had only served to furnish arms against him.

Though Melville has assured him that this is not yet an actual trial ("your examination will be transmitted elsewhere"), the hero's sudden lapse into silence can hardly help him. Moreover, he refuses to tell anything of the Mac-Ivors, for that would be a poor return for their "unsuspecting hospitality" to himself (Ch. 31). This stance, fine as it is, indirectly affirms that, where the hero alone is concerned, there can be no concealment of his activities from a duly appointed authority of civil society such as this stern magistrate. The authorities may one day be satisfied, perhaps, but the hero never. The experience is like a bad dream, in which the threat to his being—his very "life and honour"—seems to extend from the society with which he identifies. The episode is representative, for suspense in *Waverley* finally turns not on the question of whether the hero will fight for the Pretender, as he half-heartedly does for a while, but whether he can get clear again from the due and lawful penalties for engaging in such an adventure.

The career of Francis Osbaldistone in *Rob Roy*—sixth of the novels but written just four years later—is a close variant to that of Edward Waverley. Scott's first hero is arrested but never actually brought to trial: the novel itself functions as his trial, in the course of which he is absolved from guilt by circumstances, perhaps, but never quite from the sensation that a trial might still be pending. Osbaldistone, on the other hand, is several times threatened with arrest, but typically the complaint is destroyed or the warrant never presented: the tenuousness of the action, in fact, makes it seem still more a study in psychological guilt than the former novel. For *Waverley*, the historical novelist exploited the events of 1745 for their familiar detail and sequence; in *Rob Roy*, set thirty years earlier, after the Union of Scotland and England, Scott is vague about history and keeps hinting at Jacobite plots only to forget them again. An implausible scheme of commercial fraud substitutes for politics, and this plot rapidly gives way before the end to the restoration of the Osbaldistone estate to its rightful heir (Frank's father, after all, was the elder son in his generation, so Frank ought to—and does—inherit the property). For a novel composed in 1818, the treatment of capitalism is scarcely forward-looking: though Frank is made to realize that he might have saved his merchant father some anguish by joining the business, this barely convincing recognition depends on archaic motives of loyalty and filial duty. Nevertheless, the familial and personal turn of *Rob Roy*—unusually for Scott, it is narrated in the first person—permits one to glimpse more inward aspects of the hero's commitment to civil society.

Rob Roy is another novel in which mere proximity to crime is bound to get the hero in trouble with the authorities. Francis Osbaldistone is out hunting in Northumberland with his cousins and Die Vernon, when he learns that he has come under suspicion for robbery and that his supposed victim is a government agent. "And so it is high treason, then, and not simple robbery, of which I am accused!" Miss Vernon's quip that high treason "has been in all ages accounted the crime of a gentleman" only succeeds in irritating the hero, whose politics and morals, he reminds her, are Hanoverian. She advises him to flee to Scotland, but as a hero of the Waverley line he insists on confronting immediately the justice of the peace before whom the charges were made (Ch. 7). Similarly, contending with Rashleigh Osbaldistone in the college yards at Glasgow, Frank insists, "you shall go with me before a magistrate," when it is Rashleigh all along who is conspiring to have him arrested and who boasts that warrants have already been drawn up for the purpose (Ch. 25). Obviously it is not villainy alone that threatens the hero. When crimes occur around him, he has a certain propensity to appear before the authorities, or even to turn up in the Glasgow prison after visiting hours:

> At finding myself so unexpectedly, fortuitously, and, as it were, by stealth, introduced within one of the legal fortresses of Scotland, I could not help recollecting my adventure in Northumberland, and fretting at the strange incidents which again, without any demerits of my own, threatened to place me in a dangerous and disagreeable collision with the laws of a country which I visited only in the capacity of a stranger. (Ch. 21)

The novel *Rob Roy* is unmistakably of two minds as to where the danger for the individual lies. The English hero and most of the Scots outwardly fear to set foot in the highlands, where lawlessness prevails. But for all the attention directed to that danger, the hero himself is scarcely threatened except by the law. At least four times, Osbald-istone is threatened with arrest, and each time he is saved by the in-tervention of Rob Roy, whose independence of the law is notorious. In the last instance, the warrant names not only Frank but Die Ver-non and her father Sir Frederick as traitors, yet the hero insists, "Commit no violence—give me leave to look at your warrant, and, if it is formal and legal, I shall not oppose it" (Ch. 39). Apparently, a young gentleman untrained in the law can recognize at a glance the authority of a warrant. Cousin Rashleigh is once again behind this move, and all three persons—hero, heroine, and her father, as if yoked in a courtship plot—are legally taken prisoner in the moments before Rob Roy enters and this time slays Rashleigh outright.

To summarize: the hero is strictly law-abiding and fears only lawless-ness; he is threatened by law nevertheless and continuously made anx-ious on this account; and if it were not for the outlaw Rob Roy he would never be relieved from this plight. Readers of the novel suppos-edly share the anxiety with the suspense, and if they should take this repeated action seriously, Francis Osbaldistone would seem to be in constant danger of being hanged. But *Rob Roy* is far too entertaining and too tentative to permit much fear of that. Rashleigh is too devil-ish a villain, Frank's other cousins and his usurping uncle too boor-ish, and Diana too much of a sportsman for the initial mystery to be very gripping. Thereafter, Scott's own interest in the story may have been distracted by the inspiration that made Andrew Fairservice the hero's self-appointed squire and especially by composing the dialect for two other characters, Rob Roy and Bailie Nicol Jarvie.[3] In the Glasgow prison scene that ought psychologically to tell for the hero (Chs. 22 and 23), Frank hardly bothers to say a word, while Rob and the Bailie meet as old acquaintances. Frank faithfully narrates their conversation, putting in all the dialect spellings. As the narrator, he cannot really be in much danger of being incarcerated for long, let alone of being hanged: psychologically, in fact, the novel is something of a tease. But for all that, the hero's plight does count in the novel's political dimension. Much weaker than *Waverley*, *Old Mortality*, and some others as an historical novel and certainly not very impressive as a psychological novel, *Rob Roy* is nevertheless important for the persis-tent shape it gives to a myth of modern polity, and all the more so be-cause of the unexpected threat of legal constraint or punishment.

For about a hundred years the Waverley Novels were very widely read; they were exported and reprinted and translated into most

---

[3] On Bailie Nicol Jarvie, see David Brown, *Walter Scott and the Historical Imagination* (London: Routledge, 1979), pp. 98–108; and Wilt, *Secret Leaves*, pp. 54–56.

European languages almost immediately; and thus they contributed to the Western world's store of wisdom. One notable piece of wisdom from *Rob Roy*, familiar to Victorian readers if not to us, is Bailie Nicol Jarvie's distinction between honor and credit:

> "I maun hear naething about honour—we ken naething here but about credit. Honour is a homicide and a bloodspiller, that gangs about making frays in the street; but Credit is a decent honest man, that sits at hame and makes the pat play." (Ch. 26)

At this point the Bailie is reproving the young hero for being concerned with honor and at the same time clearing space for his own occupation. His measure of honor as a willingness to kill or be killed is just, however, and his put-down of honor—its reduction to a brawl in the streets—is very quick. When Scott writes at his best, dialect—that is, the low style—is subversive of most pretensions. So the Bailie's boast about credit is exaggerated somewhat: he means it but means it as a joke, just to be safe. Credit always remains in doubt, if only in the sense that it ought to be open to examination, like a Waverley hero. Even personification sits a little less easily with credit than with honor; and on his own side of the comparison the Bailie's put-down is more of a come-down, reflecting a determination to stay out of trouble and tend to the profits. Historically speaking, this particular come-down amounts to something like a feminization of culture, for it is traditionally women who sit at home and make the pot boil ("the pat play") while the men are out fighting.

The comparison of credit and honor is far from being an isolated witticism in this novel. That the Bailie's meaning is cultural is proved by a misunderstanding of the clerk Owen, who naively begins to interrupt the conversation with a bookkeeper's definition of "credit." That the sense is also historical—credit taking the place of honor over time—is borne out by the subsequent discussion of the survival in the highlands of a less pacific form of government conducted by chiefs like Rob Roy.

> "Ah, but ye judge Rob hardly," said the Bailie, "ye judge him hardly, puir chield; and the truth is, that ye ken naething about our hill country, or Hielands, as we ca' them. They are clean anither set frae the like o' huz;—there's nae bailie-courts amang them—nae magistrates that dinna bear the sword in vain ... like mysell and other present magistrates in this city—But it's just the laird's command, and the loon maun loop; and the never another law hae they but the length o' their dirks—the broadsword's pursuer, or plaintiff, as you Englishers ca' it, and the target is defender; the stoutest head bears the langest out;—and there's a Hieland plea for ye."

Owen groaned deeply; and I allow that the description did not greatly increase my desire to trust myself in a country so lawless as he described these Scottish mountains. (Ch. 26)

Obviously Jarvie is enjoying himself. Like Odysseus telling of his close escape from the land of the Cyclops, he goes out of his way to remark the absence of any modern system of justice among these strange people. Scott treats the tale lightly but also has a serious historical purpose. Jarvie next produces statistics on the demography and economy of the highlands that, if they are not actually culled from the Earl of Selkirk's *Observations on the Present State of the Highlands of Scotland* (1804), are compiled just as anachronistically in the same spirit.[4]

A strong indication of the success with which Scott touched on his culture's myth of the yielding of violence to law can be found by placing Nicol Jarvie's witty distinction between honor and credit side by side with Henry Maine's famous distinction between status and contract, first published in his *Ancient Law* in 1861 and influential in sociology to this day. The latter distinction arises from Maine's principal idea of progress in society, from the ties of birth and family to those of individual obligation. "The movement of the progressive societies has been uniform in one respect," he wrote. "Through all its course it has been distinguished by the gradual dissolution of family dependency and the growth of individual obligation in its place. The Individual is steadily substituted for the Family, as the unit of which civil laws take account." Accompanying this replacement of the family by the individual is the increasing clarity and sway of contract, "which replaces by degrees those forms of reciprocity in rights and duties which have their origin in the Family." Then, in the final paragraph of his chapter on "Primitive Society and Ancient Law," Maine offers the word "status" as summarizing rights and duties derived from the family and concludes as follows:

All the forms of Status taken notice of in the Law of Persons were derived from, and to some extent are still coloured by, the powers and privileges anciently residing in the Family. If then we employ Status,

---

[4] That these matters are central to Scott's conception of *Rob Roy* is evident from the opening paragraphs of his 1829 introduction to the novel: Rob Roy "owed his fame in a great measure to his residing on the very verge of the Highlands, and playing such pranks in the beginning of the 18th century as are usually ascribed to Robin Hood in the middle ages,—and that within forty miles of Glasgow, a great commercial city, the seat of a learned university. . . . It is this strong contrast betwixt the civilised and cultivated mode of life on the one side of the Highland line, and the wild and lawless adventures which were habitually undertaken and achieved by one who dwelt on the opposite side of that ideal boundary, which creates the interest attached to his name."

agreeably with the usage of the best writers, to signify these personal conditions only, and avoid applying the term to such conditions as are the immediate or remote result of agreement, we may say that the movement of the progressive societies has hitherto been a movement *from Status to Contract.*[5]

It would take me too far afield to explore the many correspondences between what Maine calls "status" and Jarvie calls "honor." In "credit" the Bailie necessarily includes the obligations implicit in Maine's conception of the modern but also a sense of character—character at least commensurate with earlier notions of honor—for "Credit is a decent honest *man.*" It could be argued that Maine's distinction is as self-serving as the Bailie's, since the Victorian wrote for an era when freedom of contract was at its highest bent. By the end of the nineteenth century, that freedom had been constrained somewhat by social legislation and by the courts.[6]

The premise of Maine's progression from status to contract, a weakening of family ties and rise of the individual, was available to political theory well before Scott's lifetime. In attacking Robert Filmer's patriarchal defense of the monarchy in 1694, Locke demolished one set of rights based on family, and the second of his *Two Treatises on Government* became the favorite discourse on contract theory in English. Distinctions between force and voluntary agreement, acquisition and institution, patriarchy and a commonwealth, had been sharply defined in Hobbes's *Leviathan* of 1651:

> The attaining to this Soveraigne Power, is by two wayes. One, by Naturall force; as when a man maketh his children, to submit themselves, and their children to his government, as being able to destroy them if they refuse; or by Warre subdueth his enemies to his will, giving them their lives on that condition. The other, is when men agree amongst themselves, to submit to some Man, or Assembly of men, voluntarily, on confidence to be protected by him against all others. This later, may be called a Politicall Common-wealth or Common-wealth by *Institution*; and the former, a Common-wealth by *Acquisition.*[7]

Hobbes had allowed that the laws of honor obtained in a state of nature. Locke's position is much closer to Maine's, however, since in

---

[5] Henry Sumner Maine, *Ancient Law: Its Connection with the Early History of Society, and Its Relation to Modern Ideas*, 4th ed. (London: Murray, 1870), pp. 168–70. See also p. 126.

[6] For a short account, with references, see A. H. Manchester, *A Modern Legal History of England and Wales, 1750–1950* (London: Butterworths, 1980), pp. 264–80.

[7] Thomas Hobbes, *Leviathan*, ed. C. B. Macpherson (Harmondsworth: Penguin, 1968), p. 228.

contending against the derivation of political power from that of fathers Locke effectively depreciated the need for any justification of government based on its origins. It did not finally matter how civil society came into being if its authority was based on continuing consent.[8]

Maine was not offering a theory of origins, let alone a justification of government. As a modern historian he scorned the fiction of "contractual origin" for the rule of law. He is especially hard on Rousseau in this regard and only somewhat less so on Montesquieu. "The point which before all others has to be apprehended in the constitution of primitive societies is that the individual creates for himself few or no rights, and few or no duties. The rules which he obeys are derived first from the station into which he is born, and next from the imperative commands addressed to him by the chief of the household of which he forms a part." Maine is not writing primarily about government, but about changes over time in relationships enforced throughout any group or nation. So also has Scott in *Rob Roy* played down his favorite dynastic plot and focused on two *kinds* of law so different that they represent two different states of social life. These are, in Jarvie's words, "the laird's command" enforced by the clansmen and the Glasgow "bailie-courts" manned by such respectable persons as himself. The eschewal of high theory by Scott and Maine scarcely diminished the cultural and historical claims of either writer. I would submit that Maine's characterizing "individual obligation" as peculiarly modern, or his writing of "the habit of mind which induces us to make good a promise," or of "the mental engagement" in promises that supersedes mere rituals of law,[9] take him beyond this imputed kinship with Bailie Nicol Jarvie, in the direction of a study of personality helpful in understanding the readiness of Waverley, Osbaldistone, and other Scott heroes to meet their commitments and even subject themselves to examination.

Before I return to this propensity of modern heroes, however, I wish to call up that figure in the novels who may well represent for youth the old law—the figure without whom, since mothers are such a rarity, there would be no family to discuss. "I feel sure that Power over Children was the root of the old conception of Power," Maine remarks at one point.[10] Undeniably the action of *Rob Roy* is framed by a

---

[8] See Gordon J. Schochet, *Patriarchalism in Political Thought: The Authoritarian Family and Political Speculation and Attitudes, Especially in Seventeenth-Century England* (Oxford: Blackwell, 1975), pp. 271–76. "After 1690, genetic justification and the identification of familial and political power were becoming dead issues" (p. 276).

[9] Maine, *Ancient Law*, pp. 308–14.

[10] Ibid., p. 319.

struggle between the hero and his father, who strives to exert his power over Frank by all means at his command—superior knowledge and fortune, love, ridicule, and command itself. The pair are stubborn enough—Frank bent on poetry and his father insisting he join in the commercial house of Osbaldistone and Tresham—that they reach an impasse before the end of chapter 2, at which time the hero is both disinherited and somehow compelled by his father to wend his way north, for purposes as thoroughly concealed from the reader as from the son. The action of this novel is certainly baffling or dreamlike, punctuated occasionally by recollections of "the perverse opposition to my father's will," which "rose up to my conscience as the cause of all this affliction" (Ch. 22). Without making much difference to the action one way or the other, but demonstrating love and still greater competence, Osbaldistone senior eventually returns to the scene. As in *Waverley* and *Redgauntlet*, other novels thought to be close to the author's personal history, there are also surrogate fathers in *Rob Roy* and a potential father-in-law to contend with, since "Father Vaughan" turns out to be the heroine's paterfamilias.

"*Rob Roy* is Scott's variation on the parable of the Prodigal Son," Robert C. Gordon's discussion of the novel begins.[11] The same has often been said of Schiller's first play, *Die Räuber*, a tragic analogue and likely inspiration of *Rob Roy*. Scott's earliest literary experiments were translations and imitations of German drama; John Gibson Lockhart, his son-in-law and biographer, believed that *Die Räuber* provided a special stimulus, because it figured in literary gatherings of lawyers in Edinburgh and was translated by Alexander Fraser Tytler, an older friend who subsequently became a judge in the Court of Sessions.[12] Some comparison of the play with Scott's novel is worth making, since my argument has to do with the appeal of this kind of material for the nineteenth century and even how such literary father-and-son relations weighed on Freud's thinking.[13] I have no idea whether Freud was acquainted with *Rob Roy*, but he certainly knew and was moved by Schiller's play. Though the tragic mode is more congenial

[11] Robert C. Gordon, *Under Which King? A Study of the Scottish Waverley Novels* (Edinburgh: Oliver and Boyd, 1969), p. 67. Gordon is an excellent guide to father-son relations throughout the Scottish novels.

[12] J. G. Lockhart, *Memoirs of Sir Walter Scott*, 5 vols. (London: Macmillan, 1914), 1: 176.

[13] In "Freud and Literature," Lionel Trilling argued for a "reciprocal" relation but mainly remarked on the influence of romantic literature on Freud: see *The Liberal Imagination* (1950; rpt. New York: Anchor, 1957), pp. 32–36. Terence Cave, citing Trilling, remarks on "the extent to which [Freud's] readings of literature actually predetermine his theory." As Cave puts the case earlier, "psychoanalysis is the elaboration of a plot structure according to rules which are already demonstrated by literary texts." See *Recognitions: A Study in Poetics* (1988; rpt. Oxford: Clarendon, 1990), pp. 176, 166.

to psychoanalysis, and may seem more romantic, the strict rules of behavior assumed by both works reflect the bourgeois morality of the time. As indexes of repression the works are similar.

The blocking characters in the two fictions, Osbaldistone senior and der alte Moor, are simply fathers—their given names are never used. Each fiction also presents a lone female character—Amalia and Die Vernon—as a love object and proceeds to surround her with an all-male cast. The foremost sexual rival to the hero is in one case a brother, Franz Moor, and in the other a cousin, Rashleigh Osbaldistone—both are distinctly villains and not fathers. These villains, however, insidiously side with the fathers, while the youthful heroes mix with outlaws. In fact, both works succeeded famously in creating outlaws, the social bandits Karl Moor and Rob Roy. In Schiller's tragedy this outlaw *is* the estranged son, who adopts the life of a Robin Hood. Karl Moor is repeatedly slandered and betrayed by his brother, he and his band are hunted by the army, and eventually he surrenders to the authorities, to be punished for his transgression. In order to sustain a similar action within a comic plot, Scott's novel necessarily employs some displacement or division of labor: Frank Osbaldistone, slandered and betrayed by his cousin and threatened by the law, remains innocent and even ignorant of crimes; Rob Roy, a career bandit, befriends the hero and looks out for his interests, even kills on his behalf. The rules are the same, but the character is doubled: the hero can safely surrender himself and the outlaw remains free. Transgression is still transgression.

The relation of *Die Räuber* to the development of Freud's thinking is well documented.[14] Most often the play is cited to demonstrate the romantic side of Freud, or even to depict him as radical thinker, though it might equally point to conservatism and repression. Schiller importantly mediated Shakespeare for German culture, as Scott to a certain extent did for English. If *Rob Roy* has scatterings of *Hamlet* within it—the Bailie, for example, scolds the hero for playing "Hamlet the Dane" where his father's business is concerned (Ch. 23)—*Die Räuber* contains some more blatant borrowings from *King Lear*. Franz's betrayal of Karl Moor is so patterned on Edmund's betrayal of his brother Edgar in *King Lear* that Schiller freely incorpo-

---

[14] See *The Interpretation of Dreams* (1900), in *The Standard Edition of the Complete Psychological Works of Sigmund Freud*, ed. and trans. James Strachey et al., 24 vols. (London: Hogarth, 1953–1974), 5: 421–25, 480–87; Alexander Grinstein, *On Sigmund Freud's Dreams* (Detroit: Wayne State University Press, 1968), pp. 292–316; and William J. McGrath, *Freud's Discovery of Psychoanalysis: The Politics of Hysteria* (Ithaca: Cornell University Press, 1986), pp. 66–78. Schiller's heroine, Amalia, had the same name as Freud's mother.

rated both Edmund's philosophy and his address to Nature. Though Freud may not have needed Schiller to mediate Shakespeare for him, patently the play had that effect.[15] Without the intervention of a romantic sensibility, it is hard to imagine either Shakespeare's Edgar or his Edmund metamorphosing into a celebrated social bandit. Contributing to this new possibility, however, is not only a romantic idea of the self but a modern notion that the state ought to be consensual, hence seriously open to challenge from competing systems. An interiorizing or Freudian reading of Schiller's play would, in its turn, suggest displacements that only thinly disguise an Oedipal plot: Amalia, the only woman in the cast and singular love object, is the mother; Franz, the rival brother, is actually the father; social banditry equals the hero's ambivalence toward his parents. But for all the ease with which such interpretations can be spelled out, thanks to Freud, they tend to collapse the historical and political dimensions that have made them possible. Here I wish to look out upon Freudianism from Schiller's stage, which chronology informs us was constructed first. Or to put it another way, I would read the political fiction of Freud's own *Totem and Taboo* as a guide to his psychology, which in great measure depends on social history and theory.

Steven Cohan has written very persuasively of *Rob Roy* by calling attention to the very forms of displacement Freud teaches one to expect. Cohan reads the cast of characters and principal events of the novel as a typical family romance designed for the hero who tells it. The interpretation, for once, follows closely what Freud wrote about family romances: that the child invents an alternative family or families to accommodate the ambivalence felt about parents of either sex, and especially the ambivalence of male children about fathers.[16] Thus high treason in Scott's novel stands for the guilt Frank feels about disobeying his father, and his eventual succession to his uncle's property disguises a wish that would otherwise imply his father's death. "Rashleigh, moreover, who openly works to undermine both Sir Hildebrand and Mr. Osbaldistone, enacts the ambition and eros that Frank himself suppresses. . . . Next to Rashleigh's, Frank's behavior seems downright docile, submissive, and obedient, so Scott rewards Frank with what Rashleigh consciously wanted all along—Osbaldistone Hall

---

[15] Thus Freud detects the "cadence" of Shakespeare's Brutus and the theme of ambition in his "Non Vixit" dream, but his boyhood experience was of reciting the part of Brutus in the ballad from *Die Räuber*, act 4; Schiller's lines restore the relation of Caesar and Brutus as father and son that Shakespeare utterly neglects. See *The Interpretation of Dreams*, pp. 424, 483; and for a translation of the ballad, Grinstein, *On Sigmund Freud's Dreams*, pp. 300–301.

[16] Freud, "Family Romances" (1909), *Standard Edition*, 9: 237–41.

and Diana Vernon." All this is excellent, and more nuanced than an excerpt can suggest. Notice, however, that Cohan, as a critic of the post-Freudian era, accepts the unconscious feelings of the son as primary. It is equally possible that tensions between fathers and sons displace some less easily expressed social anxiety, or that, historically, a fantasy of being charged with high treason finds expression in the family romance. "As we have seen," Cohan writes, "the hero cannot avoid his guilt, no matter how much the narrative structure of this novel may seem willing to soothe his anxiety."[17] But there ought to be some explanation of why such stories proliferated in the nineteenth century. Cohan's interpretation, which seems right enough, may be circular if the psychoanalytic grounds for it owed as much as I think they do to nineteenth-century novels and to the myth of progress from status to contract, or from undisguised patriarchalism to a self-restraining individualism.

In his reading of *Waverley*, the same critic calls attention to three instances of the word "parricide" in the novel, on two different occasions when the hero's thoughts are engaged with characters who serve to him as fathers. When on the battlefield Waverley sees his former commanding officer threatened by Callum Beg, he feels "as if he was about to see a parricide committed in his presence" (Ch. 46). Later, once his identification with the Jacobite cause has run its course, he reads in an out-of-date newspaper that his father has died in London, and, more distressingly, that his uncle Sir Everard is likely to be tried for high treason unless the nephew "shall surrender himself to justice." Of the first item, Waverley exclaims, "Good God! . . . am I then a parricide?" But this improbability—that a father "who never showed the affection of a father while he lived, [could not] have been so much affected by my supposed death as to hasten his own"—he quickly dismisses. As to the threat to his uncle, it would be "worse than parricide to suffer any danger to hang over my noble and generous uncle, who has ever been more to me than a father" (Ch. 61). The latter occasion bristles with displacements that are at least partly conscious, while the word "parricide" might be blurted from a reservoir of unconscious hostility. Cohan cites these relations as well as the hero's coming to rely on still another father-figure, Colonel Talbot, to conclude as follows:

> In *Waverley* the hero has enough father figures to give him the luxury of
> committing acts of parricide in thought but not in action, so he never

[17] Steven Cohan, *Violation and Repair in the English Novel: The Paradigm of Experience from Richardson to Woolf* (Detroit: Wayne State University Press, 1986), pp. 87–91.

has to see himself consciously as a heinous criminal. His relationships with these men thus serve as the main index to his maturation . . . In working out his resistance to parental figures of authority created in response to his absent father, Edward comes to accept an institutionalized figure of authority: society.[18]

I have cut short this valuable interpretation of Scott's novel as a bildungsroman in order to come to rest, as Cohan does, on that word "society." Though Waverley's feelings of guilt anticipate Osbaldistone's feelings toward his father, *Rob Roy* affords much more discussion of society. Suppose one approached such texts less from the assumption of depth psychology and the family romance and more from their coincidence in history with new social institutions that, in effect, define maturation as self-repression. Suppose the relations of fathers and sons change over time, in this culture, but not nearly as swiftly or as demonstrably as political institutions and economic doctrine have changed. These latter changes occurred, not before there were families of course, but before family romances became the staple of popular imagination and the object of analysis. "Am I then a parricide?" Waverley's question speaks for the nineteenth century, and therein speaks to Dickens, to Dostoevsky, and to Freud. When first social theory and then social mobility left fathers behind, it may be supposed, an Oedipus complex needed to be discovered.

A few of the novels capture very well the quarrel between old-time fathering and modern manners, as status gives way to contract. The evidence recovered by Steven Cohan from *Waverley* and *Rob Roy* delineates a struggle that is only more pronounced in *Redgauntlet*, published in 1824 when Scott was fifty-three. With few exceptions, of course, all the novels are comedies, and the number of fathers serving as blocking characters who are somehow got round by the end is not too surprising. *Redgauntlet*, however, with its two heroes, the friends Alan Fairford and Darsie Latimer, multiplies the possibilities. Like *Rob Roy*, the novel promotes a broad historical myth instead of portraying a single historical event. Fairford is a young advocate in Edinburgh, whose father is readily identifiable as a Writer to the Signet determined that his son shall follow in the profession of the law.[19] The comedy of this relationship pits parental dominance against

---

[18] Ibid., pp. 83–86.

[19] Lockhart, *Memoirs of Sir Walter Scott*, 1: 152, 156–58, accepts the traditional identification of Saunders Fairford with Scott's own father. One way *Redgauntlet* seems to enact fantasies close to the life of its author is simply in the split between the two heroes, Fairford the promising young advocate and Latimer the wandering romantic, uncertain of his identity and captive of a violent past.

youthful, though respectful, resistance. Latimer, the roving friend, fulfills a romance convention, for he has no idea who his parents are and keeps up a brave front on that account. As dubious compensation for this lack, Scott endows Latimer with a harsh and forbidding surrogate who turns out to be his uncle Redgauntlet. (Since Darsie is a Redgauntlet also, the title of the novel itself might be said to contain the struggle of the two generations.) In his wanderings, which are even less specifically directed than Waverley's or Osbaldistone's, Latimer encounters still other fathers: the Quaker Joshua Geddes offers him a home briefly; and "Father Buonaventure"—the Stuart Pretender again—holds him under house arrest. Even the life history of a minor character, Nanty Ewart, tells of a son who has disappointed his father, who subsequently died one night after preaching on seven Sabbaths against his son's "falling away." The seafaring Nanty has been advised that, if he should ever return to his village, "the very stones of the street would rise up against me as my father's murderer" (Ch. 14). Of this novel, Gordon has remarked, "One cannot help being amazed at the sheer narrative energy and motivation that Scott finds in the impercipience of fathers."[20]

More than any other novel by Scott, *Redgauntlet* situates fathers politically, and Darsie Latimer's family romance—which at times has the aspect of a nightmare—situates fathers well in the past, before status gave way to contract. As in other Waverley novels, both heroes are threatened with arrest at one point or another, but in each instance the law is being manipulated by Hugh Redgauntlet or his agents. This Redgauntlet is the heavy in the plot, who with a show of force kidnaps his nephew, as if in a child-custody struggle. Significantly, the uncle's politics are as repressive as his manners are oppressive. Even before his identity is revealed to Darsie, a pitched argument develops between them. When the younger man claims "the privilege of acting for myself" as an Englishman's right, the older denies this principle and counters with an archaic appeal to honor. "'The true cant of the day,' said Herries in a tone of scorn. 'The privilege of free action belongs to no mortal—we are tied down by the fetters of duty—our mortal path is limited by the regulations of honour—our most indifferent actions are but meshes of the web of destiny by which we are all surrounded'" (Ch. 8). The note of fatalism accompanies the man's brooding presence whenever he appears. Later, in his own name, he holds up for his nephew "a more worthy object of ambition" than a career in the law: a thoroughly anachronistic plan for restoring the Stuarts to the throne. "Men of honour, boy . . . set life, property, fam-

---

[20] Gordon, *Under Which King?*, p. 161.

ily, and all at stake when that honour commands it!" (Ch. 19). In this novel, such commands oppose not merely the Hanoverian establishment but the very constitution of society, including its freedom of contract or "privilege of acting for myself," as Darsie puts it.

Anachronistic politics are thus bound up in *Redgauntlet* with a decided ferocity of fathering. The uncle himself informs Darsie of their medieval ancestor Alberick Redgauntlet, who struck the life from his estranged son. That only son "shared so much the haughty spirit of his father, that he became impatient of domestic control, resisted parental authority, and finally fled from his father's house." In a subsequent struggle for the Scottish crown, the son opposed his father in arms. Alberick recognized him on the battleground, possibly wounded, but attempted to leap his horse over him: "The steed made indeed a bound forward, but was unable to clear the body of the youth, and with its hind foot struck him in the forehead, as he was in the act of rising" (Ch. 8). Not surprisingly, in the present action of the novel, Darsie wonders whether his fierce uncle might "use unfair measures toward a youth whom he would find himself unable to mould to his purpose" (Ch. 12). In truth the uncle uses everything short of violence, and browbeats Darsie in the name of his actual father, who now appears to have been executed—like Fergus Mac-Ivor—after the rebellion of 1745, and whose skull is still suspended above the walls of Carlisle. When the nephew protests against another such vain attempt to revive the fortunes of the Stuarts, he is told angrily:

> I will not hear you speak a word against the justice of that enterprise, for which your oppressed country calls with the voice of a parent, entreating her children for aid—or against that noble revenge which your father's blood demands from his dishonoured grave. His skull is yet standing over the Rikargate, and even its bleak and mouldered jaws command you to be a man. (Ch. 19)

Redgauntlet here seems a crazy version of *Hamlet* in which Claudius exhorts the hero to avenge his father. The nephew's reluctance is palpable: in the novel, the older generation are alike usurpers of the sons' prerogatives and Hugh Redgauntlet a usurper of the modern state.

In the famous ending, Redgauntlet and the Pretender are defeated by the magnanimity of the present government, in the person of General Colin Campbell, who allows all the conspirators to go unpunished. Even before this graceful denouement, the uncle has been advised that he never could succeed without "the authority of your nephew" (Ch. 22), and the whole of the ending rests upon the younger generation, political and personal. During the course of the novel, the murky outdated Stuart business has been overshadowed anyway by the oppressive claims of patriarchy, registered sometimes as a terror and sometimes as an embarrassment for Darsie Latimer, also a Redgauntlet. Now, with a breath of fresh air, the terror and embarrassment—which has extended so far that Latimer is forced to wear skirts in the final chapters—have been lifted.[21] Most significantly, Darsie is reunited with his friend Alan, who has been searching for him in the west of Scotland. The female dress unexpectedly facilitates their embrace as Darsie's feet catch in "the extreme folds of his riding-skirt" when he tries to dismount, and "it was his friend Alan Fairford in whose arms he found himself"—though with his uncle standing by he dares not yet reveal who he is. If cross-dressing brings the friends together this way, it has also introduced Darsie to his sister Lilias, whom he has admired as the mysterious Green Mantle: while he is in skirts she reveals to him their relationship. The solution, predictably, is for Alan to marry Lilias. The game of bonding played out by Scott attains a mythical dimension comparable to the imagined role of General Campbell. Mutual attraction and exchange in the marriage of a sister unite the friends, now brothers, and reprove the patriarchy. In vain has the older Redgauntlet interposed "his person betwixt the supposed young lady [Darsie] and the stranger [Alan] of whom he was suspicious" (Ch. 19). This is one novel in which courtship emphatically does not mean the exchange of a daughter, for Saunders Fairford has no more to do with the arrangement than uncle Hugh; Lilias is given to Alan by Darsie. *Redgauntlet* begins as an exchange of letters between the friends; at a point where the narrative shifts from Latimer's diary to a third-person account of Fairford's adventures, Scott writes that "Alan doted on his friend Darsie, even more than he loved his profession" (Ch. 10). In that love he is opposed by Saunders, who is trying to marry his son to the law.

If *Redgauntlet* seems oddly personal, as Scott's novels go, it too is constructive of a political myth. At bottom this is another version of the progress from status to contract like *Rob Roy*, but its relentless attack on father-right suggests a myth closer to Freud's idea of ancient history than to Maine's. In reading Freud, too, the projection of his per-

---

[21] Darsie's uncle forces him to wear female dress, to discourage him from attempting to escape. Later he advises his nephew not to blush at this disguise: "It is when female craft or female cowardice find their way into a manly bosom, that he who entertains these sentiments should take eternal shame to himself for thus having resembled womankind" (Ch. 22). Wilt, *Secret Leaves*, pp. 146–50, has some interesting things to say about the episode.

sonal stake in any story has to be sorted out from its claims to univer-
sality. So it is with the myth of society with which the fourth essay of
Totem and Taboo concludes. The Freudian reordering of society begins
with the sons killing and eating the primal father, but when the author writes of "a sense of guilt" and "the remorse felt by the whole
group," we remember the close bearing of his own father's death on
the discovery of the Oedipus complex. Fifteen years after that event,
in the myth Freud composed, "the dead father became stronger than
the living one had been—for events took the course we so often see
them follow in human affairs to this day."[22] In *Redgauntlet* the treatment of fathers and their surrogates is less savage, but Scott was casting his imagination back only a hundred years or so, and it was
enough for him to render the older generation powerless. With Scott,
the crime to be sorry for was Alberick's, and that effect descends to
successive fathers and uncles[23] until Hugh Redgauntlet "bit his lip"—
more in chagrin, perhaps, than remorse (Ch. 22). For all their differences, these myths have much in common. Neither is strictly a myth
of origin but of progression from one source of authority to another.
Scott and Freud both reject the fiction of a state of nature more be-
nign than civilization; they are Hobbesian rather than Rousseauistic
in characterizing the general pacification of society. Furthermore,
in their different accounts of this pacification, they both perceive a
necessary self-control or repression. In Philip Rieff's summary of
Freud's position, "civilization begins when the paternal taboos are
self-imposed" and "culture is established through a series of renun-
ciations."[24]

The near brother-sister incest in *Redgauntlet* seems an echo of the
Restoration drama that Scott knew well, and which he may have consciously introduced in the novel for its period flavor. Freud's discussion of incest in *Totem and Taboo* reflects his sources in late Victorian
anthropology; but though he is undoubtedly thinking of mother-son
incest as he narrates the myth in the fourth essay, his words might
apply to the end of the novel:

> Sexual desires do not unite men but divide them. Though the brothers
> had banded together in order to overcome their father, they were all

---

[22] Freud, *Totem and Taboo* (1914), *Standard Edition*, 13: 143.

[23] The different assignment of guilt parallels the difference between Shakespeare's
Hamlet and Freud's interpretation of the play. Roughly speaking, Shakespeare and
Scott assign the guilt, including guilt feelings, to uncles and ancestors, Freud to the
son and nephew.

[24] Philip Rieff, *Freud: The Mind of a Moralist* (1959; rpt. New York: Anchor, 1961), p.
217. Rieff also makes the comparison to Hobbes (p. 242).

one another's rivals in regard to the woman. . . . Thus the brothers had no alternative, if they were to live together, but . . . to institute the law against incest . . . In this way they rescued the organization which had made them strong—and which may have been based on homosexual feelings and acts, originating perhaps during the period of their expulsion from the horde.[25]

Two friends in *Redgauntlet*, even augmented by Green Mantle, sister of one and sometime sexual object of both, do not add up to a horde, but the conflict of generations clearly matters in the novel, and of the two generations the younger has become representative. The two friends and brothers, that is, resemble others of their time and class, and readers are bound to identify with them. Elsewhere, Scott was not above introducing in his myth of society a primal horde. Just as Schiller, by evoking social banditry, was able to introduce a more primitive form of organization in the present time of *Die Räuber*, Scott half-mockingly introduced in *Rob Roy* a band of brothers so brutal and untouched by modern manners that they could very well be a horde. Perceval, Thorncliff, John, Dickon, and Wilfred Osbaldistone, cousins of the hero, are said by Die Vernon, cousin on their mother's side, to be sot, bully, gamekeeper, jockey, and fool respectively. None is a gentleman except, of a sort, the sixth brother Rashleigh, who is a consummate villain. The brothers devote themselves solely to hunting and drinking and require guests to do the same. The narrator-hero does not fail to express his scorn for them all; of course, Thornie is his overt rival, and Rashleigh the secret rival, for Diana. Suggestively, and unusually for Scott, Rashleigh has endeavored to seduce the heroine. Though the novelist reserves Rashleigh for Rob Roy's justice, he kills off the five boorish brothers in separate actions told on a single page—with a facetiousness like that of the Robert Hame film *Kind Hearts and Coronets* (1949), in which Alec Guinness plays all eight rivals for the hero's fortune.

Scott was undoubtedly distancing himself, as well as his readers, from the wish-fulfillment designed for the end of *Rob Roy*, as he had done by referring matters to Miss Buskbody at the end of *Old Mortality*. In a second rush of events, the hero tells of his wooing and marrying Die Vernon and of her death in exactly three sentences. Some ambiguity was attached to the hero's relation to Die from the start. She first crosses his path as "a vision" and "my beautiful apparition," expressions that suggest he is daydreaming or that she is too attractive to be real. The narrator recalls from that time her "coat, vest,

[25] Freud, *Totem and Taboo*, p. 144.

and hat, resembling those of a man, which fashion has since called a riding habit" (Ch. 5). He nevertheless is overcome by her womanly beauty, while she urges him to "forget my unlucky sex; call me Tom Vernon, if you have a mind, but speak to me as you would to a friend and companion" (Ch. 6). As they become better acquainted at Osbaldistone Hall, where she is the only woman, she places emphasis both on her "masculine accomplishments that my brute cousins run mad after" and on her learning, "which you men-scholars would engross to yourselves." Diana runs through a long catalogue of female art work that she will *not* have in her quarters. Yet, "there stands the sword of my ancestor Sir Richard Vernon, slain at Shrewsbury, and sadly slandered by a sad fellow called Will Shakespeare" (Ch. 10): she collects the sorts of memorabilia, armor and weaponry, that Scott collected at Abbotsford. There is certainly cross-dressing in *Rob Roy*, as later in *Redgauntlet*, but this time it is voluntary and in the person of the woman. Frank expresses a good deal of uneasiness at Diana's forwardness with him, just as Darsie worries about his loved one's behavior during the time they are both dressed as women and only she is aware of their relationship. Unless a point is made that first cousins come under the interdict, near-incest is missing from *Rob Roy*. A subtext of "homosexual feelings" such as Freud imagines for the primal horde, though, is a reminder of the degree to which both novels celebrate bonding among the young rather than marriages with the aim of perpetuating a patriarchy.

There seems to me little question that Scott conceived of society within the general picture of contract theory from Locke to the present day. He depends on this theory and constructs imaginative versions of it, in some novels more noticeably than in others. Freud evokes this tradition as well, though in *Civilization and Its Discontents* he tends to contrast the brute strength of individuals with law-abiding communities rather than families and freely contracting individuals.[26] Freud is more imaginative—that is, he throws around a good many fictions—in *Totem and Taboo*, and those earlier essays were formative in his thinking about society. Similarly, I believe, a widely read fiction called *Rob Roy* was formative of our thinking, as well as informed by the contract idea. Largely with reference to *Totem and Taboo*, Rieff summarizes Freud's position this way:

> In Freud's version, the social contract appears as a counter-revolutionary response to the overthrow of patriarchal government. It does not implement the prudence of the group; only in a carefully defined sense does

---

[26] Freud, *Civilization and Its Discontents* (1930), *Standard Edition*, 21: 95.

it represent the majority will of the citizen-brothers. Social-contract myths may be reinterpreted psychoanalytically as a reassertion of the will of the father against the rebellious impulses of a chastened son-ship. The law of primal ambivalence is conveniently at work, matching rebellion with guilt, aggression with submissiveness.

I shall come back to the matter of "a reassertion of the will of the father." Scott would have had little difficulty accepting the view that "all social relations, whatever their variety, are mechanisms of authority"; whereas he might reject, as applied to himself, Rieff's earlier statement that "all social relations, in Freud's view, are coercive."[27] Nevertheless, dramatically his novels suggest that the social contract can be experienced as coercive.

Since Locke, at least, contract theory has seemed antipatriarchal. This emphasis did not result from any antipathy to fathers, obviously, but from opposition to Filmer's *Patriarcha*. Filmer had attempted to justify the inherited authority of monarchs by analogy to the father's authority in the family, supported by the Bible and tradition. Locke rejected this analogy, since the family had little bearing on the principle of founding government on the consent of the governed. The heat of the argument, nevertheless, moved him to insist on the equality of fathers and sons once the latter had come of age: "After that the father and son are equally free, as much as tutor and pupil, after nonage, without any dominion left in the father over life, liberty, or estate of his son, whether they be only in the state and under the law of Nature, or under the positive laws of an established government." Locke did not write so of daughters, because they had no political rights when they came of age or any significant independence from the family. Though marriage is said to be "a voluntary compact between man and woman," it was no different in a state of nature.[28] Aside from Locke's rhetoric about male equality in successive generations, then, family relations are unaffected by civil society—though a subtext favoring sons eventuates in fictions like the Waverley Novels and Freud's account of the primal horde.

Because the attitude of exponents of the social contract seems so evidently filial, Carole Pateman has recently redesignated it "the sexual contract," in order to expose a continuing assumption of male dominance and elucidate the meaning of fraternity as a revolutionary slogan. Pateman accepts the historical demise of patriarchy as a reality but challenges the loose and often self-serving notion that con-

[27] Rieff, *Freud*, pp. 244–45, 216.

[28] John Locke, *Two Treatises of Government*, ed. W. S. Carpenter (London: Everyman, 1924), pp. 145, 155.

tracts join equals or are freely entered into. That freedom is a fiction, in her view, for "contract always generates political right in the form of relations of domination and subordination." She has chiefly in mind the subordination of women, which is implicit throughout Locke's remarks about the marriage compact, but the observation can easily be extended to other relationships. This is Pateman's summary of contract theory over time:

> The classical patriarchalism of the seventeenth century was the last time that masculine political right was seen as father-right. Classical contract theory is another story of the masculine genesis of political life, but it is a specifically modern tale, told over the dead body of the father. In civil society the two dimensions of political right [dominion over Eve and her descendants, in effect] are no longer united in the figure of the father, and sex-right is separated from political right.[29]

From all such narratives about the formation or reformation of society, a distinct theory of repression follows. Even if one assumes that repression was a fact of life in the earliest of human communities—or speculates with Freud that Polynesian taboos confirm this fact—there remains the question of why civilized thinkers in the nineteenth century became aware of repression. When Nietzsche observes the internalization of aggression that accompanies the pacification of society or Freud later conceives of the superego to account for something very similar,[30] they are bemused by behavior exactly like that depicted in the Waverley Novels and later nineteenth-century fiction. Freud's superego perfectly explains why Waverley and Osbaldistone typically rush off to submit themselves to examination—were it not for a suspicion that the theory merely describes, as novels do, modern behavior together with feelings of how one ought to behave. An adequate basis for a theory of repression, it seems, can also be found in Maine's high Victorian text:

> It is just here that archaic law renders us one of the greatest of its services and fills up a gap which otherwise could only have been bridged by conjecture. It is full, in all its provinces, of the clearest indications that society in primitive times was not what it is assumed to be at present, a collection of *individuals*. In fact, and in view of the men who composed

---

[29] Carole Pateman, *The Sexual Contract* (Stanford: Stanford University Press, 1988), pp. 8, 88–89.

[30] See Friedrich Nietzsche, *On the Genealogy of Morals*, trans. Walter Kaufmann and R. J. Hollingdale (1967; rpt. New York: Vintage, 1969), pp. 162–63; and Freud, *The Ego and the Id* (1923), *Standard Edition*, 19: 28–39. The concept of the superego appears earlier in Freud's writings under various guises: see the editor's note, pp. 4–11.

it, it was *an aggregation of families.* The contrast may be most forcibly expressed by saying that the *unit* of an ancient society was the Family, of a modern society the individual.[31]

Maine also claims he has the evidence, embedded in ancient laws like fossils in a rock formation (the primitive, for him, is generally pre-Roman). As in other versions of the story, it is the unit of the individual that counts here.[32] If society is truly a collection of discrete individuals, then individuals must exercise all necessary authority by exerting pressure on others and more commonly *re*pressing themselves. If power is widely distributed, most of it will be internalized, since power cannot be exercised externally by everyone at the same time.

The results of the devolution of authority upon the self are legion. To repress desire seems to take more energy than either satisfying it or finding it suppressed. Repressing desire may be distinctly less satisfying than resenting one who suppresses it. Either way desire is frustrated, and if one lets up or lets go, no one else is to blame. Thus guilt attaches to the contract, discontent to civilization. Freud's myth of society assumed that psychological guilt was of primordial origin, but I would judge that it is modern. If social history and political theory are taken as prior to psychology, the observation that "the human sense of guilt goes back to the killing of the primal father" takes on a significance not intended by Freud. His sentence need not refer to inherited guilt or to personal feelings projected back in time, but simply to the history of guilt *since* the demise of patriarchy. Fathers, after all, may even forgive children at times, but children, as sovereign individuals who have the last word, may not forgive themselves so easily. Anxiety also resides in the individual unit by contract, as in the very "assurance that a law once made will not be broken in favor of an individual."[33] Scott's heroes were among the first to experience this assurance as a threat, and their story was not without its effect.

The political and social nature of repression has been the study of Michel Foucault. Even Foucault's writings about knowledge are grim, since knowledge too has the negative connotations of discipline. It

---

[31] Maine, *Ancient Law*, p. 126.

[32] Pateman, for example, locates the conflict between Filmer and Locke in "the question whether political power and subjection were natural or conventional, that is, created by the individuals themselves" (*Sexual Contract*, p. 82); Schochet believes that Locke's achievement was to turn contract theory away from "how men become subject to political authority" toward "a doctrine based on consent" (*Patriarchalism*, p. 271); Rieff credits Freud with shifting the perspective of political science from institutions to "individual psychology" (*Freud*, pp. 241–42).

[33] Freud, *Civilization and Its Discontents*, pp. 132, 95.

may be asked whether the thrust of his research was finally political or anarchist.[34] As a publicist of repression, Freud obviously came first, for only an era that already takes repression for granted could produce or comprehend a Foucault. The latter has read repression back into political theory and into the social history now associated with his name. Of all things to be learned from *Discipline and Punish*, the ways in which individuals are expected to participate in their own disciplining may be the most telling. For all the searing descriptions of social institutions, Foucault is one of those political theorists—again following Freud—most concerned with individual life. One test of the difference of modern social organization from the past is "the reversal of the political axis of individualization," from the minutiae of the lives of a few rulers to the minutiae of many lives gathered by surveillance. "And if from the early Middle Ages to the present day the 'adventure' is an account of individuality, the passage from the epic to the novel, from the noble deed to the secret singularity, from long exiles to the internal search for childhood, from combats to phantasies, it is also inscribed in the formation of a disciplinary society."[35] Obviously this is no eager celebration of individualism, as one might expect from Foucault's many accounts of oppressive institutions, but a mordant contemplation of the repressed individual along parallel lines. The practice of "panopticism" extends to the persons subject to it, without suggesting what they can do to remedy their situation.

The main historical ground of this thesis is the reformation of criminal justice in the late eighteenth and early nineteenth centuries. Foucault vividly demonstrates how the purpose and practice of punishment changed, from public execution and the spectacle of vengeance upon the criminal's body to measured terms of imprisonment supposed to change the criminal's ways. Systematic incarceration is seen to resemble other institutions, the hospital and school, which Foucault has already studied, and "the carceral" rises from an adjective to become a substantive, a condition of life. The advent of the penitentiary in the nineteenth century, obviously, depended as closely on technology and marshaling of labor as the factory system: Foucault's fascination is with the techniques and mechanisms of control, within and outside the prison. He does not associate contract itself with subjection, as Pateman does, or with repression, as I do here. He

---

[34] See especially Michael Walzer, "The Lonely Politics of Michel Foucault," in *The Company of Critics: Social Criticism and Political Commitment in the Twentieth Century* (New York: Basic Books, 1988), pp. 191–209.

[35] Michel Foucault, *Discipline and Punish: The Birth of the Prison*, trans. Alan Sheridan (1977; rpt. New York: Vintage, 1979), pp. 192–93.

allows a Rousseauistic contract to be a good thing, but finds it supported by some very dubious mechanisms: "Although, in a formal way, the representative régime makes it possible . . . for the will of all to form the fundamental authority of sovereignty, the disciplines provide, at the base, a guarantee of the submission of forces and bodies." Thus "the contract may have been regarded as the ideal foundation of law and political power; panopticism constituted the technique, universally widespread, of coercion." Contract was the ideal, in short, but panopticism is what we have (compare "formal" thought to practices "universally" in evidence). Foucault decides that discipline is "entirely different" from contract. While "the acceptance of a discipline may be underwritten by contract," he suggests,

> the way in which it is imposed, the mechanisms it brings into play, the non-reversible subordination of one group of people by another, the "surplus" power that is always fixed on the same side, the inequality of position of the different "partners" in relation to the common regulation, all these distinguish the disciplinary link from the contractual link, and make it possible to distort the contractual link systematically from the moment it has as its content a mechanism of discipline.

Foucault apparently wishes to keep the social contract, and freedom of contract, pure. But if a given discipline is "underwritten" by contract, the latter would seem to be implicated with the former after all. Again, in an argument that introduces this one, disciplines "extend the general forms defined by law to the infinitesimal level of individual lives; or they appear as methods of training that enable individuals to become integrated into these general demands."[36] In such case, the law and its demands would seem to require the repression necessary to be "integrated" as well as the nuisances suggested by "infinitesimal."

The shift in civil punishment delineated by Foucault occurred roughly in Scott's lifetime. It is not surprising, therefore, that a novelist so attuned to history and to politics should register many of the effects theorized by the historian a century and a half later. Foucault writes of the new paradigm that "the guilty person is only one of the targets of punishment," and that "everyone must see punishment not only as natural, but in his own interest."[37] The innocent Francis Osbaldistone, as we have seen, discovers himself to be such a target. Nor does he fail to appreciate that the system of punishment is in his

[36] Ibid., pp. 222–23. See also p. 194.
[37] Ibid., pp. 108–9.

own interest. On one occasion in *Rob Roy*, Frank at once protests his innocence and adds that robbery is a crime "which would . . . deservedly forfeit my life to the laws of my country" (Ch. 11). Though little if any attention has been paid to such reflections by critics who apply Foucault's ideas to the history of the novel, Bruce Beiderwell has recently made up for this by reading the Waverley Novels in close conjunction with expressed theories of punishment from the eighteenth century to the present day.[38] From the Tower of London to village strongrooms, the prisons described in the novels are old-fashioned affairs, remote from the modern penitentiary, but the same can be said of nearly all the prisons in the novels of Dickens, written after the building of the first penitentiaries. In *The Heart of Mid-Lothian*, moreover, Scott addressed some aspects of imprisonment that antedate the prison's technological and theoretical transformation as an instrument of punishment. A prison provided the title of the novel, and since the title refers both to the gaol in the High Street of Edinburgh and to the organic center of an urban site known as Midlothian to this day, the ironies could not be more Foucauldian.

The Tolbooth, as it was called, abutted the cathedral, parliament, and law courts of Scotland's major city. As an old-style prison, it functions paradoxically in *The Heart of Mid-Lothian* as the center of everything that is marginal: the relations between the law and outlaws, force and violence, order and disruption. Though some of the same issues are raised elsewhere by Scott—in the social banditry of Rob or the wrongs of Helen MacGregor, for example—it is as if in this novel he could not lay them aside. Not only is the great Porteous riot treated in such a way that readers are led to share the mob's sense of justice, but the trial of Effie Deans casts doubt on the justice of a particular law and ultimately on the Court of Sessions. To prepare for the Porteous narrative, the novel begins with a smuggling case—always of interest to Scott. Here is how he generalizes the matter:

> Contraband trade, though it strikes at the root of legitimate government, by encroaching on its revenues,—though it injures the fair trader, and debauches the minds of those engaged in it,—is not usually looked upon, either by the vulgar or by their betters, in a very heinous point of view. On the contrary, in those countries where it prevails, the cleverest, boldest, and most intelligent of the peasantry, are uniformly engaged in illicit transactions, and very often with the sanction of the farmers and inferior gentry. (Ch. 2)

[38] Bruce Beiderwell, *Power and Punishment in Scott's Novels* (Athens: University of Georgia Press, 1991).

As such marginal activity gravitates to the center of the novel, established power and authority come into question. Partly this subversion is effected once again by the dialect voices of Scott's low characters. Daddie Ratcliffe, a completely marginal thief and thief-taker, gets a good deal to say, such as "I have kend the Law this mony a year, and mony a thrawart job I hae had wi' her first and last; but the auld jaud is no sae ill as that comes to—I aye fand her bark waur than her bite" (Ch. 13). More memorably, when a magistrate named Middleburgh comes from the city to confront Davie Deans, he is met with an out-pouring of dialect, a sermon in fact, denying the jurisdiction of the court over any cases whatever. (One has to recall that Scott was clerk to this same Court of Session for most of his adult life.) But authority is also called into question by historical matters: the statute that created a presumptive proof of infanticide, and the pardoning power vested in sovereigns and others.

Scott should be thought of as a great political novelist as well as an historical novelist. In English, he may be matched in this regard only by George Eliot in her last novel and by Conrad at his best, though he wrote when the English novel was more politicized than in any other era and there are many exemplary political novels by Disraeli, Gaskell, Trollope, and others.[39] Scott understood contract theory and was able to express better than philosophers what it meant to live in a contractual society. For all his heroes' self-surrenders, he does not leave the impression that individualization was a bad thing. In his most problematic treatment of society, *The Heart of Mid-Lothian*, the possession of individual presence of mind, not to say stubbornness, descends all the way to "the Celtic obstinacy" of Rory Bean, the pony (Ch. 13). Readers come away from the novel, after all, not immediately concerned with the limits of authority but impressed by the redoubtable talent for having one's way exhibited by the female protagonist Jeanie Deans, by her father and her sister, by the Edinburgh mob itself, and even by such as Dumbiedikes, the owner of the pony. The magistrate Middleburgh, emerging from his struggle with Davie Deans, captures this side of the novel's politics perfectly: "that is to say, Mr. Deans . . . that you are a *Deanite*, and have opinions peculiar to yourself" (Ch. 18).

Neither Jeanie nor David Deans is quite at home among Scott's usual heroines or heroes. Though Jeanie will marry the schoolmaster

---

[39] Marilyn Butler, *Jane Austen and the War of Ideas* (Oxford: Clarendon, 1975), is the most enterprising account of political novels of the time, if only because Austen's novels were customarily regarded as apolitical. See also Gary Kelly, *The English Jacobin Novel, 1780–1805* (Oxford: Clarendon, 1976).

Reuben Butler and achieve a small independence of the propertied kind, her native independence derives from folklore on the one side—the story of Helen Walker—and Scott's adaptation of the contrast of styles on the other—her father's side. Thus the Deans are not called upon conspicuously to support the social contract or property in land. Deanism, nevertheless, appears in one form or another in most of the novels, and expresses in a comic vein the freedom that repression allows and particularly values.

INDEX

Characters in the Waverley Novels are indicated by a dagger (†).